COVERDALE
on Management

The Coverdale Organisation was founded in 1965 to help people develop skills, with the emphasis on the need to put training to use at work.

The Coverdale Organisation plc
Dorland House
14–16 Regent Street
London SW1Y 4PH
Tel: 071 925 0099

COVERDALE
on Management

Second edition

MAX TAYLOR
MA, MPhil., FCA, MIPM

BUTTERWORTH
HEINEMANN

Butterworth-Heinemann Ltd
Linacre House, Jordan Hill, Oxford OX2 8DP

 PART OF REED INTERNATIONAL BOOKS

OXFORD   LONDON   BOSTON
MUNICH   NEW DELHI   SINGAPORE   SYDNEY
TOKYO   TORONTO   WELLINGTON

First published 1979
Reprinted 1987
Second edition 1992

British Library Cataloguing in Publication Data
Taylor, Max
    Coverdale on management. – 2Rev.ed
    I. Title
    658

ISBN 0 7506 0150 7

Composition by Genesis Typesetting, Laser Quay, Rochester, Kent
Printed and bound in Great Britain by Billings & Sons Ltd, Worcester

Contents

Foreword by Sir John Harvey-Jones   vii
Preface   ix
Acknowledgements and sources   xi

Part 1   INTRODUCTION

1 The development of Coverdale training   3
2 Training – theory and practice   11

Part 2   THEMES OF COVERDALE LEARNING

3 Discovering purpose   29
4 Purpose and action   37
5 A systematic approach   53
6 Observation   65
7 Process planning and skills   70
8 Listening   81
9 Authority and leadership   87
10 Building on success   99

Part 3   ORGANIZATION DEVELOPMENT

11 The need for change   113
12 Managing an OD project   119
13 The process consultant   128
14 Functional training – workshops, leadership,
    negotiation, project management   137

Part 4   THE THEMES IN ACTION

15 Some detailed problems   149
16 Coverdale on the shop floor – Whitbread Cheltenham
    and Shell Carrington   162
17 Architects and scientists – John Brunton and
    Courtaulds Research   171
18 Work with children's charities   180
19 Coverdale and education   190
20 Bangladesh – the agricultural management
    development programme   199
21 Training across frontiers – ICI and
    'Hygrowth Electric'   206

Appendixes
I   Charting   211
II   Human behaviour and purposes   216
III   Some results of training   218
IV   Coverdale, ethics and Christianity   222

Further reading   225

Index   227

Foreword by Sir John Harvey-Jones

In the late 1960s, I was faced with a major problem of remotivating a disparate group of managers who desperately needed to be formed into a coherent team. It was plain to me that the probable solution lay in some form of joint training exercise and I, therefore, looked at every training system that I could find in Europe and America. Luckily for me, I alighted upon the Coverdale system which had been developed by Ralph Coverdale himself in order to ensure that managers would actually manage. Quite apart from the fact that the training majored on teamwork and cooperation, which were problems that I faced then, and which are even more prevalent today, the attraction of the Coverdale system was that it was heavily action orientated and could be adapted to the needs of any organization. It also incorporated a system of continuous learning, something which is now broadly recognized as being a necessity but in those days was considered to be a novel thought. It was, moreover, British in as much as it did not promise success from a programme, but rather that the continuous application of principles of self-improvement for individuals and organizations would lead to better operations. The Coverdale course also involved some sensitivity training, some training in the necessity and art of listening, and lessons in the fact that everyone has a value and can contribute in their own unique way.

I found the theory of the course and my actual experience with it entirely congruent with my own values and ideas and indeed it played an important part in the development of them. Many of the ideas which were novelties in the 1960s are now accepted as truism. Nobody, for example, would seriously dispute that industry and business face major problems of change, and that the limitation on change is the ability of individuals to maintain and improve their skills. Nobody would now contend that business is a one-man band. Progress is made by working together as groups and ensuring that the skills and abilities of every man and woman are involved for the achievement of the common aim.

In common with its philosophy and beliefs Coverdale training has adapted and developed its techniques over the years. These have been applied in many organizations in Britain and elsewhere, and some of the more recent ones are described in this book. There is no question that technology offers major new opportunities, but the usage of these opportunities depends totally on developing the human skills of management. The need for the lessons which can be learned from working with Coverdale have not diminished in any way.

I share their dream to change the face of British industry and make it more effective by motivating and inspiring every man and woman in it. I hope you will find this Coverdale book on management as useful to you in your chosen career, as I have found their ideas to be for me during my business career.

Sir John Harvey-Jones

Preface

The purpose of this book is to improve the performance of people at work.

It describes the work of Ralph Coverdale – both the methods of training and organization development that he and his colleagues devised, and the training's content.

Ralph Coverdale, who died in 1975, was in turn a Jesuit novice, a soldier, a psychologist, and a management consultant. In this last role he founded the Coverdale Organisation, which since his death has continued to prosper, and whose clients have included bodies such as the World Bank and the International Monetary Fund, as well as many major companies, some of which are the subject of detailed case studies here. The training has been experienced by over 100,000 managers in a dozen countries, and this is a full-length description of its methods and effects.

The book can be used by an individual manager as a guide to improving his own work, or that of his team: it can also be used by those responsible for improving the performance of an organization as a whole.

The basic content of the training is not knowledge, but skill – skill in teamwork, planning and other aspects of getting a job done. The emphasis is on the things a manager has to do every day or every week. It is not so difficult to buy in advisers, and get grand strategy right; but the most significant way in which thriving companies differ from ailing ones is in their greater effectiveness all the way down the line, at low levels and in the management of specific detailed activities. It is in this that the book may help.

Acknowledgements and sources

My main source in writing this book is the continuing tradition of Coverdale Training, the course notes (written by Ralph Coverdale and others) and the verbal inputs given by many course directors and coaches. More data has come from interviews with Coverdale consultants who have particular knowledge or experience.

The next most valuable source has been the papers left by Ralph Coverdale, including complete drafts for two books (one on philosophy and one on team formation in sport), some chapters of a third, and the texts of a number of addresses given to courses and conferences. I have drawn on these particularly for the history of the training (Chapter 1) and for some of the themes of training (especially Chapters 5 to 9).

I am most grateful to the companies who have allowed me to use their material for the various case studies, and to the people in them who have given such kind and tolerant consideration to the various drafts. I would like to thank especially in The Children's Society, Ian Sparks; in Courtaulds, David Giachardi; in ICI Europe, Peter Pay; in the London Borough of Greenwich, Rod Sharman; in the London Borough of Newham, Christine Archer; in the NSPCC, Christopher Brown, and in Whitbread, David Hudson.

Among those connected with the Coverdale Organisation, I should like to thank in particular Bernard Babington Smith. He was co-inventor with Ralph Coverdale of the system of training from which the material in the book is drawn and has done much valuable work since, particularly in the field of organization development. He gave me a mass of perceptive notes and comments on drafts of the book. Among my other colleagues it is very difficult to single out individuals for thanks, since all have helped in some way, but those who read the draft and made suggestions or those from whom I obtained particularly valuable points include Harry Barnes, Tony Birbeck, Leonard Bridge, David Claridge, Wally Cork, Christopher Coverdale, Denis Cummings, Gavin Duncan, Robert Gordon, Jack

Forester, Elaine Gold, Olwen Haslam, Peter Harris, Rosemary Jackson, Nancy James, Candace Keenan, Ian Keenan, Kevin McCourt, Dwilla Mortimore, John Nye, Hilary Pinder, Jill Revie, David Robinson, Carrie Spender, Basil Thatcher, Alan Thomas, Alan Trotter, John Waterston and Gary Willis.

This book is an interpretation of many people's experiences. While there is nothing here with which I disagree, I have tried to give a fair picture of the views of Ralph Coverdale and his colleagues.

London   *Max Taylor*

PART 1

Introduction

1   The development of Coverdale training

And art made tongue-tied by Authority,
And Folly, doctor-like, controlling Skill,
And simple Truth miscall'd Simplicity,
And captive Good attending captain Ill.
                                        Shakespeare, *Sonnet 66*

- Why do meetings go on for ever, circling round a problem without getting to a decision?
- Why are mistakes repeated by mature people, who learn nothing by the experience?
- Why are staff afraid to speak their minds – or if they do, no notice is taken?
- Why are elaborate schemes devised, which anyone could see won't work?
- Why do people who have to co-operate, go on wrangling over trifles?
- Why don't staff hear what you tell them?
- Why are petty failures crawled over with a magnifying glass – and successes neither examined nor praised?

The purpose of this book is to suggest answers to questions like these, and point to practical ways forward. Its main theme is *getting things done in co-operation with other people*. A second theme is *learning from experience*, based on the analysis of success.

Why 'Coverdale on management'?

Ralph Coverdale was a pioneering psychologist and philosopher, who died in 1975. 'Coverdale' is the name both of the system of training he developed, and of the organization he founded – now a flourishing international consultancy. The courses concentrate on ways of working together, and methods of getting the job done; the only aspect of a manager's job that is excluded is professional expertise – accountancy, engineering, sales, teaching, or whatever. Coverdale learning is not so much concerned with management policy, as with management *behaviour* – setting objectives, briefing subordinates, tackling a job that must be done.

This may sound of secondary importance, but it can make the difference between a good manager and a bad one, or between potential fulfilled and a stunted career.

Although the training was originally designed for managers, it is now used far more widely. Its method is to put groups of people into a situation that simulates working life, and encourage them to experiment and build up a repertoire of successful practices. From the start of Coverdale training (over 30 years ago) it became clear that successive training groups were rediscovering the same working methods, and these repeated 'discoveries' were codified by Ralph and his colleagues. Moreover methods that worked in training proved to be just as successful in real life; clients could transplant them back to the work place, and do their job more effectively as a result. The training has now been undergone by over 100,000 men and women, and this book reflects their combined experience.

If the training is valuable for individuals, it is even more powerful when a whole team is trained. A systematic project (as described in several case studies) can transform the behaviour of a whole organization. Projects of this sort, and work with boards of directors, have led to Coverdale's methods being applied to questions of systems and strategy. Here the huge advantage of training-based consultancy is that the consultant does not impose his own ideas on the client: rather he helps clients to apply principles learnt on the course to their own problems. The outcome is the client's own, created with his own local knowledge (which is bound to be greater than that of an outsider); the client understands the reasons that underlie the solution, and is committed to making it work.

Coverdale training started in large companies (Esso, ICI, Unigate) but its use has spread far beyond them. Case studies describe its use with charities, with professional firms, inside a research department, and on a huge development project in the Third World. Recently its use has spread to the world of education, not only with officers and head teachers, but even with children themselves. Indeed the methods described here are universal: the same kinds of skill are needed by a managing director handling his board, a foreman handling his shift, or a teacher handling an awkward child (or *vice versa*!); and the most striking evidence for this is that they can all be trained in the same fundamental way.

Ralph Coverdale was trained as a Jesuit, and in his work he was expressing strong moral convictions, which he bequeathed to the organization he founded. One conviction was the duty to help people fulfil their potential; another was the value of co-operation – people who set out to help each other will often find a far more valuable solution than if they act as rivals or impose their will on the other side. However, the choice of whether to co-operate, compete or dominate is theirs: a trainer's job is not to impose values, but to enable clients to do what they want, in the light of well-thought-out and consistent aims. (The argument is discussed further in

Appendix IV, in the sermon preached by A. L. Birbeck at Ralph Coverdale's memorial service.)

Why write a book?

Coverdale training concentrates on developing skill, enabling participants to apply what they have learnt. Unfortunately, though you can learn understanding from a book, you cannot easily learn skill. However, not all management principles need skill to apply – some things can just be done (see, for example, the aiming techniques in Chapters 3 and 4), while new skills can be developed on one's own by trying things out, reviewing and improving. Other readers may be less interested in improving their management performance than in finding out about training methods, or developing organizations as a whole.

Ralph Coverdale and his work

Ralph was one of the most striking and influential figures England has produced since the Second World War; yet to the public, and even the business world, he was almost unknown. A hundred thousand men and women, most of them in positions of authority, have undergone his training, and few of them have not been influenced by it. But Ralph never published a book and had no talent for publicity, and his attention was absorbed by the product and organization he founded.

Ralph Coverdale was born in 1918. He was educated by the Jesuits at Beaumont College and went to Heythrop College in Oxfordshire, with a view to becoming a Jesuit novice. In 1942, however, he left the college and went into the army, serving in the 10th King's Royal Rifle Corps. He stayed in the army until 1947, when he left with the rank of captain. It will be seen that until he was 30 Ralph's life was spent in organizations where direction is laid down from the top, and which are distinguished for obedience and discipline.

In 1947 he went up to St Catherine's College, Oxford, to read psychology. There he was on varied terms with his tutors. One of them said to him, 'You'll only get a third, but you might do quite well as a social worker.' In fact he got his diploma with distinction and went on to take an advanced degree. In 1950 he came down from Oxford, and spent 5 years working for a number of organizations in the fields of opinion surveys and psychological research. Finally he joined the Steel Company of Wales as Executive Development Officer, and his life's work began.

How Coverdale came to develop his training is described below. After 5 years with the Steel Company of Wales, he transferred to Esso Petroleum, as Head of Management Studies, and spent 4 years developing his courses until they reached approximately their present form. In 1965 he and Esso realized that the company could not absorb all his energies. He set up on his own, with Esso as his first client, and developed what is now the Coverdale Organization.

Ralph's last activity as a manager was in October 1974, when he visited the United States to inaugurate a series of courses for clients that included the World Bank, the International Monetary Fund, the Governmental Affairs Institute, and the United Nations Development Programme. On his return he was affected by a series of blinding headaches, for which no explanation could be found. Eventually lung cancer was diagnosed, and he died in February 1975, aged 56.

The development of Coverdale training

In 1955 Ralph was given a broad brief to set up an executive development programme for the Steel Company of Wales. With the help of his department head, Kenneth Dauncey, he began to survey the difficulties that executives in the company seemed to find in doing their job.

The first problem was a human one. The company tended to promote the best technical steelmakers to be managers, but they seemed to find it hard to realize they were not managing steel but people. One symptom of this was a constant demand for better staff: 'four good men – and they must be technical graduates, with industrial experience'. The company was spending a fortune on recruitment and was full of able young graduates. Coverdale was daunted by the prospect of taking on still more, to make the grim transition from university to working on equal terms with supervisors who had less education but far more skill in getting people to work for them. What managers needed was to recognize the strength of the staff they already had, and make proper use of them.

A second problem was that managers seemed unable to free themselves from the immediate pressure of work, and take a long view of their job. However much they were pressed by their seniors to think ahead, there never seemed to be time.

Managers, then, needed two kinds of skill: first, in handling human relations in their work groups; second, in organizing themselves – becoming more aware of long-term problems, knowing when to act, when to ask permission first, and when to spend more time planning. What they certainly did not need was more teaching in their own technology, for they were already highly competent. In fact the only difficulty they seemed to find here was in presenting their ideas logically, so as to gain the support of their seniors.

Obviously a training programme to fit these problems would be very different from the usual sequence of lecture and study. What had to be put across was *skill*; and this could only come through practical experience. Yet it is evident that experience on its own does not necessarily teach anything at all. You can find people on report-writing courses who have been writing bad reports for 15 years, and experience has done nothing to help them write better ones. What these managers needed was to *learn how to learn* – to acquire the actual skill of learning, so that they would go on improving, even after they left the training course and were back at work.

There had been a lot of research on how to convey technical knowledge, but very little on how to teach skill. While Ralph was casting around for sources of ideas, he attended a seminar on group dynamics, and this led him to look at the systems known as 'sensitivity training' and 'T-groups'.

Sensitivity training was originally a development of psychoanalysis – the theory and treatment of mental illness devised by Sigmund Freud. The purpose of psychoanalysis is to help the patient gain an understanding of himself, his drives, and the difficulties he has in expressing them. The assumption is that this understanding will give such a release of tension that he will be able to face life maturely. Originally psychoanalysts treated mental patients one at a time, but during the Second World War there were so many men in need of treatment for battle fatigue and other psychological disturbance that the small number of analysts began to treat them in groups. Soon it was found that this method was not at all a second-class substitute, for the cures were both quicker and seemed to last longer than with the traditional form of psychotherapy. After the war the work was developed for other purposes, including training managers. The student was placed in a group of strangers, and encouraged to dwell on his feelings about himself and the group, in order to develop self-understanding.

Ralph was convinced that, for training line managers, a small group was the right medium. After all, every manager is bound to interact with at least one subordinate, and with colleagues and superiors as well; in each of these relationships he is part of a team working with other people to achieve a result. But Ralph came to see that for his purposes T-groups and sensitivity training had grave drawbacks:

1 They concentrated on looking backwards, and analysing the past; but a manager's job is to look ahead, and make sure that action takes place.
2 They concentrated entirely on feelings. Feelings are of course extremely important, and have to be taken into account, but a manager is more concerned with thinking and doing than with emotions. He has to be pretty ruthless with his own feelings, and occasionally with other people's as well.
3 Analysis of feelings can put a lot of pressure on people taking part. At best it may be embarrassing; at worst it can do real harm.

Coverdale and Dauncey spent a year trying to find a training course which used the positive aspects of group training – giving managers a chance to talk through their problems – but which avoided the danger of leaving groups glooming for too long over the past. In the end they decided that, with their knowledge of the steel industry, they could tackle the job best themselves. But they needed a reliable psychologist to help them design the pattern of training. (They also felt a need for some academic respectability, since what they wanted to do, however well thought out, might have seemed rather odd.) Accordingly, Ralph approached Bernard Babington Smith, who had given him tuition at Oxford. Ralph had been struck by Bernard's work on the nature of human perception, and knew him as a man of quiet wisdom, not too readily influenced by current fashions of thinking. He also knew that Bernard was prepared to take his work out of the laboratory and into the real world, where not every factor can be controlled.

When he was approached for help, Bernard was attracted by the problem, but was not sure that academic psychology had a great deal yet to offer. Like Ralph, he had doubts about using psychotherapeutic methods for training managers. He agreed, however, to design and carry out some demonstrations in the fields of observation and perception that might be relevant to managers, e.g. on methods of solving problems, and the reliability of eyewitness reports.

The first courses were made up of group work, demonstrations and lectures. The group sessions were almost unstructured. The lectures dealt with psychological matters such as personality, and the prevention of accidents. The first attempts were not easy. It was found that if a group went on trying to talk through problems without doing anything about them, it could lead to frustration, and so to aggression. Sometimes several people would pick on one member to criticize, and the victim might not be able to handle it. At one of the earliest courses, at Avoncroft, Bernard remembers a frightening case of this, when Ralph had to sit up for two nights with a man whom the rest had attacked. Clearly this would not do: it is one thing to put volunteers through this sort of thing as part of a scientific experiment, or even to treat a patient in this way if it is going to help his cure, but it is quite wrong to send a manager on a course as part of his job, and then expect him to start rummaging around in his own motives and feelings.

Luckily there was another way forward. As part of his initial research, Ralph had spent much time observing and talking to those managers who were generally reckoned to be first class, to find out what they actually did. The paradox was that very often the most effective managers could not explain how they operated; and those who were definite in their ideas about management tended not to be the best. The impression he got was that good management did not mean sticking to any particular set of rules, but choosing the right approach for the particular situation. Could this be the way to train managers – to allow them to try out different styles in a variety of contexts, and judge the effectiveness for themselves? They would need to experiment in situations where the risk was low, so that if anyone made a fool of himself, it would not cost the company much money. Why not do this on a training course? The trainees could be given a job to do – one with a result that they could assess, rather than merely a case study.

Accordingly, on the next course, three groups were given the task 'State the principles of good management'. The job allowed little enough action, but its effect on morale was remarkable. As soon as the members of the group were able to break out from inconclusive discussion to a task with an end-product, their frustration disappeared. More tasks were soon improvised, all with the same result; and Bernard recalls coming into a yard and seeing a training group at work washing cars, but looking like people who have just announced their engagement.

Ralph's transfer to Esso led to further developments. By this time the courses were engendering plenty of enthusiasm, and people felt they were learning. The trouble was that when they got back to work, they had great difficulty in applying the new lessons – or even in explaining them to other people. Ralph and Bernard cast around for a way of helping, and finally concluded that they could never foretell precisely what difficulties people would meet when they got back. The best hope was to equip them with a general method for tackling whatever came up. Ralph wanted to find a way in which people could develop their ability to learn from experience, while Bernard had ideas on the need to alternate thought with action. Combining their ideas, they evolved 'a Systematic Approach to Getting Things Done', which is described in Chapter 5 and is now a main strand in Coverdale learning.

It was found on the early courses that people could get so wrapped up in the small tasks they were set that they were incapable of learning; indeed Ralph felt that he himself learned more by watching from the sideline. The answer seemed to be to pull out students in turn, give them a chance to observe their colleagues, and feed back suggestions for improvement. Since then this has always been done, and is one of the most valuable learning experiences. It gives the student a chance to take an overview of the team's progress, and suggest ways of working together more effectively – precisely as a good manager does for his department.

At Esso the objectives of the course gradually evolved. At the beginning the emphasis had been on 'forming a group'. A change came from the introduction of tasks, when people were encouraged to form not merely a group but a team, capable of setting and achieving objectives. However, it was obvious that teams formed on courses were going to break up as soon as the week was over; the point must be to equip each individual with the skills of teamwork that he could use when he got back to work. But in most industrial environments a team is not self-contained, but carries out its functions within a wider organization. Too tight a team can be a menace, if the people in it are blind to the needs of outsiders. In any case, most managers work in several teams, and switch from one to another quite rapidly. Accordingly, a second training course was designed, one in which members move from group to group, practising their skills in each of them.

During 1964 the concept of a 'project' was developed. The idea was that if the learning helped individuals, it would have an even stronger effect if it was shared by all the members of a department, unit or organization. The first project, in which some 300 people took part, was launched in 1964 at the Irish Refining Company's plant at Whitegate; and it was followed in the next year by a much larger project at Esso's refinery at Fawley.

2   Training – theory and practice

Psychology is a science, and teaching is an art: and sciences never generate arts directly out of themselves.

William James, *Lectures to teachers*

Psychology and human development

To understand how original Ralph's work was, one must recall the state of psychology in the 1950s and 1960s★. There were several competing schools – trait psychology, psychoanalysis and behaviourism – as well as a widespread assumption that 'attitudes' were the real determinants of behaviour. These theories conflicted with each other, but about the one thing they could all have agreed on was that Ralph's approach would make no real difference to the way clients behaved. (Trait psychologists, for example, maintained that personality was too stable to be seriously affected by training; psychoanalysts that training was tinkering with symptoms, rather than dealing with real causes.)

Ralph's approach was anything but naive; he was a trained psychologist, and had regular discussions with Bernard Babington-Smith at Oxford. However, he consciously chose an older model of behaviour – that derived from his Jesuit training, and ultimately from Aristotle. He believed that behaviour depended largely on habits, which could be changed for better ones, through personal planning backed up by review. He believed in the importance of qualities like courage, determination and a sense of justice, which we might call 'virtues' (or 'character strengths', to use a name with less misleading overtones). Above all he believed in the importance of free will: people could choose their own behaviour – for example, whether to compete or co-operate – and use skills and intellect to put their choice into practice. It must have taken unusual stubbornness or genius to follow this line of development, when the weight of scientific opinion argued the opposite.

We can see now that the theories of the 1950s were, if not wrong, at least so much over-simplified as to be seriously misleading. (They are still

★ For references for psychological points discussed in this section, see p. 25.

influential today, since some of their assumptions underlie a good deal of training and counselling.) They have, however, been largely superseded by later research, particularly by the discoveries known as 'social learning theory', and the work of David McClelland and others on psychological needs.

Social learning theory is an adaptation of behaviourism, and its findings are now generally accepted. Unlike trait psychology, it argues that personality is not particularly stable, and can be modified by many kinds of experience. Unlike old-fashioned behaviourism, it recognizes that the way people behave is largely determined by what goes on in their minds. The most important factors are:

1 *Expectations* – what people think they will gain or lose.
2 *Competences* – the range of things that they are able to do.
3 The way they *interpret* their experience of the world.
4 The *systems and plans* they employ for controlling their own behaviour (like getting oneself 'psyched up' for a big occasion).

Successful training can affect all these factors. Its main job is teaching new competences – people learn to do things they couldn't do before – but it can also introduce new systems and plans for self-regulation, and new ways of looking at the world. All three are deliberate components of Coverdale training. In combination, these changes can have a profound effect on people's expectations of whether they will succeed or fail. From the trainer's point of view, the most important conclusion of social learning theory is that behaviour can be profoundly modified, through the development of skill.

A second, complementary, body of research is that initiated by the American psychologist David McClelland, based on the study of *psychological needs*. McClelland worked particularly with the three needs for 'achievement', 'power', and 'affiliation' (i.e. comradeship), all of which are important in working life. Some people are motivated by their need for achievement, and work in order to get worthwhile results. Others enjoy human society and are motivated by the satisfactions of teamwork. Others again are stimulated by the exercise of power, or by related rewards such as status.

These 'needs' are a fairly stable part of personality, but they can be modified by training. McClelland went on to show that they are closely associated with what we have called 'character strengths', such as persistence, courage and justice. He established that a character strength is not, as many psychologists argued, merely a sort of attitude or value; one can *value* achievement very highly, but still not *behave* in an achieving way. Although attitudes obviously have a strong effect on the way people do their jobs, they are not the only determinants; competences, skills and character strengths are at least as important, and more appropriate, targets for training.

Behaviour, then, depends on a number of different factors. One model that fits them all together is based on the three fundamental kinds of human experience – *thinking, doing,* and *feeling* (emotions). Effective behaviour needs a combination of these, turning raw emotions into sensible thoughts, and moving from thought to action. This can be shown by three interlocking circles, as in Figure 2.1.

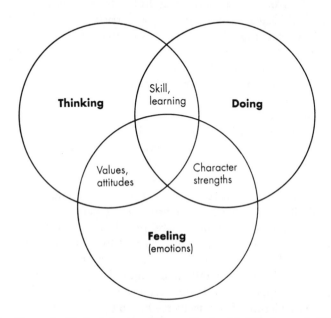

Figure 2.1   *Factors in effective behaviour (Source: Taylor, M. Effectiveness in Education and Training, Avebury, 1990)*

The factors we have been discussing occur where two circles overlap. The overlap between doing and thinking is the area of intelligent action, resulting in learning and skill. The overlap between thinking and feeling is the area of attitudes – you both *think* your job is worthwhile, and *feel* strongly committed to it. The overlap between of feeling and doing is the area of 'character strengths': the feeling of determination is what gets the job done.

Coverdale training is primarily concerned with the thinking and doing circles, and does not directly tackle emotions (except when feelings are running high in a group, so that action gets blocked). However, where a client suffers from emotional problems (such as lack of confidence), the training can often help: first, through the development of a strong training group, in which all participants feel valued; and, second, through giving

practice in learning from experience, which allows participants to tackle
problems of this sort for themselves.

How skill is learnt

Research has also thrown light on why the pattern of training that Ralph
devised proved to be so effective in practice. The main problem with
learning skill is *transfer*: a piece of skilful behaviour learnt on a training
course in a particular group, during a particular task, first has to be
generalized, so that it applies in a range of situations, and then applied on
different kinds of activity back at work. 'Generalizing' the behaviour means
identifying rules or principles that you can follow in a whole range of
situations: 'Always check the car is in neutral before starting the engine';
'Step to the pitch of the ball'; 'If you want people to be committed, explain
what the job is for'.

Transfer has been much studied, and the rules that make for success are
well established. First, the principle which students are to apply must be
taught and recognized as a general one: e.g. *always* check the information
before you start making plans. Students must then practise the principle in a
basic situation until they have mastered it completely, and go on to test it in
a range of different situations, to prove its generality. Students will be
helped by *learning how to learn*, e.g. by practising a method for learning a
whole set of skills. They will also be helped by watching other people in
action, especially if they are made to write down or report back what they
see. Other factors apply generally in changing human behaviour. Change is
more likely to happen when people acquire new aims or values, or where
they get a new picture of themselves – finding they can do something they
thought was impossible, taking on a new role, or coming under the
influence of a new set of people.

These rules are all applied in Coverdale training. New methods of
working are suggested by the course director, or extracted by groups from
their own experience; they are then practised again and again in a variety of
tasks, in the light of a basic learning procedure called Systematic Approach
(see Chapter 5). People are given detailed feedback about their performance,
concentrating on their strengths and successes. As the training group
develops into a strong team, people influence each other and become a new
source of opinions and values on matters of management behaviour.

Although Ralph Coverdale discovered his pattern of working by
informal experiment, theory has now caught up with it, so that its success is
no longer surprising. However, for training to be successful, it is not
enough for it to be psychologically sound; skill is needed, to design and run
the course, and experience (both personal and corporate) to be able to
explain the relevance of the points being made to the people being trained.

Coverdale training today

The Part I course

The central aim of Coverdale training is to help people manage better. The job of managers is getting things done, usually in co-operation with other people, and that situation is built into the basic training course (known as Teamwork Part I, or 'Part I' for short). To enable strong teams to form, each group stays unchanged throughout the course (at least until the closing stages). To enable groups to practise working together, the groups' members carry out a series of tasks, each calling for a certain amount of action, and having an end-product that can be evaluated. To provide the repetition needed to develop skill, tasks are quite short – usually less than an hour. Each task is followed by a review, in which participants examine the way they worked together, and plan to repeat practices that helped, and avoid behaviour that hindered.

The learning comes from the way the members of the group work together – how they agree on an effective approach to the task, and how they combine their talents to build a successful team. People are encouraged to experiment. If some procedure does not work it can be thrown out, while if it proves useful, it can be deliberately used again. In this way people acquire a certain amount of knowledge of human behaviour; but, far more valuably, they begin to build up *habits* of good management that they can develop further at work. Figure 2.2 shows the basic pattern.

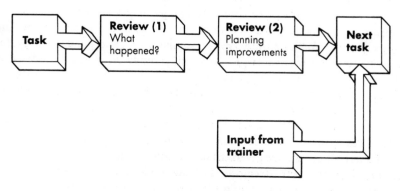

Figure 2.2   *The basic pattern of training*

Kinds of task

A variety of tasks is used to bring out the learning. Apart from the essential needs for action and an end result, tasks must allow discretion, and call for a certain amount of ingenuity. They must also be able to be completed in the fairly short time available, and not need anything too elaborate in the way of equipment or location. Tasks used are concerned with producing small objects (such as paper pads), carrying out surveys, creating artwork or a course newspaper, or acting television advertisements or plays. In a sense, the subject matter of the task is not important, as long as participants are prepared to take it as a challenge. However, experience shows that if participants are given tasks that are directly relevant to their job, they tend to become so caught up in them that they ignore the question of teamwork.

Tasks therefore have a 'neutral' content. This doesn't normally worry managers, who are used to the idea that whether a company makes airliners or ping-pong balls, the job of management will have a great deal in common. However, it sometimes arouses doubts in specialists such as teachers and social workers, who are more apt to regard their problems as unique. But it is essential for them to learn that the principles apply in a range of different tasks and contexts; the *same* cluster of skills are used by a salesman trying to understand the needs of a customer, and a social worker trying to understand a young offender – even though the aims of the discussion and the way the dialogue goes may be very different. Although 'neutral' tasks are always used for the first two or three days, it is possible later on to use tasks that relate to the job, particularly when courses are run in-house for a particular client ('workshops' on this pattern are discussed in Chapter 16).

Training groups

Groups normally consist of five to eight participants, with two to four groups on a course (variant programmes have been developed for dealing with larger or smaller numbers). This makes a group small enough for everyone to take part, and large enough to provide problems of interaction – e.g. people have to agree on aims and procedures, and avoid over-talking. This size of group is also large enough to bring out a differentiation of roles, such as chairman, ideas generator, timekeeper or conciliator. In some well-known work, Meredith Belbin examined the mix of roles that make up a successful team, together with the kind of personality that each role requires (based on the four psychological scales of dominance, intelligence, extrovert – introvert, and emotional–stable). He found that a strong team does not necessarily consist of the ablest people, but the best spread of different types. A team needs, for example, one intelligent and dominant introvert to produce the ideas, but if you have three or four people with this personality, they will find it difficult to stop arguing and move into action. Coverdale does not select groups to conform to Belbin's ideal mix (after all, the training is a preparation for real life, where ideal groups are rare); instead it is the random mix of the group that provides the challenges from which learning comes. If a group has too many ideas, and not enough action, it must do something about it, e.g. persuading the idea-generators to stop competing and agree on one workable idea, perhaps sacrificing a degree of creativity in order to get the job done on time.

The development of a group follows no set pattern. Some groups adopt formal leaders, others choose to work without them. Some are steered by one individual from the start, others remain a democracy. One can go on a course several times and enjoy quite different experiences, depending on the mix of people. These experiences are never wasted: you can learn as much from a docile team as from a rowdy one, from a team with a strong chairman as from a leaderless one. Some (by no means all) of the lessons will be different, but all of them are valid, and will be useful in some management context.

The Part II course

It was recognized early on that the pattern of the Part I course – a team working on its own, with no changes of personnel – corresponds to only part of management life. Much of the time managers move from group to group, playing a different role in each, depending on their position in the hierarchy and the knowledge and expertise they have to contribute. Accordingly a 'Part II' course was designed, in which individuals have more defined roles, and move between groups. This introduces a new range of skills, as well as consolidating the understanding and techniques learned on Part I. Later other courses were added, dealing with specific *applications* of skill, such as leadership, negotiation and project management (see Chapter 11).

Characteristics of training

The courses have certain other characteristics that play an important part in their success. First, they take place away from work, in contexts that are nothing to do with participants' normal business. This means that people can experiment with their own behaviour, and try out things they could not risk doing among their colleagues at work.

The second point is that the issues and results are all real. People easily become absorbed in a game or any other co-operative activity, and the feelings and behaviour that come out of it are as authentic as any that arise in the office or factory. That is why case studies are not used. People who are given a theoretical exercise, ending up with a cliff-hanging decision like 'Do we or don't we sack the marketing manager?', behave quite differently from the way they would in real life. After all, the manager does not really get sacked, market share does not really fall through the floor, and no one has to carry the can. This does not mean that case studies are useless; they are fine for exploring the theoretical effects of a range of options, but they do not develop skill in getting things done.

Thirdly, tasks result in action. People need to spend just so long in planning, before they actually get up and do the job. Planning has to be done, but much of the discussion that goes on in meetings is not real – it is daydreaming, or recrimination, which may satisfy people's feelings, but gets them no nearer action. Action itself is like a cold plunge – fine when you are in, but too easy to put off – and most people need practice in judging the moment to dive.

Groups are helped by a consultant, who is known as the 'coach', which is in fact a precise description of the role. Any skill, from football to management, is acquired most quickly by a mixture of coaching and practice. Learners must experiment, make their own mistakes, find out what does and what does not work. The coach's job is to observe and help them to see what they did that was different, what it was that actually got the football into the net or the task finished on time. Good coaches pay at least as much attention to what went right as to what went wrong. In each case learners must be helped to identify the cause; but harping on mistakes leads people to lose confidence, and often to repeat them. If a disaster happens, the coach must stop the group from delving endlessly into who caused it, and get them to find a way of preventing it from happening again.

Coverdale coaches advise, but do not prescribe what people should learn. Out of the enormous variety of events that can occur when teams are doing tasks, one cannot guarantee that any particular one will crop up, or that it will make any impression on the team if it does. Nearly all the learning is inductive: the coach and the group pull lessons out of what actually happened and devise their own procedures for the future. A few techniques are taught in a conventional way, but each technique is then tested by the group in action, and discarded if its members find for some reason that it does not work. This is the great difficulty of coaching, compared with straightforward teaching, for while teachers can come into their class and deliver a prepared text, confining discussion to what they have talked about, the coach must be ready to respond to whatever occurs – and make the point when the issue is red hot, rather than pull the group's mind back to something that happened two or three minutes before.

Syllabus of skills

The syllabus of the Part I course was built up empirically, over many years: the same issues came up in group after group, until eventually a standard catalogue was established. (This list of skills, together with their underlying principles, is itself a contribution to our understanding of how teams operate.) The main themes that occur on Part I are:

- Clarifying aims.
- Setting measures of success.
- Working methodically.
- Co-operating and getting co-operation.
- Listening.
- Speaking and proposing.
- Reviewing.
- Building on success.
- Planning – to improve one's own contribution, and the way the group works.
- Identifying and using people's talents.
- Leadership and authority.
- Time management.

Each of these broad 'themes' is made up of a number of procedures and principles of behaviour, which are discussed in detail in Chapters 3 to 10.

The Part II course added the themes of motivation and induction; it also has a more formal look at leadership (developed further on the specialized Leadership course), and the co-ordination of separate teams within a hierarchy.

Although the lessons of Coverdale have been applied in many work situations, they are largely derived from experience of courses. How far does this limit their generality? To the extent that the pattern of the training – groups of men and women working together to establish and achieve common objectives – is the basic building brick of the working world, the lessons are universal. There are, however, a number of factors that receive less emphasis on courses than their importance in the world outside might seem to deserve. One of these, financial reward, needs little discussion; although courses do not deal with it directly, they do deal with the reconciliation of group and personal objectives, of which financial reward is normally one. Three other factors need to be considered in more detail: they are *conflict, creativity,* and *competition.*

Conflict

In our society we are used to regarding conflict as inevitable. Many of our institutions – party politics, industrial relations, the conduct of trials – are based on it, and even in civil affairs we have come to admire the fighters rather than the peacemakers and trimmers. It is argued in this book that apparent conflict often masks wide areas of common interest, and that action to achieve the common good can itself take the bitterness out of the conflict, even if it does not resolve it. Within training teams, people naturally have their differences, and valuable learning can come out of resolving them. However, the training does not try to equip people for the more extreme forms of conflict. In some organizations people have to fight or intrigue in order to survive, but these are rare, if only because they do not usually prosper in a competitive market. In any company bitter disputes occasionally blow up, and there are a few individuals who are regularly aggressive or employ underhand methods. Coverdale does not deal with such situations in training (though it may do in individual consultancy), first, because it is hard to design any training that would not risk putting the participants under unacceptable pressure, and, second, because it is not in the interests of any client organization (even if it suited individual staff members) to increase the ability of people to fight each other.

Creativity and thinking skills

The emphasis in Coverdale training is on getting a workmanlike job done, on time, with the resources available. This is what is normally required of middle and junior managers. Lateral thinking is developed (see pp. 42–43) but the thinking skills that receive most emphasis are those of getting from thought to action, rather than engendering radically new ideas. Where highly creative solutions are needed, this is usually in the technical field (of research scientists, designers, engineers, etc.) and creativity will be part of their professional rather than their managerial role. What Coverdale has a lot to say about is the *management* of creative people, and the circumstances that allow creativity to flourish (for the management of scientists and creative workers, see Chapter 17).

Many people believe that conflict is the essence of creativity. Harry Lime in the film of *The Third Man* said something like 'Look at the Italian Renaissance; a hundred years of bloodshed, civil war and treachery produced the greatest works of art that have ever been seen: and what did the Swiss produce in four hundred years of peace and prosperity? The cuckoo clock!' In fact, Harry Lime's history was shaky: the Swiss were too poor and too busy fighting as mercenaries in the thick of every European war to have much time for the arts, while the Florentine Renaissance was built up under the Medici in a period of rare peace and stable, open government.

In fact what engenders creativity is not conflict but contrast – the light thrown on a problem by someone else's way of thought, or the comparison with what they have done. This is more likely to be fruitful in a context of teamwork than in one of conflict or rivalry. One can see this, for example, in the circumstances in which Shakespeare's plays were written – the relationship between patron, poet and a tightly knit team of actors. For an account of this, see Leslie Hotson's *The First Night of Twelfth Night* (Hart-Davis, 1954).

Competition

Co-operation and competition are kinds of behaviour that are often seen as opposites. Some people approve of one or the other on ideological grounds, seeing competition either as wholly destructive, or as the engine of progress. In fact the two are not necessarily so far apart: compared with working on one's own, both competition and co-operation provide excitement, stimulus, and new information. In many situations they are both present: two boxers may be competing like fury, but they are co-operating in keeping the rules and making a match of it. A management team may be a superb example of co-operation, but its members still know that only one of them can succeed to the boss's job. Some of the contrasting effects are shown in Table 2.1.

Table 2.1 *Competition and co-operation*

Effects of competition	*Effects of co-operation*
Cuts out or reduces inefficiency	Pools information and resources
Acts as a spur to action/improvement	Creates synergy
Differentiates, creating contrast and choice	Tends to assimilate (people do the same)
Sets high standards	Creates warmth and (sometimes) complacency
May cause insecurity and stress	
Creates losers	Allows all to be winners
Is sometimes inevitable (only one place in the lifeboat)	Is sometimes essential (we can't move the wagon unless we *all* push)

Coverdale courses do not deliberately make use of competition, although where a number of teams carry out similar tasks, it is apt to creep in. Competition has two great advantages: first, it acts as a motivator; second, it sets standard of performance. However, both benefits can be had by other means: e.g. people who learn to set stretching targets for their own performance can compete just as vigorously against these; and competition certainly makes it more difficult to co-operate, even where co-operation is the key to success. Suppose a tough manager takes over a team of salesmen, and runs it on the basis that the one who sells most gets a bonus, and the one who sells least gets the boot. He may well increase sales very quickly, especially if before he arrived nobody really cared. His policy will cause tale-bearing and jealousy, and a good deal of stress, but he may still get sales. However, if instead he had led the salesmen to co-operate, he would find them reallocating their rounds to give shorter travelling and more selling time; he would find salesmen comparing their approaches and becoming more perceptive at judging how to tackle a particular kind of interview. He might find that one or other of them turned out to be the expert with a particular product or type of customer, and sales blossoming from the proper use of talents.

The drawbacks of competition, and the benefits of co-operation, are strongest among a small group of people. Competition within one department, unless it is treated as a game, can be destructive. Competition between factories or regions may inhibit a useful exchange of ideas, but is less likely to create bitterness or stress. As systems get larger, the benefits of co-operation get less; two heads are better than one, but 100 heads are not that much better than fifty, and the benefit of competition as a setter of standards begins to outweigh its damaging effects as a source of conflict (Figure 2.3). This is particularly true of a whole national or international market, where co-operation between companies (or between producers and trade unions) can only too easily be at the expense of the third party, the general public. One can support a free-enterprise system without wanting to turn the individual firm into a rat-race.

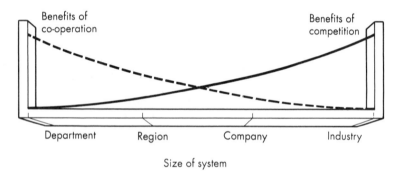

Figure 2.3   *Co-operation v competition*

Self-development and teamwork

In its basic form Coverdale training is about development of individuals (even though the *group* is the vehicle for learning). Many companies send people to be trained in ones or twos, either because they are facing a new challenge, such as promotion, or because their performance is falling short. Through practice in reviewing, these participants learn the skill of continuous self-improvement, and over a period may transform their own management ability. See Figure 2.4.

The training has greater value still as a way of developing *teams*. Sometimes a working team is trained together, which has the advantage of giving them a shared experience. Sometimes, however, people who know

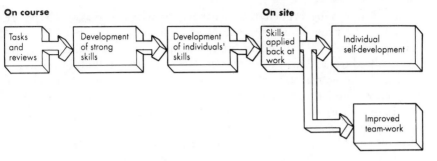

Figure 2.4   *The pattern of development, on and after the course*

each other well may be burdened with assumptions about what their
colleagues can and cannot do, or know each other embarrassingly well, so
that it is better to send individuals on separate courses. Whichever approach
is chosen, there is an extra bonus for the team in which all the members
have been trained. First, members encourage each other to use what they
have learned, and to keep up the standards that were achieved on the course.
Second, they have a common language, and common procedures for
dealing with problems. Third, a trained team is at once a supportive and a
challenging environment: there is a constant search for improvements in the
way the job is done, while people know that if they have problems, their
colleagues will help them. Individuals feel valued, since their particular
abilities are recognized, and they are put in roles where they can shine to the
best advantage.

Systems, strategy and behaviour

These benefits occur on a larger scale where training extends across a whole
organization. Conflicts between groups can be quickly resolved, or if they
spring from some inherent problem in the organization, the people
concerned can themselves take steps to see that the system is changed.
Although Coverdale has wide experience in systems thinking and design, it
has usually found that the best systems work is carried out, with
consultants' help, by participants themselves. After all, they know the facts
and have to live with the results, and it is their aims, not the consultant's,
that will be pursued in action. For these reasons, the bulk of Coverdale's
work is in training entire managerial strata of departments or companies,
including the board of directors; and though the skills that senior managers
and directors learn from Coverdale may sometimes be simple ones, the
resulting improvement in board performance has a striking impact on
policy.

Indeed it can be argued that whenever companies make bad policy decisions, the usual cause is not intellectual misjudgement but defects of management *behaviour*: directors are too arrogant to listen to their staff, too disorganized to have time to master the facts, or lack the skills of clarifying aims and setting realistic targets. Coverdale would argue that faults like these *always* underlie the well-known occasions of corporate disaster that feature in the case studies of business schools. Business education would be more useful if, instead of aiming to teach strategy, it concentrated on the way in which managers should conduct themselves. Often the grand decisions are not all that important; where there is a choice of equally attractive alternatives, any one of them can be made to work, provided it is carried through with consistency, realism, and above-average mastery of the basic elements of management behaviour. It is this mastery that Coverdale aims to develop.

To sum up, training can bring the following benefits:

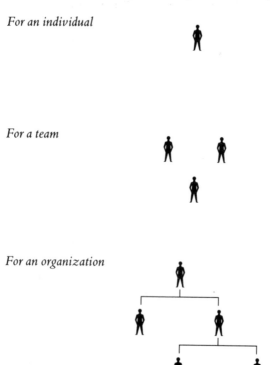

For an individual

- Personal skill.
- Self-knowledge.
- Self-development.
- Insight into other people (aims and skills).

For a team

- Common language.
- Common approach to problems.
- Establishing common aims.
- Appreciation of individuals' skills.

For an organization

- Self-improvement of team.
- Common language and approach to problems.
- Corporate aims and values.
- Encouraging staff to grow.
- Self-improvement of systems and strategies.

Sources of psychological statements

For social learning theory, see Bandura, A. (1977) *Social Learning Theory*, New Jersey: Prentice-Hall. For factors that determine behaviour, see Mischel, W. (1973) *Towards a Cognitive Social Learning Conceptualisation of Personality*, Psychological Review, pp. 252 ff. For the factors in effective behaviour (and the three circle diagram), see Taylor, C. M. K. (1990) *Effectiveness in Education and Training*, Aldershot: Gower Publishing. For transfer of learning see Ellis, H. C. (1965) *The Transfer of Learning*, New York: Macmillan. For behaviour change generally, see Atkinson, R. L., Atkinson, R. C., and Hilgard, E. R. (1983) *Introduction to Psychology*, 8th edition, San Diego: Harcourt Brace Jovanovich. For psychological needs, see McClelland, D. C., Atkinson, J. W., Clarke, R. A., and Lowell, E. L. (1953) *The Achievement Motive*, New York: Appleton-Century-Crofts; and McClelland, D. C., and Winter, D. (1969) *Motivating Economic Achievement*, New York: The Free Press. For achievement skills and character strengths, see McClelland, D. C. (1975) *Power, the Inner Experience*, New York: Wiley.

PART 2

Themes of Coverdale Learning

Managers, or almost anyone with a responsible job to do, need four main kinds of skill:

1 The professional expertise of their job – accountancy, marketing, teaching or whatever.
2 Setting direction – establishing the purpose of what they are doing and the stages of getting there.
3 Working methodically.
4 Giving and gaining co-operation.

Professional expertise is not dealt with here, but the last three types of skill are the main themes of Coverdale training, and are dealt with in Part 2. Chapters 3 and 4 deal with setting direction, Chapter 5 with a methodical way of working, and Chapters 7 and 9 with improving co-operation, by deliberate planning and by the use of authority and leadership. Chapters 6 and 8 deal with observation and listening – the essential feedback from other people which makes it possible to co-operate with them. Chapter 10 deals more generally with the way to develop these skills, by the deliberate analysis and reproduction of success.

For most managers, professional life includes both working on one's own, and being part of a team. However, most of life falls between these extremes – you encounter other people, with whom you have to collaborate, negotiate, and occasionally dispute. The skills discussed in this section apply in any sort of interpersonal transaction, and many of them (particularly those discussed in Chapters 3–5, and 10) apply to solo work as well.

These themes are dealt with largely in the context of one manager and his immediate working group – his own boss, peers and subordinates. Within these relationships, the principles one needs to follow are very much the same, whether the work group consists of a foreman and a gang of labourers, a chairman and a board of directors, or a convener and a group of shop stewards. The wider context of management – the development and use of these skills throughout an organization – is dealt with in Part 3, 'Organization Development'.

Part 2 does not attempt to give a complete survey of the human side of management. Because of the manner in which Coverdale experience has been built up, there are gaps in the subjects covered. There is nothing here about remuneration, not much about long-term planning or career development. The emphasis is on those things that a manager has to do every day or every week, rather than on the decisions of grand strategy. This is after all what most of managerial life consists of, even for people at the highest levels.

The emphasis is strongly on teamwork. This is partly because of the way Coverdale's experience has been built up, partly because good teamwork requires all the skills of collaboration in their highest form. The main reason, however, is that good teamwork gives one of the highest assurances of an organization's success. When companies fail, it may on the surface be because of bad strategic decisions, guessing the market wrong, etc. But underlying bad decisions, there is nearly always bad management practice, and/or lack of skill: being unclear about aims, too busy to review the facts, or too arrogant to listen. One man on his own is never going to get everything right – he is not a universal expert, and he doesn't have all the skills. But a good team, working to common aims, and sharing information and responsibilities, will have few weak points; and an organization in which teamwork is strong, all the way up to board level, will have the same virtues. It must be noted that though strong teams do in fact create emotional bonds, this is not what the book is mainly about: teamwork is created by *skill*, and its main effect is that the joint skills and abilities of all concerned are aimed at the most pressing and fundamental problems.

3   Discovering purpose

I want it, these are my orders: for what purpose? My pleasure!
Juvenal, *Satire* vi.

Aiming and foresight

Almost anything we do has a purpose. Sometimes we begin with the purpose in mind and deliberately plan what action we should take towards achieving it. More often perhaps, action is the starting-point: we know what needs doing – because we are told, because it is obvious, or because we do it every day. It can sometimes be vital to ask ourselves, 'Why?' Is what we have always done still valid? Does the obvious step really help us in the direction we want to go? Committees continue to meet regularly, reports are written and circulated, years after the purpose for which they were started has ceased to be valid (or even to be remembered at all).

A note on terminology

The terms in which we talk about aims are often confused, and vary from speaker to speaker and from company to company; for that reason, it is often safer in conversation to replace a single word by a phrase. I shall use the various terms as follows:

1 *Task.* The immediate job we are tackling. What we have chosen or been ordered to do.
2 *Purpose.* Why the job is being tackled: 'I am doing this job *in order to* . . .' The purpose is usually outside and beyond the job itself, and may be a continuing need ('in order to satisfy hunger') or a long-term objective ('in order to win the war').
3 *Objective.* A specific end-point, whose achievement fulfils or contributes towards the purpose. An objective may be a subdivision of the task, or the task may merely contribute towards a longer-term objective.
4 *End-product.* A description of what will have been achieved when the job is done (a clean floor; a fifty-page typed report, dealing with . . .).

5 *Success measure.*★ A visible sign or indication that success has been achieved – preferably something that can be quantified (a 10 per cent increase in sales).
6 *Target.* A broad term, including 3, 4, and 5.
7 *Aims.* A general term, covering all the above.

How aims arise

Aims arise from some stimulus or piece of information that makes us feel that action is necessary. One of the recurrent human drives (like hunger) may erupt into consciousness, or fresh information may make corrective action necessary, or call a brand new aim into existence. When Rutherford was asked what made him take up physics, he replied that he first became interested as a boy, when watering cattle in New Zealand. He noticed that where a stick enters the water it appears bent, and wanted to find out why. Similarly, if someone overhears a Stock Exchange tip, it may trigger off a latent desire to make money.

In employment, the most usual stimulus is that higher management wants something done. In itself this is only information; one cannot wish an aim into someone else's mind, and we can all choose whether or not to adopt our superior's aims as our own. A piece of information becomes an aim when one feels impelled to do something about it. In any job requiring co-operation, the normal sequence is: information $\longrightarrow$ formulation of aim $\longrightarrow$ commitment of those taking part.

Aims and timescale

Aiming needs foresight and imagination, and people differ widely in how complex a chain of cause and effect they can imagine, and how far they can think ahead. If you ask several people to identify the purpose of some activity, they may come up with a range of answers, some relating to the immediate future, some two years or twenty years ahead. The directors of a company decide to carry out a survey of salaries. If they were asked the purpose, their answers might be:

1 To let us know what people earn
2 To bring our salaries in line with the market
3 To prevent staff leaving because they are underpaid
4 To make sure we have a pool of able middle management, from which we can select the next generation of directors.

★ Or 'success criterion'. Strictly speaking, the criterion is the kind of result in terms of which the measure is expressed. If the criterion is 'profit', the measure may be a 20 per cent increase within six months.

These are all valid answers, and in fact all perfectly compatible with each other; but there is scope for misunderstanding between the someone who thinks three months ahead in terms of answer 1 and the someone who thinks ten years ahead in terms of answer 4.

Some people find it hard to give a clear picture of where they want to be even 24 hours ahead. Their symptom is a constant manoeuvring to deal with the here and now, which makes them good at improvisation, but very bad at holding direction. They may be able and honest, but their constant changes of tack make them seem devious, since one assumes that they have some deep purpose. Ralph Coverdale himself was at the other extreme, with a disconcerting tendency to think over a very long timescale. For example, Ralph might say, 'What we need is a full-time man on promoting sales.' The consultant who was doing the job part-time, and naturally felt threatened, might reply, 'But we're fully booked for the next three months.' It might take some probing to discover that Ralph was envisaging a much bigger company 3 years ahead.

Open and closed aims

Just as objectives can be nearer or further into the future, so they can be more or less certain, definite or 'closed'. 'To set up a production line for our *XY* engine' is a fairly closed objective; 'to design a successor for our *XY* engine' is rather more open; 'to find a new product' is more open still. Objectives can be 'open' in a number of different ways:

1 Where you are not clear about the *purpose*. Take, for example, an instruction to 'carry out an opinion survey and find what the staff really want'. Is the purpose to decide the next pay rise, or to design the new canteen?
2 Where you are not clear about the *method*. 'You'll just have to make the shop steward co-operate.' Yes, I know exactly what you want, but how?
3 Where you are not clear on what the end-product will look like, or how much is expected. 'I want much more profit from this branch.' Is £1000 satisfactory – or £2000 – or £5000?

Openness may be caused by the nature of the job itself (for example, when one is breaking new ground) or by the imprecision of the instructions. It also depends on the training and experience of the person doing the job. I might see getting my car to start as a highly open task, but a trained mechanic will have routine procedures. If someone is faced with an open task which they cannot close down, the effect is that they do not know where to start. There will probably be indecision, frustration, and eventually a drop in morale. A good deal of the art of management consists of closing down open objectives (both for oneself and one's subordinates) and the next chapter deals with some ways of doing this.

Instructions an.' purpose

After the 1966 seamen's strike, a commission was set up to enquire into their pay and conditions. One day the general manager of a shipping company received an enquiry from the commission: 'How long do your ships spend in port?' As it happened, the head of the section that kept the records was out, but in his absence his staff got on with it. Now ships are 'at sea' only while steaming from sea-buoy to sea-buoy, and all the rest of the time counts as 'in port', which therefore includes steaming time in harbour, time at anchor, time in the Suez Canal, as well as the fairly short periods spent alongside. So, a great deal of work was necessary. When the section head got back, he was told what was going on. He rang the general manager and asked why? The general manager said that really he had no idea. The commission wanted it, so be a good chap. The section head got on to the secretary of the commission and asked what the purpose was. He was told, 'To find out what opportunities seamen have for going ashore.' 'But even while they're alongside,' he said, 'seamen are far too busy to leave the ship. The answer, for your purpose, is "none".'

This sort of aimless instruction is very common – partly perhaps because until recent years, standards were set by managers who had served in the forces, where you do not ask why. In civil life, in the rare cases when you cannot tell a man the purpose of a job (for reasons of secrecy or whatever) you need to give him extremely precise and detailed instructions, which he cannot misinterpret.

Lack of aims is most dangerous when the briefing is in writing, so that there is no chance to ask. Instructions for manufactured goods are often at fault in this way. 'After use, it is essential to rinse thoroughly with Barker's Patent Sludge.' 'Essential' for what purpose? What happens if I don't? And (given that the shops are shut) won't anything else do instead?

The other important question in framing instructions is the level of training. If someone has done or practised a job many times before, he will have the right response at his fingertips; giving him the instruction will be merely flipping a switch. An important use of training is to make unfamiliar tasks familiar, turn open tasks into closed ones, and make it possible to operate with no obstructions at all. This is why the services have long been the experts in training, because in battle there may be no opportunity for long briefing, and complicated manoeuvres have to be carried out on receiving a code word – or hearing a bugle call.

Aims and commitment

Understanding the purpose of a job has a powerful effect on the commitment of people carrying it out. The relationship is a complex one, but it can be summarized in the following way. People employed by someone else bring neutral motivation to their work; they are neither naturally idle, nor naturally committed. They will become more committed if:

1 The objective is clear (and they understand why they are doing the job); specific (either the task itself is closed, or the person briefed can close it down himself); apparently attainable (otherwise frustration sets in).
2 The objective is accepted (the person wants to finish the job for its own sake, rather than merely to avoid blame).

They will become highly committed if:

1 The objective is self-set, or they are allowed to determine the means.
2 The objective contributes towards a personal aim or value (or the means of achieving the objective contribute, for example, by giving a chance of practising a new skill).
3 The means of achieving the objective are socially rewarding.

They will become less committed if:

1 They suffer from *frustration*. People get frustrated when:
   (*a*) Changes in the environment (for example, their manager's decisions) follow no rational pattern. (A problem for company boards is how to respond to changes in the market or in technology, without seeming to their subordinates to be merely capricious.)
   (*b*) They are set two or more objectives of equal priority, which they see as mutually exclusive: they believe they can only fulfil one at the expense of the other. An example might be when an old-fashioned foreman is told to encourage 'participation', but still get the job done!
   (*c*) Superiors continue to insist on something that seems to be hopeless being achieved.
   (*d*) The task brings insignificant results in terms of effort employed or of a man's standards (for example, a genius makes a bad clerk).
2 The objective clashes with personal aims or with psychological needs – for example, for the approval of colleagues.
3 The objective appears to spring from objectionable motives on the part of the boss (even if the objective is itself acceptable).

Commitment is not necessarily the same as interest or enjoyment. One can be grimly (and effectively) committed to a task which one loathes.

Commitment is easier to gain than to keep. In the short term one can buy it with salary increases – or even with a splash of generosity like a few rounds of drinks. The trouble with these methods is that people soon see through them; then if the other causes of commitment are not there, the reaction can be disastrous.

One symptom of low commitment is that people go through the motions of carrying out the job, without concerning themselves with the purpose, or whether what they are doing is of any use. Another is that they skimp the job, only doing the bits they see as contributing to their own private concerns.

Aims and co-operation

Any human organization consists of a network of co-operation, based on reconciling the aims of individual members. The most common device for doing this is the contract of employment: *A* wants a job done, *B* wants a livelihood, so *A* pays *B* to do it. Money is often the only basis of co-operation, although the job gets done more effectively if *B* is led to share *A*'s aim and is interested in doing the job for its own sake. An organization is most effective when individual members grasp every opportunity for combining their several aims into one course of action, and one of the benefits of training can be to encourage people to look for ways of doing this. A maintenance foreman, for example, landed with a big cleaning job that would take a squad of men about a week, discovered that the works fire station, was planning a high-pressure hose practice; by combining forces, they cleared the job in a day.

When you ask people to support or collaborate in something, they will often agree. However, this verbal agreement may have one of a wide range of meanings, such as:

I *share* your aim – and together we will do all we can to achieve it.
I *support* your aim and I am ready to help you.
I *sympathize* with your aim and I hope you succeed.
I *acquiesce* in your aim – though I do not really care either way.
I *reject your aim* – and I will have nothing to do with it.
I *oppose* your aim – and I will see you damned first.

The most common response is acquiescence. If you work with people regularly, it can make life easier if you have some sort of convention for finding out, when they say they agree, what they actually *do* mean. And it is much more helpful if someone who rejects or opposes your aim actually says so (rather than secretly dragging his feet) since he and you may be able to work out together some approach he can accept.

Important as it is to set aims that are right from the organizational point of view, it may be just as important to set aims that people can agree on. There are times where the need to get the consent of other people – staff, partners, suppliers, customers – makes it necessary to modify corporate aims, and settle for the best you can get.

Conflict

Conflict – the situation where one person can only win if the other loses – can crop up in a number of ways. Simple dislike, for example, can make one oppose someone else's plan, although people who spend their lives in business usually learn to avoid the grosser forms of provocation. More often, conflict arises because one person sees another apparently threatening something he values or intends to do – in other words, from a clash of aims. This conflict can be a real one, or it can spring from misunderstanding. The trouble is that whatever started it, the conflict itself soon becomes real, as emotion takes over. Both sides forget their true interests and concentrate on the negative aim of doing the other lot down. The best way out may be for both sides to go back to the original purposes, and this is where a third party can be useful; probing often discloses an area of common interest – something at least that can be done to help both sides. If people once start co-operating, even on a side issue, suspicion will tend to dissipate, and they are far more likely to come up with a solution that benefits both.

Personal and group aims

Even if people who work together share a common aim, they will also have aims of their own – social, political, culture, spiritual, and what have you. In practice a team can work quite well together, even though their reasons for doing the job are quite different. Consider four people involved in extending a factory. Their respective aims may be:

A To get the approval of my colleagues.
B To get promotion and power.
C To provide work in a depressed area.
D To improve the environment for staff.

They are not likely to announce their aims publicly, but it will be easier to work with them if each has some insight into what the others are really after. For people will go on pursuing their own aims, whatever lip service they may pay to yours, unless you can either persuade them to abandon their aims and go for yours (which is very difficult) or find a course of action that suits you both.

Managers need to understand the personal aims of subordinates. They can do this by building up an informal personal relationship, using their imagination to put themselves in another's shoes. They can also discuss aims more formally through appraisal interviews ('Where do you want to be in 5 years' time?'). When giving an assignment, one can sometimes relate the subordinate's aims to those of the task. ('This job should give you experience in . . .'). When one is dealing with a sophisticated man or woman who has strongly held personal objectives, it may be useful to draw up together a formal network of aims (see the next chapter) showing how his aims and the company's interrelate. It is equally important to know if a colleague has strong and peculiar moral views, with which his job might conflict.

In all this the risks are fairly high, particularly for the subordinate. The manager may be affronted when he discovers what his subordinate's ambitions are, or it may provoke conflict that could otherwise lie dormant for years. But the possible gains are far greater; if the subordinate understands that his personal aims will be taken into account in any future work he is given, he will be far more committed to the job as a whole.

Aims in society

Most human objectives can only be met through co-operation, often between people whose aims are divergent. Investors, managers and unions have quite different views on how the company's profits should be spent, but unless they can co-operate, there will be no profits for anyone. One trouble with old-style industrial relations was that it made negotiation continuous: 'productivity bargaining' meant that co-operation itself was an issue to be haggled over, and conceded only at a price.

People in working life should discipline themselves to ask, 'How can my proposals be adapted so that they benefit the other party as well?' Looking out for ways of co-operating for mutual benefit is a way of looking at the world – but also an improvable skill which we all need to work at. The next chapter describes one technique for doing so.

4 Purpose and action

In considering what ought to be done in the next hour or day or perhaps week he was superb. But anything approaching a long-term plan was outside his scope. If I tried to talk to him of such things he would droop the corners of his mouth and make his long yellow face still longer and say, 'Your Lordship may have these intentions. But I would remind Your Lordship that the man who stares too hard into the fog before him, trips over the stone at his feet.'

Nigel Balchin, *The Borgia Testament*

The why/how network

The first part of this chapter describes a technique for clarifying aims. It is one of great flexibility, effective both for simple personal problems and complex ones such as setting direction for a large organization. Some of its uses are:

1 Where one is faced with action, and wishes to be clear on its purpose.
2 Where one holds a long-term objective, and wants to establish stages for getting there.
3 Where one is faced with a vague, 'open' task, and needs to know what it implies, or where to start.
4 To discover a range of solutions, or the best possible solution.
5 As a means of inducing 'lateral thinking'.
6 Where the aims of two parties need to be reconciled – for example, a union with management or a production department with marketing.
7 As a way of resolving conflict – provided there is any common ground.
8 As a way of exploring the intentions of people with whom one is negotiating or competing.

Opening up by asking 'Why?'

1 Take a sheet of paper and write in the middle of it a statement of the job that needs to be done – for example:

Survey salaries within the company

(If the job presents itself as a problem – 'We don't know what people earn' – then turn the sentence round and make it purposeful.)

2 Ask *WHY* the task needs to be done – what the purpose of doing it is. There will frequently be more than one purpose: write down each one in a balloon above the statement of the task.
3 Take the purposes you have recorded, and ask why each of them is desirable. Go on asking *WHY* until you come to some ultimate purpose which you regard as self-evident, or at least not worth exploring further today, such as 'In order to increase profits'.

In Figure 4.1, each of the statements leads reasonably into the one above: for instance, the purpose of letting the board know what people earn is to bring salaries in line with the market.

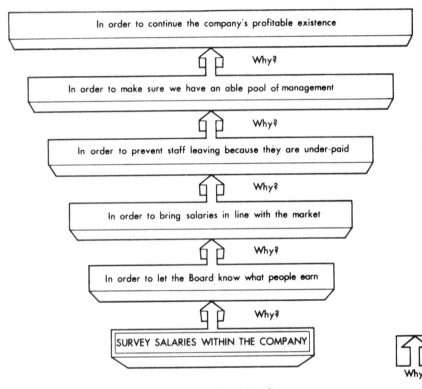

Figure 4.1   *A hierarchy of aims*

Figure 4.2 shows an example of extending a factory: here the different individuals' aims do not contribute towards each other, beyond the execution of task itself. They do not therefore form a hierarchy, but spread out laterally from the original statement of the task.

Note that the question 'Why?' is asking for an answer in the format, 'In order to . . .', *not* in the format, 'Because . . .' 'In order to' expresses a

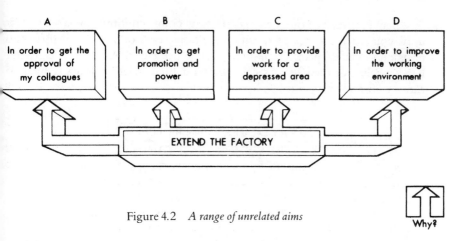

Figure 4.2   *A range of unrelated aims*

purpose, while 'because' merely provides a piece of information. 'Because the working environment is terrible at the moment', does not tell you anything about your aims. Either rephrase it and turn it into an aim – 'In order to improve the environment' – or, if no purpose is contained in it, record it as information at the side of the network.

Why-because is a question that pushes back into the past, into the origins of the situation. Why-in-order pushes into the future, to uncover what you are trying to achieve. The contrast is shown in Figure 4.3

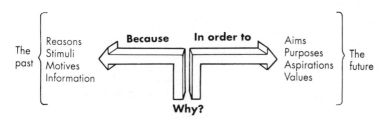

Figure 4.3   *'Because' and 'in order to'*

Closing down by asking 'How?'

So far the network has been developed upwards, by asking 'Why?' The next stage is to develop it downwards on the page, by asking the question 'How?' Starting at the top of the chart, take each statement and ask *HOW* it is to be achieved. One answer should be the statement immediately below it: 'How?' going downwards = 'Why?' going upwards.

For example, in Figure 4.1 (the salary survey), *how* do we 'continue the company's profitable existence?' *By* 'making sure we have a pool of able management . . .' This process tests the logic of the existing network.

When you reach your original starting point, continue to ask 'How?', until you reach a series of specific intentions, each of which can form the basis of a detailed plan (*or can just be done*). See Figure 4.4. In this case, the left-hand line of the network ends with a definite brief for Jones, which he can go off and carry out.

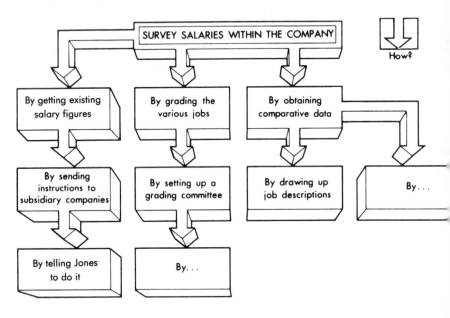

Figure 4.4   *Closing down by asking 'How'*

Information

The why/how network has no formal stage of recording or seeking information. Often this does not matter, since all the relevant information is in one's head. But if the network seems to be getting stuck, it may be necessary to make a deliberate stage of jotting down what you know, and what you need to know, about the problem. This information should be recorded on the side of the chart (not included in the network). It is convenient to record *information known* on the left of the chart, and *information needed* on the right (Figure 4.5).

Lateral thinking

It may be that by asking '*HOW*' about the level of the task, you will find some alternative way of achieving your higher-level aims. Occasionally the original task itself is seen as no longer necessary.

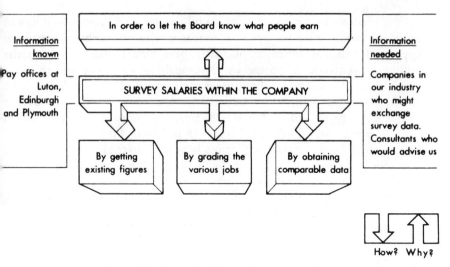

Figure 4.5   *Recording information in a network*

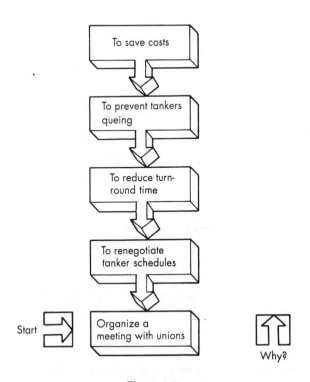

Figure 4.6

One example of this comes from an oil refinery that drew its supplies of crude oil from the sea by tanker. A manager who had fairly recently been appointed was instructed to negotiate new tanker schedules with the unions. He regarded the prospect with some dread, since industrial relations were precarious, but he set about organizing a meeting. Before doing so, he checked through the aims in a routine way. At present, tankers were having to queue up to unload, and it was essential to improve their turn-round time. The network he produced is shown in Figure 4.6.

It then occurred to him to try asking 'how else?' to the higher level boxes. Were there any other ways of improving tankers' turn-round time? Yes, by installing a second feed valve, which would allow two tankers to be unloaded at once. This was done, at relatively trivial cost, and the threatened disruption was avoided.

Used in this way, a how/why network can produce the same results as what Edward de Bono calls 'lateral thinking'. The solution does in fact appear laterally on the chart, beside the original intention (Figure 4.7).

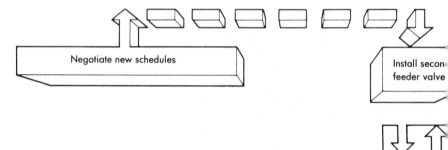

Figure 4.7   *Lateral thinking*

Its opposite, 'vertical thinking', occurs when you ask 'how' only to the original intention, so that the answer appears as shown in Figure 4.8.

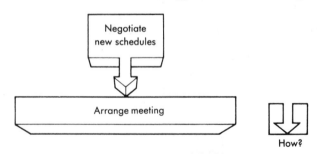

Figure 4.8   *Vertical thinking*

Another example comes from a food distribution company. The starting point was the need to build an extension to the central warehouse, which would cost about £1m. Once again, the manager responsible charted the aims in a routine way, and produced the network shown in Figure 4.9.

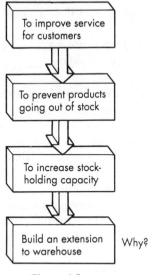

Start

Why?

Figure 4.9

Again he asked 'how else?' to the highest level box, and came up with 'by rethinking the distribution pattern'. He followed down the chain of hows and came up with a scheme for having fewer but larger vehicles – in effect, mobile warehouses. The new system was put in at a cost of £700,000 and improved the service even more than expected, in that customers could come up with extra orders at the time of delivery.

Open and closed tasks

A why/how network can be used:

1 To make an open task manageable by closing it down (Figure 4.10).

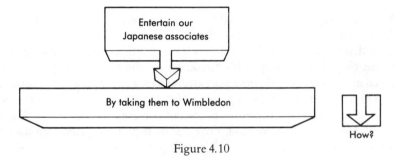

How?

Figure 4.10

2 To open up a closed task where:
   (a) You can see no answer.
   (b) None of the apparent answers is good enough.
   (c) The risks are high, so you need a range of solutions from which to select the best.
   (d) You feel that you may not have grasped the full implications or reasons for what you are doing.

Here are two examples of opening up a closed task.

1 Where the obvious answer was unsatisfactory

In a plant producing polymer, a Pitot tube was being used to measure the rate of flow, by recording the amount of glycol being given off.. The tube kept going wrong, and was taken out and put back a dozen times. In effect, the problem was being diagnosed as shown in Figure 4.11.

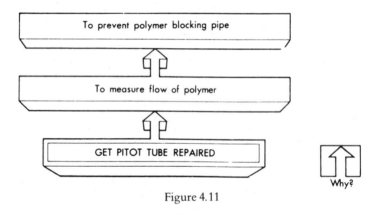

Figure 4.11

A blocked pipe would take eight to ten men two days to strip down, as well as causing loss of production during that time. The foreman began to suspect that he was treating as a closed task something that needed opening out. He therefore expanded his thinking, as shown in Figure 4.12. He checked and discovered that the polymer was of a type not often processed, low in glycol content. At the beginning of the process there was not enough glycol to measure. He therefore proposed the solution shown in Figure 4.13. This was an older method, now out of use. It was reintroduced and worked.

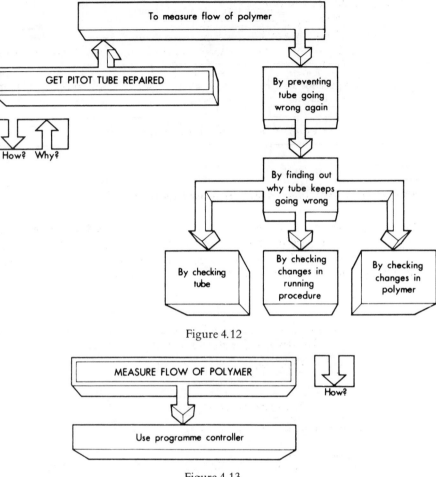

Figure 4.12

Figure 4.13

2 Getting a range of solutions

A transport officer had the problem of reducing damage to the batteries of conveyancer trucks. Each battery cost over £1,000 and weighed more than a ton. The network of solutions he came up with is shown in Figure 4.14.

Having a range of solutions, you still need to compare them, consider the various pros and cons (including cost) and select the best. In this example it was possible to pursue them all (except for photographing the damage, which was not thought necessary). Some by-products of improving the design of the trucks were to cut down the time and effort taken to reload batteries (from 15 minutes to 3) and to reduce injuries.

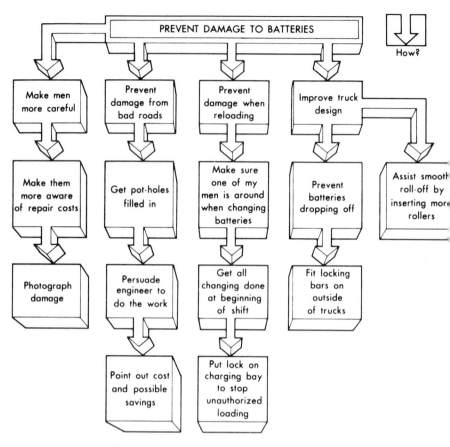

Figure 4.14   *A network providing a range of solutions*

Even if a network produces no fresh solutions, it can still help to establish the relationship between various objectives – which of them can be combined or reinforce each other – and to assess priorities. It can also indicate whether or not a task really does contribute towards a valid aim.

Personal networks

At the beginning of this chapter we talked about exploring aims upwards until you come to one that seems to you self-evident. Most networks if carried far enough branch into organizational benefits ('increase profits') and personal benefits ('job satisfaction' or 'more pay'). Obviously it is not worth exploring these levels every time you draw up the network of some commercial problem. However, once a year or so it is well worth pushing a network upwards as high as it will go – in order to make explicit your assumptions about society, and to explore the relationships of your present activity with your own long-term aims. You can use the technique to audit your present career or to select a new one. You can use it to reconcile the different roles you have to play in business and in family life, to test whether your job really does help your family or leave the world a better place; or to examine the relationship between your own actions and whatever purpose you believe there is in life.

Measures of success

If you are given an instruction, the first thing to establish is the purpose; the second is what sort of end result is expected. If it is a report – do they want reams of appendices, or half a sheet of paper? Sometimes the purpose may make it obvious; or whoever is briefing you may not know, but may (quite reasonably) leave the task open and expect you to think it through and find something that suits the broad aim given you. But one must be sure that the job is not already closed down in the boss's mind – he knows exactly what he wants but has not bothered to say, perhaps because he thinks it is obvious.

Another of the ways in which a task can be open is by not specifying the standard or quality of result that is expected. People tackling a job need some way of telling how well they have succeeded. Either they or their manager must set *success measures*: that is, ways of judging whether the task has been completed successfully. Apart from the practical advantages of knowing that a job is out of the way and that resources can now be switched elsewhere, consciousness of success gives a burst of confidence, so that success tends to breed more success. Measures need to be specific and not capable of being disputed, or their effect will be lost. For this reason they should, where possible, be quantified, though factors that cannot be quantified should not be ignored. One measure nearly always present is that of time for completion. Another is usually financial, relating to cost or profit. All measures must, of course, be set in advance: it is not very convincing deciding what constitutes success after you have got there! Setting success measures can also help close a task, where there are many possible outcomes – for instance, choosing a career. You may decide you want a minimum income of so many thousands a year when you are 40: this cuts out a fair range of jobs. Your work must be in the country – this cuts out a few more. Such measures will suggest what information you need to look for, as well as giving a quick way of deciding between options.

A success measure can either be an actual aspect of success – like £1000 profit – or it can be some sort of sample or test. This latter may be particularly valuable where the results of the task are not capable of being measured directly. Suppose the job is to 'improve communications within this department', how do you measure that? Not, at any rate, by the number of bits of paper going round. You may, however, devise a test like, 'Once a week I will ask Joe what Fred is working on: my measure of success is that Joe should give the right answer three weeks out of four (instead of one week in four, as at present).'

One way of setting success measures for an indefinite task is from a why/how network. Each why or how statement branching from the central task may suggest a result that can be measured.

By using success measures, you can close a task down to the point where it is manageable by whoever is set to do it. It is no good giving a trainee secretary a year to purge all the files: the end-point is too far off and the task will be neglected. It is much more practical to give her 3 months to clear one cabinet, or a month for one drawer. A network for improving communications is shown in Figure 4.15.

A service department can often use success measures to demonstrate its usefulness. A works medical department found itself regarded as an unproductive overhead. The sister-in-charge did some work on quantifying

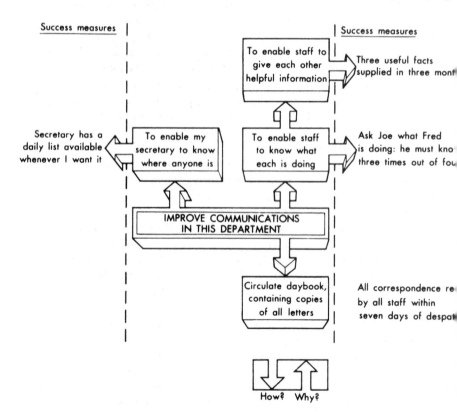

Figure 4.15   *Deriving success measures from a network*

past results and used them to set measures for the future – for instance, targets for the physiotherapy unit in terms of money saved each month through reduction of sick-leave. Before long the department found itself quite popular with even the most hard-nosed managers.

Defining purpose through a series of whys carries you further into the future, where the picture is necessarily more blurred. Defining the end-product and setting success measures has the opposite effect. It brings the future sharply into focus, so that you know, in essence, what you have to achieve, at what cost and by what date.

Aims and the organization

So far the examples have dealt with aim-setting at a fairly low level, indicating, if nothing else, that the foreman and the junior manager need to be aware of them. But the higher up the organization you go, the more important aim-setting becomes. At the highest level, the main function of the board of directors is setting direction for the company as a whole, while management is concerned with the means of getting there.

Figure 4.16 shows the why/how network drawn up by the management of a small milk factory, at a time when the plant was under threat of closure. The network's starting point was, 'Improve the efficiency of plant operation'. One important factor was that milk, the basic raw material, was allocated to factories by a central department. In this factory the attitude of management had always been, 'How do we get rid of all this milk they keep sending us?' There was no feeling that they were in any sense in control of their own destiny. But when they looked at the problem in the context of the factory's survival, the aims became to maximize use of plant by getting *more* milk – and therefore to influence the head office department to channel extra milk their way.

A department that is allowed to pursue mistaken aims is condemning itself to death. The central laboratory of a large food company had long traditions of fundamental research, its standards were high, its results were impeccable. It gradually assumed the duty of testing, to a superb degree of accuracy, samples of every batch of food produced by every factory in the group. The results came back four days later – four days too late to be any use. A half-trained chemist in each factory did a crude on-the-spot test and management worked to that. The laboratory has been broken up and its staff dispersed around the divisions.

When you set objectives for individuals, you have of course to take account of their own needs for personal development. In the same way, when objectives are set for branches and departments you have to consider their future role in the developing organization: not just what needs doing, but who ought to do it. One company set up an industrial relations

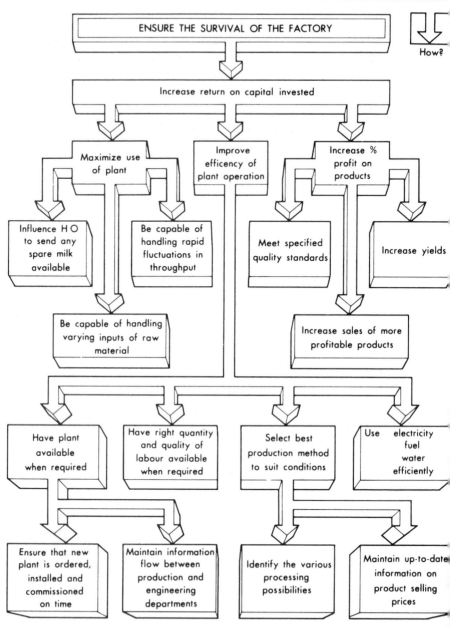

Figure 4.16   *Aims network of a milk factory*

On a chart like this, the final statements are themselves fairly open, and each one of them needs to be developed by the particular departments responsible before they can be broken down into workable plans. There is also an obvious need to quantify and set measures of success: 'maximum' use of plant means having it running for how many hours a day? You may find that 'maximum' use of plant does not square with maintaining quality – so that concepts such as 'optimum' creep in. An aims network is no substitute for mathematical analysis, but it may be the essential starting point.

department, manned by very able young officers. These people rushed round the company's depots at the least hint of trouble, and stamped it out before it could develop or spread. The result in the first year was a sharp fall in industrial disputes. The aims network the company worked to, might have been drawn as in Figure 4.17.

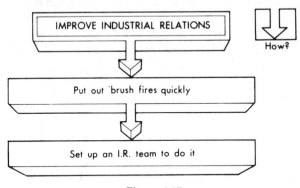

Figure 4.17

But the director responsible realized that depot managers were losing both the capacity and the authority to deal with industrial relations on their own account. Shop stewards were ceasing to regard them as people worth talking to: they were in effect ceasing to manage. The network was faulty – through not considering which aim was related to which department. The IR officers were withdrawn to a training and advisory role, and the network in effect redrawn as in Figure 4.18.

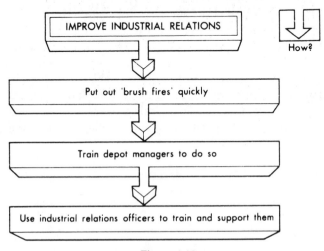

Figure 4.18

Corporate aims

Setting aims for a company calls for basic questions such as 'What business are we in?' to be answered. The example often quoted of an industry getting its aims wrong is that of the American and Canadian railroads, which thought they were in the business of running trains when really they were in transport. However, the thing that railroad companies could do better than anyone else was to run railroads – not fly aeroplanes, which would have needed a totally different expertise. Sometimes a more useful formation of the question is to break it in half and ask:

1 What do we as a company do as well or better than anyone else?
2 What are the aims of our actual or potential customers?

Then the art is to reconcile them. One can draw up a notional aims network for customers, and see to which of their aims one can provide a 'HOW'. The aims of railroad customers were to get themselves and their goods across country quickly, cheaply and conveniently. By the end, probably the one skill the railroads had to offer that people wanted was in cheap, long-haul carriage of goods.

Another example, quoted by Robert Heller in *The Naked Manager* (Barrie & Jenkins, 1972), is that of the gaggle of large companies that went into computers. Every single company had excellent reasons, based on realistic definitions of its business, for adding computer capacity. Yet every single one suffered untold grief as a result. They failed not by misunderstanding what business they were in, but by not seeing what business computers were in – and that, overwhelmingly, was the replacement of punch-card machines. Their own aims were impeccable – but it was misunderstanding the aims of their potential customers that got them into trouble.

Compared with, say, critical path analysis, an aims network is a simple technique. A large sheet of paper can contain the most elaborate network that is likely to be of much use: it can illustrate the interaction of customers, unions, government and the company's own objectives. It is a technique that the chairman or the foreman can use on the back of an envelope. It can force a man to ask the right questions, and by concentrated practice develop the skills of foresight, imagination and identifying what is really worth doing.

5 A systematic approach

The need for a system

The process of doing any job of work can be broken down into a number of
stages. First, obviously there must be a stimulus to do something – an order
from a boss, an opportunity or a danger seen, or a desire to be filled. This,
the question of aims, was dealt with in the last two chapters.

But once the stimulus is received and the objective is set, the job will
normally be tackled in at least two stages: *preparation* and *action*. The
preparation stage may be short or long, according to the complexity of the
task, but some information-gathering or planning is still essential.
Sometimes the objective can be achieved in one bite. More often perhaps,
work is carried out as a series of sub-tasks. If I am decorating a room, I strip
the walls (preparation/action), paint the woodwork (preparation/action),
and paper the walls (preparation/action). When a stage of action is
complete, a useful, though not an inevitable, step is to review the results,

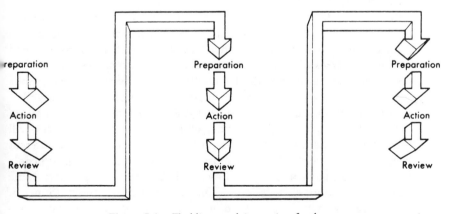

Figure 5.1   *Tackling a task in a series of cycles*

and check what has been done and what is still to do. This is almost inevitable when a job is broken into a series of sub-tasks, since the results of the first stage must be reviewed to provide information for the second. In this case the sequence of doing a job becomes as shown in Figure 5.1.

The preparation stage itself comprises two or three distinct kinds of activity: first, assembling the *information*; second, determining from the information *what has to be done*. In a job of any size there is a third stage, of making detailed plans – specifying how, when and where the various activities are to be carried out, and who is going to do them. These stages of doing a job form a sequence, which is called '*a systematic approach to getting things done*':

- Preparation:
    Information.
    What has to be done.
    Planning.
- Action.
- Review.

If the job is being tackled in a series of bites, the review stage of the first cycle leads naturally into the information stage of the next.

Some professions have codified this sequence, labelling the stages and expanding them to suit the way they work. Some examples are shown in Table 5.1.

Given this broad uniformity of approach, it should in theory be quite simple for a group to work through a problem together. In practice we all know that it can be very difficult. Some of the reasons are:

1 Different people have different time perspectives; as we saw in the last chapter, one may be thinking about tomorrow, while another is thinking 3 months ahead.
2 Different people tend to dwell on different stages of the sequence – either because of their natural disposition, or the way in which they have been trained. Some people, those who make good directors of companies, tend to think in terms of aims; an accountant is likely to spend a lot of time assembling and analysing the facts, while a salesman will have rushed straight off into action. If three such people are forced to work together on the same job, there could well be chaos. Certainly they will all go through the same cycle of preparing, acting and reviewing, but they will each start at a different point and probably go through it at a different pace. (One can verify this by a short experiment: get a group of people together and ask them to write down their immediate response to some simple instruction, such as 'move this table out of the room'. Some of them will ask why it is to be done, some will ask for information –

Table 5.1 *Comparison of systems for getting things done*

A SYSTEMATIC APPROACH	MILITARY: APPRECIATION OF THE SITUATION*	MILITARY: ORDERS	PRINCIPLES OF WORK STUDY
Aims	Aim		
Information	Factors Own courses	Situation	Select Record Examine
What has to be done	Plan	Mission	Develop
Plan		Execution Administration and logistics Command and signals	
Act			Install
Review			Maintain

* Described as 'an orderly sequence of reasoning, leading logically to the best solution to a problem'.

where, when, who else will help? – or will offer information, such as that it looks heavy. Others again will come up with more or less detailed plans for getting the job done, while a few may actually get up and do it.)
3 There is also the impact of emotion. When everyone knows they have got the answer but cannot get the rest to see, they may become frustrated and aggressive.

The 'Systematic Approach' used in Coverdale training is not so much a prescription of how people ought to think, but a description of how they actually do think. It is a way of co-ordinating the thinking of a group, so that they all arrive at the same stage at the same moment.

The stages of systematic approach

Aims

These have already been discussed in Chapter 3.

Information

This stage consists of specifying all the information relevant to your aims, which you either know already or need to find out. Some types of information are: *facts* (their probability, and the evidence on which they are based); *ideas* (including possible ways of tackling the job); and degree of *risk* (How high are the stakes? What do we lose if we go wrong?) Sometimes the highest risk lies in inaction, delaying so that nothing gets done at all, and that too must be weighed.

Although the matter dealt with in the information stage is not really homogeneous (ideas, for instance, are quite distinct from facts), for most operations it can all be dealt with in one stage. However, when one is dealing with matters of policy, the stage can become highly complex. It may consist, for example, of using basic information to engender a series of ideas, assembling further facts relevant to each of them, evaluating them in the light of aims and the degree of risk, and passing the preferred solution down the line for lower management to push into action.

What has to be done (WHTBD)

This stage consists of stating from the information, the main steps that have to be taken to meet the objective, and establishing their priorities. Sometimes this means fixing on an idea that was produced in the information stage. As long as an idea is merely a possibility, it remains information. But when you decide to follow it, it becomes as it were an order to yourself or to the group – in other words, something to be done.

Note that the word is *stating* what has to be done – not *asking*; Systematic Approach has no stage for taking decisions as such. Decisions are one of the great hang-ups of Western industry. In nine-tenths of the jobs one does at work, there is no need to take any 'decision' at all; once the facts are assembled, the lines of action are obvious. If one does have to take a decision, it is often a sign that the information stage is not complete. Of course there are some variables (including people's motives and behaviour) that one cannot determine with any certainty; to that extent one is working in the dark and has to take 'decisions', since the 'information' is no more than intelligent guesswork. Most decision-taking techniques (cost-benefit analysis and the like) are basically ways of quantifying uncertainties, in such a way that they can be treated as facts. If you estimate that you have a 90 per cent chance of taking £1000 a week in your new shop, you can treat the £1000 as a 'fact', making suitable insurance for uncertainty, and state what has to be done accordingly. But often in daily working life, when you have a choice of approaches, there is nothing to choose between them; the best bet is to follow the first reasonable proposal that comes up, get on and do the job, and review afterwards in the light of any new information the action has given you.

Systematic Approach substitutes for one big decision a series of choices all down the line. Setting objectives calls for choice, as does selecting relevant information and criteria of success. By the time one comes to state what has to be done, the range of possibilities is already narrowed, often to only one. This avoids the need for the sort of arbitrary decision-making that 'strong men' are prone to, and cuts out a good deal of the stress associated with doubt and delay.

Planning

Systematic Approach breaks down the process of specifying how a job is to be done, into two distinct stages. In the WHTBD stage the broad priorities are established; the planning stage supplies the details which are necessary to carry WHTBDs into action. The distinction is of great practical importance, especially in a complex job, since if you do not establish **all** the WHTBDs first, you may get into action on part of the job, before you realize what is involved, and have no resources left for finishing it. The resource that runs out most easily is time. I have a timetable for writing this book; if I forget that one WHTBD is to give my colleagues a chance to read it, I am likely to find the time is up and the job is not finished.

In the planning stage, the questions to ask are those in Rudyard Kipling's poem:

> I keep six honest serving-men
> (They taught me all I knew);
> Their names are *What* and *Why* and *When*
> And *How* and *Where* and *Who*.

'Why' is the aiming question and should have been answered already (though this is the time to check that the plan will in fact contribute to the aims). The other questions are those that the plan should answer – exactly *who* is going to do *what*, and *how*, *when* and *where* they will do it. In a complicated project, the planning stage will call for an elaborate timetable and marshalling of resources. In a simple job, the only plan needed may be for Jack to volunteer to get on with it, using his own discretion as to how he does it.

Without a plan to implement it, a WHTBD may end up as nothing more than a good intention. This is especially true in committees; a job without a name attached to it has a poor chance of getting done before the next meeting.

Action

The action stage is where the plan is carried out. One benefit of systematic approach is that it leads directly and methodically from aims to action, so that someone who follows it is carried along the stream and is much less likely to surrender to inertia, and discover reasons for doing nothing. Everyone knows how great a problem this can be: one can think hard about digging the garden for most of the weekend, but the garden is still horribly likely to remain undug!

Review

When the action is complete, it should be reviewed. Two sorts of questions need to be asked:

1 *About the job itself.* Have we achieved what we set out to do? What more has to be done? Can we improve the result?
2 *About methods of work.* Can we improve the way we worked? Where were the snags and how can they be avoided another time? What were the successful parts of the exercise, which we can adopt and use on other occasions?

In this second part of the review stage, Systematic Approach becomes a basic method of learning. Experience, by itself, may teach very little: improvements come only from reviewing what happened, understanding why, and pulling out lessons that one can use for the future. If the review is carried out consciously and deliberately, the learning will come much faster. This is indeed the basic way in which skill (as opposed to knowledge) is learnt – by a cycle of *thought – action – thought*, which corresponds with *preparation – action – review*. Ten minutes' review at the end of a job or at the end of a day can save many hours for the future; it makes sure that one actually learns from the experience – which is not something which nature provides on her own, or there would be fewer old fools in the world.

In any review, the emphasis should be on what to do next time, rather than merely what to avoid, and it is at least as important to identify what went well as what went badly. Of course, failures must be traced and avoided; but time must also be deliberately spent on analysing success, if only because a review that dwells mostly on failure is destructive of morale. This theme is developed further in Chapter 10.

Ways of using Systematic Approach

Systematic Approach can be used in a number of ways – either as a once-through procedure, or as a series of cycles (Figures 5.2 to 5.4). Which

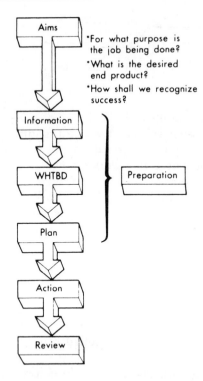

Figure 5.2 *Formal, once through method (used when trial and error is difficult, or the risks of failure are high)*

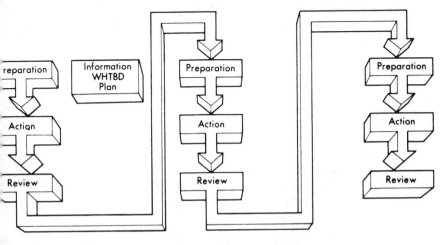

Figure 5.3 *Learning from experience (used when the risk is low)*

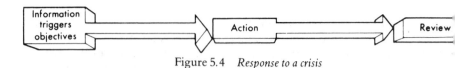

Figure 5.4   *Response to a crisis*

approach to use is bound up with the degree of *risk* – that is to say, how much you stand to lose if you get it wrong first time round. If the job is something like choosing a site for a distribution depot, the risk really is high, and you cannot conceivably work by trial and error. However, most of the time, in most people's lives, the risk is pretty low – at any rate in the incidental jobs they have to do. An industrial chemist may be engaged in a project where the risk is enormous – if he gets his answer wrong the plant may blow up. But within this project, there may be half a dozen ways of carrying out a particular experiment, and it may not be worth dithering over which is the best.

Often the worst risk is that of inaction – getting nothing done at all. On occasions you may need to crash into the action stage without any plan, and think later in the review stage. This approach is right either when the risks of action are very low, or when the risks of inaction are very high; if a child is drowning, you jump straight in, without debating whether or not to take off your socks.

When a task has high risk attached to it, the best way to reduce it may be to go through a series of dummy runs or small-scale cycles first. This has three advantages: it provides practice, so that the job is done more efficiently; it reduces tension, making the job familiar when you have to do it in earnest; and it shows you what can go wrong, and gives a chance to adjust your approach.

Used in this last way, systematic approach becomes the pattern of *learning from experience*. The basic method is to try a task (either in simulation or in earnest) or undergo an experience, review the results, and plan to reproduce behaviour that worked, or improve behaviour that didn't. The improvement may be technical ('Let's try with a high-pressure hose'), or in one's own behaviour or skill ('I won't lift my head' or 'I will keep my temper'). In the simplest form of learning from experience, behaviour is merely repeated or avoided. 'Next time, I won't ask permission – I'll just do it.' In the more complex form of learning you look, in the review stage, for the *causes* of success or failure, and draw out principles of more general use: 'If your boss is a ditherer, and you are confident of success, get on and use your initiative.'

In this form, Systematic Approach comes to resemble scientific method, as formulated by Sir Karl Popper. Scientific method starts in the review stage, with a 'problem' – typically experimental evidence that doesn't square with the current theory. There is then an expanded information stage, which consists first of hitting on a new theory or model, then devising a way of testing it. What Has To Be Done is the experiment, which then has to be planned and put into action, and finally to be reviewed, to see if the new theory stands up, and the problem is now solved. (For a fuller account, see Max Taylor's *Effectiveness in Education and Training*, Gower, 1990.)

Systematic Approach and other techniques

Systematic Approach is not a substitute for specialized techniques such as critical-path analysis or brainstorming, but a framework within which they can be applied, each at the proper stage. Brainstorming, for example, is a method of engendering ideas – and so usually part of the information stage; critical-path analysis establishes priorities and is part of WHTBD, while decision-making techniques, such as discounted cash flow and cost benefit analysis, come late in the information stage – where the risk has to be weighed up and probabilities assessed.

Systematic Approach and aims

Establishing the aim is not necessarily part of the Systematic Approach cycle: a long-term aim may remain valid while one goes through a whole series of cycles, each getting closer to it by achieving some interim objective – which is why it was given the name Systematic *Approach*. (You need to check in each cycle, that the work really does contribute towards the aim.) Sometimes it is impossible to define the aims at the outset. It may be necessary to get into action first and try things out, before the right direction becomes apparent. I may set myself some broad aim like 'running an effective department', but it may not mean much till I have done the job for a couple of months first.

Again, without experimenting, you may not know what is possible: some aims may not be worth pursuing, while others may be unexpectedly easy. It may be that the uncertainty is in your boss's mind: he may suspect something is wrong, but not know quite what it is or what should be done. In a case like this you may need to try something out and get feedback from him before you know you are on the right lines.

There is also no set place in the cycle for setting measures of success, since one may well need information before one can decide what sort of target is reasonable. Often the best procedure is:

1 Establish the purpose.
2 Get enough information to know what result is needed and what is practical.

3 Define the desired end-product and set measures of success – high enough to stretch you in the light of what you know.
4 Continue the information stage: assemble whatever detailed information you need to do the job to the standards you have set.

In the last chapter we looked at why/how networks, which, like Systematic Approach, can be a way of getting towards action (although their main function is to clarify purpose). They are in fact a different presentation of the same material, since the higher-level 'hows' are WHTBDs, and lower-level 'hows' are plans (though they may lack the necessary detail).

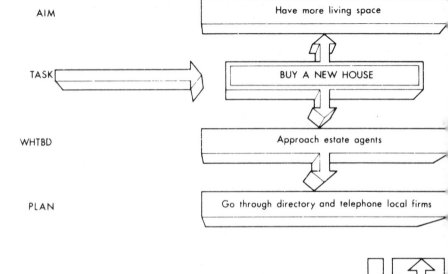

Figure 5.5   *Comparison of how/why network with Systematic Approach*

A why/how network (Figure 5.5) is less rigorous, since it lacks a formal information stage, and this can sometimes make it unsatisfactory and even misleading. However, it can be a useful starting point, even though one may need to revert to Systematic Approach to get the job into action. Occasions when a network may be particularly useful are:

1 When tackling a job where the facts are clear but the objectives are not (this may often apply to personal problems).
2 When you need to satisfy a number of different aims (your own and other people's).

3 When you want to be clear what effect one course of action has on another.
4 When you need to find an ingenious solution to a familiar problem (that is, to break assumptions).

A method for teamwork

A group of people who work together regularly may find it useful to apply Systematic Approach as a regular procedure. Systematic Approach becomes a kind of sub-agenda for handling each item on the main agenda. However, if it is misapplied, it can become merely a ritual, and certainly there is no point in imposing it if a group is getting on quite well without.

Using the approach needs skill, which can be developed at first by practising it consciously and deliberately 'in slow time'. Gradually the habits of thought become ingrained, so that one follows it without needing to label the stages, though it can still help to do so whenever you run into difficulty.

Systematic Approach provides a common language, which allows even strangers to work together effectively. That is one benefit that large companies expect from training the whole body of managerial staff, since people from a diversity of regions or departments can come to a meeting, establish their respective aims and tackle a problem together, using common standards of relevance and ways of judging progress.

Since Systematic Approach describes the natural sequence in which work gets done, a manager can use it to regulate his own contributions at a meeting, even if no one else there has ever heard of it. If, for instance, he sees that most people are at the stage of gathering information, he knows it is the right time to come out with facts and ideas, and to be ready with proposals of what has to be done. If people's contributions are all over the place, one can use Systematic Approach to pull them together: 'I'm sorry, I'm still not clear exactly what we're trying to achieve', or, 'Is there any point in making these plans, till John has given us the facts?' The important thing is to avoid jargon, and use terms that other people will understand.

Summary

Systematic Approach is valuable for individuals, but it comes into its own when it co-ordinates the work of a team. Its main benefits are:

1 It ties action to thought, so that thinking leads naturally into doing.
2 It lets one tackle large, complex problems in small bites, and so build up confidence from progress.

3 It provides a deliberate method of learning from experience.
4 It helps one discover what stage other people are at, and keeps one's contribution in phase with the meeting.
5 It enables a group to co-ordinate their thinking and focus all their minds simultaneously on one aspect of the topic.
6 It allows people who work together regularly to identify what stage of systematic approach each does best, and so move forward at the pace of the fastest.
7 It provides a pilot for uncharted waters; when one is faced with a situation right outside one's experience, it provides at least somewhere to start.
8 Since it can be applied to open problems, it can be used on the very open problems of human interaction (see Chapter 7).

6 Observation

'The curious incident of the dog in the night-time.'
'The dog did nothing in the night-time.'
'That was the curious incident,' remarked Sherlock Holmes.
    Conan Doyle, *The Memoirs of Sherlock Holmes* – *Silver Blaze*

Perception and purpose

One of the curious things about falling in love is that the impressions of one's senses become far more vivid. Trees seem more green, skies are bluer, birds sing more loudly and clearly. This intense awareness of one's surroundings is something managers must envy and should emulate, for there are times when their job may depend on it. It is the basis of all the learning that follows in this chapter – the skill by which a manager remains in touch with the needs and feelings of people around him, and with the essential purposes of his job.

Human beings live surrounded by a confused mass of stimuli – sights, sounds, smells, the feel of things and indefinable 'atmospheres'. From birth we begin to recognize that some of these stimuli can be ignored, while others demand attention. A baby of only a few hours old will ignore its bedding, but will react to the presence of its mother's breast, by opening its mouth and attempting to suck. As children grow older they become more skilful, both at recognizing stimuli that are significant, and at rejecting others, so as to leave the field clear for the things that matter. When crossing a road, for example, one ignores parked vehicles, and only notices the ones that are moving. At times concentration on one subject can become so intense that you become blind to the rest of your surroundings; you can be so wrapped up in some work problem that you step off a kerb into the moving traffic without being aware of doing so.

There is no perception without contrast. If you look at the sky it is one vast blue blank, and it is impossible to pick out and concentrate on any one particular spot, without the use of optical instruments, such as a telescope. But you can see a star at night, or the vapour trail of an aircraft, because these contrast with the background. In the same way, you cannot fix your eyes on a single point on a plain wall, which is why opticians sometimes choose a patterned wallpaper for their consulting rooms, to give the patient something to stare at while he is being examined. This principle of contrast is used in printing a book (black letters on a white page), in designing road signs, and in safety clothing, like the bright orange jackets worn by men working on a motorway. It is also the means by which we perceive human behaviour; when people do something that contrasts with our expectation, our attention is called to it. That is why it is so much easier to notice things that go wrong than things that go right.

The sights and sounds we encounter differ in their significance according to our purpose. If you have a letter to post, you will tend to 'notice' pillar-boxes which are nearest your home or your office. Without such a motive, they are just part of the scenery; even if you walk down a particular road every day, you will find it hard to remember where they stand, if you have never wanted to post a letter there. This facility of knowing what to look for and spotting things that are significant for our purpose, is the skill of *observation*.

Expanding awareness

Because we ignore irrelevant stimuli, we tend to over-concentrate and see only the things that are favourable to our objectives. Successful observation, however, includes spotting the piece that does not fit – the irrelevant factor that suddenly becomes relevant. A fighter pilot in pursuit of one enemy bomber, must still be aware of all other aircraft in the sky or he may miss the fighter that is going for him. While the scientist is looking out for the results he expects from his experiment, he must also be alert for the unexpected happening which may be of even greater significance – like the casual growth of a mould by which Fleming discovered penicillin. The good observer needs at once a closed mind to concentrate on what is known to be important – and an open mind to spot the unexpected. Sometimes this unexpected information may be negative – such as the fact that the dog did *not* bark, from which Sherlock Holmes deduced that the thief was its own master.

With practice, people can develop a conscious awareness of the whole situation in which they find themselves. A barrister cross-examining a witness, responds to his answers, but at the same time he will be conscious of his effect on the judge and jury. The same awareness is needed by interpretive artists, such as actors or musicians.

The manager as an observer

What do managers need to be aware of? What are the events they should be observing? The answer is whatever may affect their job or call for action, beyond the particular problem they have on their desk at the moment. The problem may need their total concentration, at any rate for short periods; they may need to lock themselves away and think about it, refusing all telephone calls and letting the rest of the job slide. While he was working on the Choral Symphony, Beethoven, they say, neither ate nor slept for three days, and no doubt it is this supreme concentration that produces works of genius. But for every hour managers do this, the risk mounts that something is happening outside the locked door that they must know about – something which may be making their present task out of date or irrelevant. Such factors may include long-term needs – of the company, of their subordinates for development, and of their own career and home life. If for 6 months on end you fail to notice your wife across the breakfast table, you may wake up one day and find her conspicuous by her absence. Managers must look out for technical aspects of their job which are not obvious – successes and opportunities, like Fleming's penicillin mould, potential disasters, like a shortage of cash flow, or a leak developing in a piece of plant. Besides this they must observe the details of human interaction – how subordinates and colleagues work together, what has got the job done or what behaviour is hindering it. Observation provides them with the information they need to keep the department on an even keel.

Learning to observe

Observing how people interact is the key skill in many transactions, such as interviewing, negotiating and interrogating, as well as in the conduct of meetings. These often provide the best place to develop it, since one has a chance to sit back and deliberately watch what is going on under the surface of discussion. To begin with, you will need to keep silent and cut yourself off from the subject being discussed. This is often difficult, since you are interested in it, or have a duty to contribute. However, there may be items on the agenda that do not directly concern you and you can practise during the periods when you are less involved. Best of all is to be allowed to attend a meeting in which you have no direct interest, simply to observe the way it does its work. The second stage is harder: coming back into the discussion, while still remaining aware of how it is being conducted. The difficulty is to keep it up, and you may need some sort of mechanism to remind yourself. One way is to note the passage of time – every minute make a tick on the corner of a scribbling pad. Sooner or later you become absorbed in the subject of the discussion and will stop ticking, but with practice you find that you can keep up the awareness for longer periods while still playing a full part.

With experience, awareness will become more comprehensive. While the beginner only spots something obvious like a snort of rage, to a practised observer the raising of an eyebrow may give just as significant information – especially about commitment or interest, which people are usually reluctant to put into words. But this sort of awareness needs constant practice, as it is quickly lost.

Using what you see

For a manager, the first use of observation is to improve the working of his team. Suppose a meeting is getting bogged down – one member keeps cutting across the discussion with a suggestion that seems to be nothing to do with the point. The manager recalls what he knows about the man; that he finds it difficult to express himself and so tends to get frustrated, which makes him even less coherent; his ideas are usually sound, but are often ignored. What can be done about it? It may be enough just to point out that the man has something to say. On the other hand, if feelings are running high, the manager may need to do something more elaborate; suggest that they break for tea, and arrange to have a talk to the man in the interval, so that they can jointly reintroduce his idea later.

When people start observing, most of what they see are faults. There is no observation without contrast, and the obvious standard of comparison is how *they* would have done the job. In training, the first observer's report is a dangerous moment for any group, since they will hear a good deal of unjustified criticism. With practice, however, one learns the more valuable skill of identifying what is going right. Suppose a manager gives out a job to do, and detects a sudden feeling of enthusiasm. It occurs to him that this has happened before, and his concern now should be to spot the common element. He may realize that the enthusiasm came when he had not time to give a detailed briefing, but just left his team to get on with it, so that they had the chance to use their initiative. If so, he has deduced a principle of success, which he can apply deliberately in future.

As others see us

One special form of observation concerns everyone, whether or not they work in groups – observing the reactions of other people to our own behaviour. Some people are naturally sensitive to the mood of those about them. Others are brashly confident that everyone loves them; often these are successful men, surrounded by toadies, and it can be a grave shock to them when people show their real feelings, when they fall or are powerless. This form of observation is also a skill that can be practised – varying our manner or our arguments till tiny signals indicate that we are persuasive or successful. A perceptive man can use people he deals with almost as a mirror, to give him a picture of his own behaviour. Perhaps one experiences the highest degree of sensitivity when attracted to someone of the other sex; all senses are stretched to determine subtle questions of mood and timing, and bold actions are based on minute signals or indications. A manager who could reproduce this sort of sensitivity would be outstandingly perceptive.

7   Process planning and skills

It is not enough just to make this resolution: one must prepare methods of putting it into practice. Suppose I foresee that I will have to discuss something with a man who is emotional and prone to anger: I will not only resolve to avoid giving him offence, but I will think of pleasant words to prevent his anger, or get help from someone who can keep him in good temper.

St François de Sales, *Introduction to the Devout Life*, II. 9.

Task and process

It is generally assumed that people either get on well together or they do not – and that there is not much that can be done about it. This chapter is based on the opposite proposition – that it is possible to improve the way people work together, by deliberate planning, using formal methods, such as Systematic Approach. A first step is to distinguish between the job itself, and the way in which it is carried out. The job itself – building a house, or repairing a machine – is called the '*task*'. The way in which people think, feel or interact in carrying it out, is called '*process*'. Process is the main subject of this book.

Some examples of task problems are:

1 A machine breaks down.
2 You run out of stock.
3 Goods are below standard and have to be scrapped.

Some examples of process problems are:

1 Where one person wants to finish the meeting and another wants to get home (a question of aims).
2 Where one person is trying to plan for 3 years ahead, and his boss wants results yesterday (different timescales).
3 Where one person is too diffident to speak, or another is too brash to listen.
4 Where two colleagues loathe each other.
5 Where the production department wants to install new plant in a hurry, and the personnel department wants to take it slow and keep the union happy.

Process issues are of two main types:

1 Impersonal matters – methods of work, such as using Systematic Approach or identifying aims.
2 Matters of human interaction – the way in which people co-operate and affect each other; their emotions, reactions, and responses. These can be internal to oneself – such as boredom with the job, or complacency. (In this chapter most of the plans discussed are concerned with meetings of one sort or another. Other forms of process plans are discussed in Chapter 9 (on authority and leadership), and Chapter 15.)

We have seen the danger of too great a concentration on the job in hand. One can also find the opposite extreme, people who are process-mesmerized – so concerned for human relations that they forget there is a job to be done. One example is the politician who is unconcerned about policy as long as the party holds together and the opinion polls are sweet. People like this may be a social success, but they are a menace in business, since all they achieve is a warm cosy glow.

Process plans and procedures

Whenever strangers within one society meet, there are conventions to regulate their behaviour. They will each try to find out more about the other, while at the same time conducting themselves in a way that is predictable and not threatening, so that the acquaintance may continue. In some societies the ritual may be long and elaborate, as it was among seventeenth-century noblemen, who, since they all wore swords and worshipped 'honour', had to be careful not to give offence. Our own society is more relaxed, being governed by the principle that one does not behave in an offensive way without having a reason for doing so; but formal procedures are still there and apply, for example, at a first meeting to discuss business. And just as individuals pass from a stage of formality to one of friendship, based on its own unique conventions, so too a group of people needs to adopt conventions of its own which all understand.

Take a training group, made up of strangers. There will be an initial period of constraint, followed by one of over-talking and contradiction; people will be jockeying for position, will be slow to take in what others are saying, and they will not have built up a sufficient respect for each other to bother to listen. The first resource is to put someone in the chair 'to keep us all in order', but even they can do no more than make people talk in turn. They cannot *force* people to keep the argument sequential or progressive; the best they can do is impose their own direction, and pull the rest of the group after them. People may accept this for a time as the only way forward, but sooner or later they will see the chairman steering them in a direction they do not want to go; they will either switch off, or begin to challenge him, so that one is back to a power struggle.

What any committee needs is not so much a chairman, as chairmanship. There must be a procedure that people will stick to; if they appoint an individual and rely on him to do it all, they ignore their own responsibility for making the meeting work. This is not to say that a chairman is of no use – he may have an important function in whatever procedures they adopt. What is critical is that he should be told by the meeting exactly how those present expect him to operate; or at least that he should explain his own procedures so that they can support him. Above all, he must be clear that his role is one of process rather than task, helping the meeting to find solutions rather than imposing his own.

Naturally there must be enough community of aims for people to want to make the meeting work. Whatever the rules, you cannot stop people manipulating them to turn a meeting into a shambles, if that is their aim – as it was, for instance, of the Irish Party in the House of Commons after the rejection of Gladstone's Home Rule bill. A procedure is a tool that must be used with a dash of common sense, since too much formality can make a meeting wooden and cumbersome. People must understand what the rules are for and when they can sensibly be bent, and conform to the spirit of them.

Besides the basic framework of who speaks when, groups need to examine their particular problems and make plans and procedures to overcome them. The plans must be tried in action and reviewed to see how well they work. One committee found it maddening if the tea trolley arrived just as someone was in the middle of explaining a point. People would jump up and start passing cups around, the flow would be broken and there would be a long interruption. One afternoon the problem was discussed and it was decided that whoever was speaking when the tea arrived, should be responsible for handing it round; he would know the right moment to break off and be in a better position to pick up the argument later. The tea lady was asked to leave the cups at the back of the room and let the meeting get on with it. They found this procedure saved about 10 minutes a time. A petty success like this can encourage a group to tackle more complex problems, such as clarifying their own objectives.

Some examples of process plans are described below (more are described in Chapter 15). It is important to note that the plans, as described, are all generalized; in practice a plan needs to be tailor-made for a particular group of people, taking account of their roles and personalities.

Silence

It seems unnatural for a group of people sitting round a table to stop talking. The fact remains that while you are talking, you do not think, and while you think, you cannot listen. Often the quickest way to begin to solve a problem is to have a set period of silence (say 2 minutes) during which everyone just thinks, jotting down their ideas on a pad. Anyone who starts talking in the middle has to be firmly shut up. Thinking time can be useful when a new item on the agenda comes up – so that everyone can assemble their thoughts on it; or when several people start talking at once, in order to allow people to decide whether their contributions are really relevant and necessary (and to slow down the tempo, so that they are prepared to take their turn). For this purpose, even half a minute may be long enough. Where a range of suggestions is needed, the quickest procedure may be silence; ask for suggestions, and record them, without discussion; examine them and select the best. Anyone with no ideas (or whose idea has already been suggested) must avoid waffling, but merely say 'pass'.

Another use of silence is to give people time to take things in. Where facts or proposals are complicated, or have strong emotional implications (risk, disaster, etc.), you need to read the items slowly and impose a pause after each one. Ignore conventional noises, indicating that people have understood; wait till they actually come up with some of the implications and add them to the plan before you proceed. With high-level work, even apparently simple statements may need a period of thought before their full implications are grasped.

The essence of these procedures is that every member must know what he is meant to be thinking about, and come up with answers to the right question.

Charting

If an issue is complex or takes time to discuss, it is helpful if all the points made are listed on a large sheet of paper or a blackboard, so that people can keep in mind the whole picture. Once everyone has had his say and seen his views recorded, a good many points of conflict are usually eliminated. On the other hand, the real difficulties stand out and the group can concentrate on them. The practice of charting is quite common, particularly in the United States, and when it is done skilfully, the impact can be very great; the person at the chart may often in practice lead the meeting. Some points of good charting are codified in Appendix I.

Physical environment

People's behaviour is influenced not just by human reactions, but by the whole environment. Experiments have been carried out to see what effect surroundings have on the way people see each other. In one, groups of students were set in two different rooms; one room was well lit and comfortable; the other was a murky hole with no view, furnished only with a table and hard chairs. The students were then shown a series of photographs of people and asked to describe their characters. In every case the descriptions given by the group in the squalid room were far less favourable. Some time later (when the students had forgotten what they had said the first time round) the results were checked by exchanging the rooms and showing the photographs again. It was found that those who moved into the pleasant room became much more favourable in their judgements, while those who moved to the unpleasant room became more jaundiced.

The same thing happens at work. A light room with a view and plenty of space helps an assembly to open up its thinking, while in bad light or a confined space, people huddle together and are less likely to come forward with ideas. Firms that move into modern offices do not always find that performance has improved as they hoped, since buildings that are austere, air-conditioned, and artificially lit can be just as forbidding as any Victorian slum.

Another effect of environment is the sharp change of mood when people get into physical action. When a group gets bogged down trying to understand some problem, the result is often frustration; those who have ideas to put across talk louder, others begin to fidget, or start striding around the room, tempers fray and people become aggressive or depressed. However, if they can actually get on and do something, especially something which demands physical movement, they often find a sharp release of tension, while the experience itself can often make the problem clearer. This is all very well in training, but for groups of managers at work relevant physical activity is not so easy to come by, though a 10-minute break for fresh air and coffee is better than nothing. (There is value too for a firm in social activities of a strenuous sort, such as football or sailing, where people can get to know each other in an enjoyable context, which demands co-operation, and where improvement is possible.)

Manipulation

You can make a process plan for yourself – 'I will behave in the group in a certain way' – and this can be a help both to you and others, particularly if they know what you are up to. In fact, making private plans for a team doesn't usually work very well – first, because the plans are based on one-sided information, and, second, because other people can't contribute if they don't know what is going on, and may obstruct. Where it can become more suspect is if your plan reflects a secret intention to shape other people's actions to your ends. Some managers spend a lot of time on political intrigue, either to get their own way or just to protect their position. In some companies one cannot help it, since everyone operates this way, and if you don't you get nowhere.

Process planning has, of course, an important place in improving one's own skills – including the effect one has on other people. You can plan to speak better, or acquire a better sense of time; you can and should plan before an important meeting how to make the best effect. Probably you will keep your preparation to yourself, and there is no question of manipulation, as long as your aims are open.

One particular sort of plan should not be discussed openly: that is, a plan to get people's commitment. It is one of the quirks of human cussedness that if you say, 'My plan to get you interested is . . .', or worse still, 'Right, now are we all committed?', the reaction will be hostile. People know perfectly well that you want their interest and their effort, but they will feel manipulated if you tell them so.

Process skills

The distinction between task and process applies also to skills. Task skills are the skills of a trade, like operating a lathe, drawing up a balance sheet or planning routes for a transport fleet. Process skills are concerned with matters like determining objectives, setting measures of success and applying the stages of systematic approach, as well as dealing with people.

In industry everyone needs skill of both kinds. Even at the lowest level, people need to be able to co-operate. Anyone in supervision or management needs a range of skills, concerned with identifying objectives, finding ways of getting there, getting people committed, and establishing rules and routines for the group to operate. At a higher level still, you have to see that your subordinates themselves apply these skills, and indeed the higher you rise, the more important process becomes.

Skill is a matter of timing: this makes it hard to observe, since when timing and design are right, things go so smoothly that the skill is concealed. Often it is hard to tell whether a successful intervention is design or chance.

No one is completely without process skills: people have them in different combinations, and one can learn new ones, just as one can learn task skills such as driving a car. Some skills are intellectual, such as those associated with the various stages of systematic approach – aim-setting, or planning. Others are skills of social interaction, such as tact, or setting the pace of work. Some people's skills are moral, in that they can lead a group into behaving with courage or justice. Others enable an emotional situation to be controlled, by humour (when tension can be relieved with a laugh), peace-making, or providing support for someone else's ideas. On training courses managers have identified over sixty different process skills, such as:

(a) Aiming

– Visualizing results to be achieved in the short term.
– Producing clear statements of purpose.
– Questioning or probing, to discover and clarify aims.
– Proposing specific, measurable success criteria.
– Keeping aims continually in sight.
– Checking the continuing relevance of aims.

(b) Systematic Approach

– Providing factual information.
– Producing creative ideas.
– Giving a balanced assessment of risks.
– Questioning to draw out facts.
– Interpreting, or recognizing the implications of information.
– Outlining things to be done, activities, sub-tasks.
– Ensuring that plans are complete and understood.
– Recognizing when action is needed and giving the lead.
– Initiating review, and checking the achievement of aims.
– Recalling what happened accurately.
– Identifying successes and their causes.
– Indicating improvements for the future.

(c) Particular functions

– Chairing.
– Co-ordinating.
– Leading.
– Listening attentively.
– Encouraging ideas.
– Creating enthusiasm.
– Observation, sensitivity to others' needs.
– Summarizing at important moments.
– Clarity of expression.
– Patience and tolerance of opposition.
– Objectivity.
– Setting and maintaining high standards.
– Judging time requirements and monitoring the use of time.

(d) Effects on morale, etc.

– Timely humour.
– Integrity, reliability.
– Courage, determination.
– Honesty, humility.
– Concern for human values.

In any group, people are likely to have a range of contrasting process skills. Faced with a problem, one person will start straight off into action, while another may be analysing its causes. They can easily clash, the doer seeing the analyst as a ditherer, the analyst seeing the man of action as a cowboy. What is necessary is that they should be brought to see where the disagreement arises, and apply their skills in the proper sequence.

Support

A group cannot make use of the range of skills it possesses unless it has built up the habit of *support*. Support means making the full use of other people's proposals and contributions, in order to advance towards a common objective. It implies that any proposal should be valued as if it were one's own – improved, the snags overcome, and helped forward into action. It is only likely to occur under the following conditions:

1 When people in the group know each other's aims, and see them as at least compatible with their own.
2 When people respect each other enough to believe that the speaker is trying to help, and is worth listening to.
3 When there is a common procedure (such as Systematic Approach) to focus everyone's attention on the same point.
4 Where there is a will to co-operate.

Supporting someone else's proposal means taking a risk, since it demands an immediate positive response. A group of people will not all see a problem in precisely the same light, since their knowledge and background will be different. The speaker's judgement may be wrong, his idea may be worthless, or at any rate not the best solution; and besides, people may have to forfeit the chance of making a better contribution themselves. But against this one must balance the risk of *not* supporting; casting around for a better idea, which can take so long that the group gets nothing done at all. When support is used successfully, it breeds further trust and confidence, and courage to use it more.

There is often a great gulf in communication between senior and junior managers, the juniors tending to conceal problems in order to avoid a row. If they succeed, the boss, who is trying to plan the overall picture, is starved of information and will therefore make bad decisions. When a breakdown does come to his notice, he will often institute a grand inquisition, which may produce plenty of dirty linen, but never the whole picture; and in any case it will be too late to do much about it. This will arise whenever people feel that they are going to be blamed for an honest mistake. If, by contrast, they are confident that their boss will support them in putting things right, they will be far more ready to admit unpalatable facts. The boss in turn must support his subordinates and their contributions to the team, and it is up to him to make the first move. Someone who encourages other people in this way will often be seen as the leader of a group, whether or not he is the official head.

Weakness into strength

Almost any piece of human behaviour can be seen in a good or a bad light, depending on whether the aims of the other party are the same as one's own. In 1935 Winston Churchill was an obstinate warmonger; in 1940 he was a tenacious bulldog, the only man with the grip to secure victory. The behaviour was very similar – only the observers' bias was different. For a manager, the important thing is that once a quality is seen in a good light, it can be used. There was once a gate-keeper in a factory who drove management mad by his obsessive concern with security, insisting on inspecting the Chairman's pass three times a day. At last the personnel manager was instructed to get rid of him. Instead, he considered whether there was any role where this characteristic could be put to use, and finally hit on the stores, where pilfering and waste had risen unusually high. Accordingly, he offered the man a last chance as a store-keeper. In a few weeks not only were the stock losses reduced, but the new store-keeper was a changed man, confident rather than surly, and even able to apply a degree of flexibility that he had never shown when he was on the gate.

This ability to see someone's apparent weakness in a positive light is a crucial skill of management. If you have a subordinate who is unsatisfactory, sit down and list his defects; with a bit of thought you should be able to identify in each of them some positive aspect that can be put to use, either by adapting his present job or finding him another one. Slapdash work may indicate speed of decision; rudeness, a capacity for straight talking; and timidity, a talent for procedure and detail.

Development of a team

Working groups can carry out process planning at three different levels:

1 *Regulatory procedures.* These tend to be fairly conventional, dealing with matters such as issuing minutes, holding weekly meetings, etc. They may cut out time-wasting, but they will not lead to positive improvement of performance.
2 *Plans to use skills.* This means getting the right person in the right role, with the right support – if necessary, cutting across the formal hierarchy.

As members build up confidence in each other, they automatically turn to the person with the appropriate skill and support him, so that the team's speed becomes, not that of the slowest, but the fastest.

3 *Plans for personal development.* In this, the third stage, whoever has the skill becomes not an executant but a teacher; his objective is not to use the skill himself, but to ensure that it is developed by others. There are risks in this, of course. When the group turn to someone who wants to develop a skill, rather than the person who has it, they risk wasting time and coming up with poor results, and they may decide because of the importance of the task, that it is just not on. Its advantage is that each member has constant encouragement to develop his own skills, which not only improves the group but fulfils a fundamental human need. In this, the mature team, self-discipline replaces the conformity that is so often associated with teamwork. A group like this is anything but conformist; it is a liberating environment, in which each wants the others to express his/her own strength, to the benefit of the community.

Emotion

Man is an emotional creature as well as a logical one, and it is dangerous to ignore it. A mature person is not scared of emotions and does not try to drive them underground, but instead recognizes and uses them.

Everyone knows people they find it difficult to get on with – usually about 10 per cent of those one meets. If a boss feels this way about a subordinate, he may be tempted to try to get him transferred or sacked, while the subordinate who feels this way about his boss must either cure it or get out. How can this kind of emotional incompatibility be overcome? The answer lies in observation: what do I do that irritates this person? How can I help him, and what are his strengths that could help me? If you concentrate on these – seeing the best in him and taking advantage of where he can be helpful – your feelings may gradually change.

If a group has emotional problems, the first need is for the members, particularly the manager, to have the courage to bring them into the open. Until they are recognized, you cannot make plans to overcome them. A good way of building mutual confidence is by facing and sharing risks together. Bringing emotions out of their holes is itself quite a severe risk, but as a team develops, people find it is a risk they can take. This is not to say they should behave like a psychotherapeutic group, and spend their time discussing how they feel. The purpose of a work group is to get things done, and emotions are its servants, not its masters. Individuals have considerable power over both their own moods and those of people round them, and they have a duty to use this influence positively; frustration has to be turned into enthusiasm, conflict into co-operation and antagonism into involvement. A team can collectively improve its morale, first by getting a move on towards action (if necessary using systematic approach to help them); second, by explicitly reconciling the aims of individuals with those of the team, so that one and all have an interest in progress.

You find this especially in small teams engaged in specialized activities such as research; to an outsider the atmosphere is informal and the behaviour unorthodox, but there is no quarrelling with the results. The group becomes much more than the sum of its members, both in terms of ideas produced and of work done. Rowers have experienced something like this, when a crew 'comes together'. For weeks, months, eight individuals oars have slogged away on practice outings, trying to co-ordinate their skills to form a crew. Then one day it happens. The boat seems to take on a life of its own; the oarsmen can forget their conscious concern with balance and getting a neat finish together, and concentrate instead in applying their strength at exactly the right moment in each stroke. Such moments, when a crew 'comes together' for the first time, are probably the sport's greatest reward.

For some people who have once experienced the effect of a group 'forming', it becomes an objective of great importance throughout the rest of their career to recreate the experience. This may be a snare, for a group may form itself on the basis of false objectives, or satisfaction may take precedence over results. Forming a team, like other matters of process, is never an end in itself.

8   Listening

First man in railway carriage: 'Is this Wembley?'
Second man: 'No, it's Thursday.'
Third man: 'So am I: let's get out and have one.'
                                                    Anon

Meaning and purpose

Listening is usually reckoned to be perfectly straightforward – if you talk to someone, naturally he will be listening to what you say. But listening effectively, that is, really absorbing and understanding what someone means, is a skill which is difficult and complex. Think of any meeting you attend: for much of the time you are preoccupied with your own thoughts; at other moments the meeting drifts away from its objectives, and the argument is hardly worth attending to. Now and then three people start talking at once and, however hard you concentrate, you do not know which voice to follow. People who have something to contribute are very often not listening at all; they are waiting, not very patiently, for the other fool to shut up.

Listening calls for several distinct activities:

1 *Noticing* that someone is speaking; this may itself involve pulling yourself away from your own thoughts.
2 *Absorbing the words* that he is using. Quite often while switching your attention across, you will have missed the first sentence or so, and have to reconstruct it.
3 Deciding *what the speaker means.* Many people are clumsy speakers, others are devious or shy, so this may not be easy.
4 Deciding his *purpose* in speaking, and how it relates to the business you are engaged in.

Of course where a statement is obviously ambiguous, you can stop the speaker and ask – or better still, repeat back the statement in your own words, to check that you understand; but most of the time you depend on your own interpretation, and the best piece of evidence is knowledge or perception of what the speaker is trying to achieve. Listening is always easiest where a common aim really is accepted, since then everyone is on the same wavelength. Another clue to meaning may be the extent to which the speaker habitually looks ahead. (When someone says, 'We've got to improve the office', if you know their normal time perspective, it will indicate whether they are talking about shifting a few desks around tomorrow, or large-scale rebuilding the year after next.) There is no leisure to ruminate on all this, because either someone else will start talking, or you have to answer yourself. In fact, although the process of thought is very quick, the time taken is still appreciable: when a group is really listening, there will be a distinct pause between one contribution and the next, even though they may not be aware of it, and may be amazed if they hear their discussion played back afterwards on tape.

Whether you take all this trouble about someone's contribution depends on what you think of him. People who are always chattering about something trivial or irrelevant, will not get the same attention as someone who speaks rarely but to the point. It is the same perhaps with social animals. 'I was delighted,' wrote Addison, 'in observing that deference which the rest of the pack paid to each particular hound, according to the character he had acquired among them. If they were at fault and an old hound of reputation opened but once, he was immediately followed by the whole cry: while a raw dog, or one that was a noted liar, might have yelped his heart out, without being taken notice of.' (*The Spectator*, No. 116.)

Supportive development

Meetings can be formal, or merely chance encounters. Formal meetings have the advantage of procedures (whose main purpose is simply to help listening) but what really matters is the personal behaviour of individuals. A meeting works best when each contribution is related to the one before, since people can concentrate without having to wrench their minds from one point to another. Each successive speaker must try to develop the last point, or correct it, but avoid killing it by changing the subject or coming up with a totally different idea of his own. This means developing the habit of identifying the useful points in any remark, however clumsily expressed; after all, unless the speaker is a complete fool, there must be some sense in it, and if his idea is strangled at birth, the sense will be lost. If you have to point out some snag which seems to you insuperable, what matters is how you phrase it: there is all the difference in the world between saying, 'That's hopeless, because . . .', and saying, 'Yes, fine, but what about . . . ?' In the first case the likely result is the loss of the idea, or at least friction between you and whoever proposed it; in the second, you have directed everybody's mind to one problem, and invited them to find a solution. In a group where this is normal practice, one can find six or a dozen contributions, each following on from the one before and each pushing a problem nearer to a better solution than any one individual could produce on his own.

This practice, which we may call 'supportive development' is one aspect of the kind of support described in the last chapter. It does not need to be verbal. If someone says 'It's hot in here', the way to support him is not by saying, 'I agree' (which gets you nowhere) but by opening the window. Supportive development will only flower when people trust each other, and are ready to assume that what anyone says is worthwhile; and when they have a positive attitude, being disposed to look for what is constructive and useful, rather than spotting the reasons why nothing can be done. Naturally, support breeds support, since if someone finds you help his ideas into action, he is ready to look for the good in yours. And once people realize that any suggestion they make will be considered seriously, and very likely adopted, they are much less likely to come out with foolish remarks they do not really believe in. (See Figure 8.1.)

In some groups, people are in competition with each other. Some companies run themselves that way, everyone at meetings striving to shine in front of the boss. Not surprisingly, this sort of atmosphere makes co-operation difficult; if everyone is out for themselves, there is not much point in listening to what the others have to say – except when they reveal their aims or their weaknesses, which one can use to do them down. So people keep their real objectives hidden, and one's interpretation of their meaning may be wildly adrift. In this climate they may talk more, but they will say less: stress causes people to be loquacious, but not to reveal what they think. Groups where members are building confidence in each other accept longer periods of silence, to give a chance to think. People who do not trust their colleagues are scared of silence, since someone else may make their point first. Silence does not of course necessarily indicate co-operation, for people may be quiet because they are resentful, bored, timid, or merely lost. The thing to cultivate is a sort of directed silence that indicates thought, and the sign of it is that after a silent period, contributions become more relevant and the atmosphere more relaxed.

Making proposals

For a contribution to be useful, it must be relevant to four separate factors:

1 To the last contribution made.
2 To the aims of the discussion.
3 To the stage of Systematic Approach (there is no worse nuisance than someone who keeps planning, when what is wanted is more information).
4 To the mood of the meeting. It is no good saying, 'Come on, let's go', if the rest of them are still deep in thought or digestion. The identical remark may strike gold 3 minutes later – but timing is crucial.

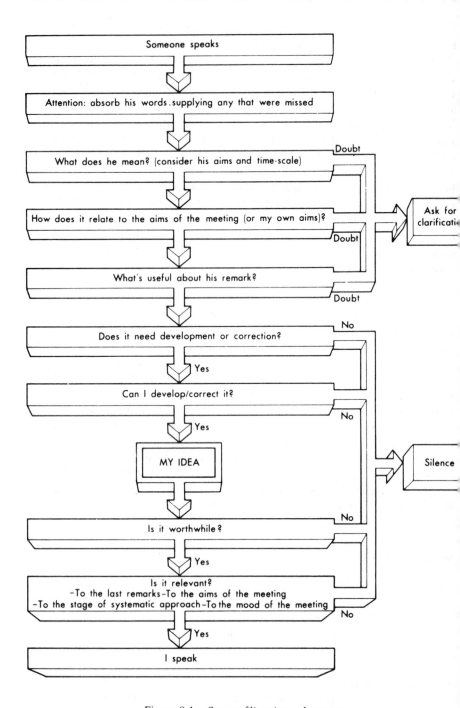

Figure 8.1   *Stages of listening and support*

What takes a meeting forward are positive proposals, so phrased that they lead to action. Contributions in the form, 'Would it be possible . . .' or 'Someone should . . .' are less likely to do this than ones beginning 'I propose . . .' The sure way of holding up the meeting is to present it with a choice. If you say 'Shall we have lunch now . . . or finish item 6?' then, sure as fate, the meeting will split fifty-fifty and neither will get done. If you say 'I propose we break for lunch now,' there is every chance that they will follow your lead. This does not mean that it is never right to present choices, but it is a matter of risk. If the risk is high, in the sense that, if the wrong choice is made, the loss will be serious, then you need to explore any possibilities: you may even need to slow down a meeting that is rushing into action too fast. But it is far more common to find the opposite fault – all talk and no action.

The problem with being positive is that you may be seen as bossy, or critical – and this is particularly true when you are making a process observation. A comment may be more acceptable in the form, 'Would it help if Jones repeated his proposal?' rather than a blunt statement like, 'Not one of you was listening to Jones.' Avoid blaming what has happened: if you think a group has been pursuing the wrong objective, propose that the objective should be changed. Obviously you may be called upon to give reasons, and have to go back into the past, but if you start off by suggesting that the group has gone wrong, this leads to dissension before your proposal is even considered. Sometimes it is helpful to show the status of an intervention by putting a label in front of it – to indicate whether it is a proposal or a piece of information or whatever. If you say, '*There is some information that* sales will have to double before we can break even,' people will realize, first, that you have facts at your disposal and are not just guessing; second, that what you are saying is not to be taken as criticism; third, that this is a point they must consider before they get to the WHTBD stage. The device becomes tedious if it is used too much, and may sound like pointless jargon to strangers, but used with discretion it can help.

Types of discussion

The form of discussion I have described – with one person speaking, the rest listening, all contributions supporting each other, and pauses for thought – is the most effective way of bringing a group towards an agreed course of action, but it is hard work, even for people who are used to it. In some cultures outside northern Europe and North America, it may be too artificial to work at all: a group of South Americans, for example, has the knack of listening while talking themselves at the tops of their voices, and can apparently make sense of a discussion that would strike an Anglo-Saxon as bedlam.

Again, if you are not pressed for time, a meeting conducted with strict self-discipline may not be the best way to get creative results. If you really do need a wide range of ideas (Figure 8.2), like advertising slogans or jokes for a comic script, it may be better to let everyone speak at once so that they spark each other off; or to use some structured form of this, such as brainstorming, whereby ideas are called out and listed on a chart without being either considered or criticized, so that they can be evaluated at leisure. Leisure will certainly be needed. If you are to handle a range of ideas, you must have some good hard criteria, set in advance, so that the group can evaluate rationally without everyone rooting for their own pet schemes. You can use these criteria to cut down a long list of ideas to a short list, bearing in mind that even an idea that does not immediately meet the criteria can perhaps be developed. You may need to consider whether two or three of the ideas can be combined, to give the advantages of all of them; and, finally, you may have to develop several of the front-runners, before you really know which is the best.

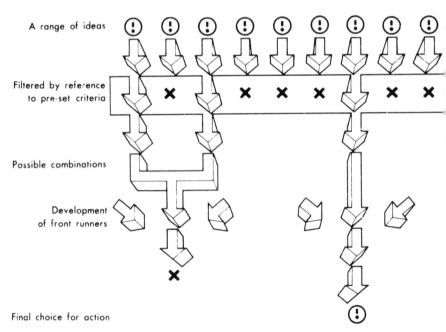

A range of ideas

Filtered by reference to pre-set criteria

Possible combinations

Development of front runners

Final choice for action

Figure 8.2   *Processing a range of ideas*

There may be times when all this is needed, but managers are usually more concerned with finding some straightforward solution and getting action quickly. Even when a high-quality solution is essential, support and development of one idea may give just as good a result as picking and choosing among a variety.

9   Authority and leadership

Therefore, if the modern world is going astray, look in your own self – the cause is in you.

Dante, *Purgatorio*, XVI. 82

Authority and leadership

Authority, the *Concise Oxford Dictionary* tells us, is the power to enforce obedience; it is used here in a positive sense, as *the power to initiate action*. Authority is always closely related to responsibility: you cannot after all hold someone responsible for a job that they have no authority to get done (though there are managers who try), while power without responsibility is what Stanley Baldwin called 'the privilege of the harlot' – and is a recipe for backstairs intrigue.

Authority can be delegated, and hierarchies are based on this. Responsibility, on the other hand, can never be unloaded on to a subordinate, since the manager remains responsible, however his staff let him down. Of course, he can blame them for it, but his superiors in turn are justified in blaming him, for assigning the job to someone who was not up to it. Naturally the manager deserves corresponding credit when his subordinates do well. In a healthy organization he will pass the praise publicly down the line (following the sound rule of complimenting in public but reprimanding in private) and it will not be seen as in any way diluting his own credit.

Since a manager has to risk his neck on the chances of his subordinates doing a good job, it follows that he ought to be allowed plenty of say in selecting, training, and rewarding them. If his department is packed with people he does not trust, perhaps because some remote personnel department deals with selection, he will not risk delegating as he should. In the same way he is entitled to a good deal of say in all the factors that may affect their morale, such as salary.

People can take responsibility upon themselves, for good or ill, even if it is not directly given to them. If I decide to solve an industrial dispute by making a special payment for which I have no authority, I must answer for the consequences – including consequences outside my immediate control, such as a stoppage in another factory when the union gets to hear about it.

There are many ways in which authority can arise. In traditional societies it depends on birth; in a police state the main source is the power of government to punish behaviour it dislikes – and even in a democracy this remains one aspect. But in paid employment, authority springs from the power to spend money – both to reward individuals and to provide resources for chosen projects.

Authority – task and process

The second definition of authority the dictionary gives is 'personal influence'. In any organization, cutting across the authority of money and rank, there is the network of influence that one person has on his fellows, which makes it possible for a rigid hierarchy and erratic human beings to co-exist. We can call the authority of rank '*task authority*', since it is based on the requirements of the job; the second kind, the power to initiate developments in human interaction, we may call '*process authority*'. Task authority is concentrated in the hands of the few – the owners and their deputies – but it can be delegated. Process authority is personal and cannot be delegated, but it is distributed much more evenly through the ranks of the organization. The doorman, for example, or the car park attendant may have virtually no task authority, but he may have the process authority to strike up conservation with the chairman and so to influence his thinking. When the Roman Emperor Trajan was riding out of the City to lead a campaign, an old woman called out after him with a petition, which he was in too much hurry to consider. She screamed after him, 'If you've no time to listen, you're no emperor.' He heard her above the crowd, and was brought back by her authority (which rested on the Roman tradition of palm-tree justice) to wait and hear her out. If such authority can be exercised at long range, over a man one has never met (who in this case was the ruler of the world and regarded as a god), it is far more potent at close range – with, say, one's own manager. Here is a man you see perhaps every day; his task authority may be considerable, but you have just as much opportunity to influence him by argument or emotion as he has to influence you, and just as much responsibility for improving the way in which the two of you work together. In the last count, it is never an absolute defence to say you could not get something done because your boss would not let you. You failed to exercise the necessary process authority. It may be that to get the results you need, you must persuade not one but two or three levels of the hierarchy above, by turning your own manager from a block to an advocate. The inertia of large numbers is very great, but it can be overcome, provided that you have the necessary information and that your aims and the company's are aligned.

Authority in a group can operate in a variety of ways. Sometimes task authority is paramount, as when the manager is the expert as well, or discipline is very rigid. Sometimes one person may exercise what is virtually a process dictatorship – often found where there is a vacuum of task authority, as in a group of students. Sometimes leadership circulates among the group, being held now by the boss (who controls the task decisions and the purse strings), now by the expert in a particular field or a particular stage of systematic approach, and now by whoever happens to feel strongly about the subject being discussed.

Steering and joining

One source of authority is knowledge. If I am the only member of a team who knows where the pub is, the rest have no choice but to follow me (or stay thirsty). Authority like this is temporary – share it, and the authority is gone. It often happens in an organization that one department sets up a project or meeting to which a number of other departments have to contribute. The initiating department does the preliminary work, and its representative will know all about it and be in a position to steer the meeting – even though he may be junior to other people there. He will obviously need the skills of presenting, informing and briefing; however, if this is all he does, he may easily fail to get his way, since he needs also to get the *commitment* of people present. After all, he 'owns' the project, they don't; he has taken decisions (if only by selecting what information to present), which they may resent. The further down the chain of Systematic Approach he takes it, the more difficult he will find it to carry his colleagues with him. If he ends with 'So my plan is . . .', he may find active hostility (unless it is an emergency, or an issue which others regard as trivial or boring – in which case decisiveness will be welcomed).

How far down the line you go is a matter of judgement, depending on the expertise and attitude of the joiners and the urgency of the job. The 'steerer' may suggest the aims but let others explore and add to them; he may present information, but invite people to correct or amplify it; he may make proposals, but in the light of other people's ideas, as well as his own. He would be unwise to assume that silence indicates commitment, but must look for signs that other people are genuinely contributing. These rules for steering apply to all sorts of people, from trainers to salesmen. They also apply to formal managers, though, because of their task authority, they can get away with rather stronger guidance.

The converse of a steerer is a joiner, and he has responsibilities too – to veil his impatience if he thinks the steerer it too autocratic, to get himself committed to the task, and to consider the steerer's proposals on their merits, however ineptly they may be presented.

Management and leadership

Leadership often has an air of grandeur or mystery, which makes it harder to have a cool look at what leaders actually do. Yet their success is based on straightforward process skills, which can be developed by training. It is true that qualities of personality, such as courage and determination, play a part, but in peacetime at least, skill is predominant.

The main job of directors, in their leadership role, is to establish the organization's mission and communicate a sense of it down the line, letting everyone see that the job they are doing is worthwhile. They must also convey a sense of the company's fundamental decency: that it is a good place to work in, allowing openness and initiative; that it expects high standards, and rewards them handsomely. Middle managers normally have to pursue aims that they must accept (though they can explore and interpret them). They have responsibility for passing a sense of mission down the line, as well as for 'managing upwards' – steering their seniors where they seem to be going wrong, and forwarding valid points from their own subordinates.

Below board level, the main leadership skills that managers need are:

- Setting or clarifying aims, communicating them down the line, and getting feedback.
- Monitoring and improving the quality of work.
- Generating energy, commitment and enthusiasm.
- Discovering and using people's skills.
- Developing both individuals and teams.
- Adapting their style to the situation.
- Deciding which jobs they should do themselves, and where they should consult, or delegate.

The three prime focuses of attention are the task, the team, and the individuals within it. Here the skills of awareness are crucial. Is the team falling apart? Are individuals under pressure? Is the task faltering at some point? One can, for instance, have a group of able subordinates who don't all pull together, or whose opinion of each other is low. Equally one can find a smooth-running team that misses its targets, being so wrapped up with its internal concerns that the task gets neglected.

But there are two other focuses of attention that are almost equally important. The first is the manager's own performance, and his skills and deficiencies. It may be that he needs to work on some weakness by developing himself. It may equally be that he can cover it by delegating some specific responsibility, and if this frees him for his main task of leadership, it is often the best way forward. The other focus is the view of senior management on his performance, often reflecting the culture of the organization. You may be managing well, in a highly relaxed style, but there are some organizations where superiors expect leaders to be autocrats – they see democracy as chaos, delegation as irresponsibility, and the manager's successes as being all to the credit of his subordinates.

The interaction of superiors, team, task and individuals is shown in Figure 9.1.

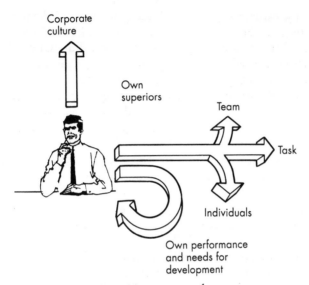

Corporate culture

Own superiors

Team

Task

Individuals

Own performance and needs for development

Figure 9.1 *Management and awareness*

A leader in the true sense, goes far beyond what merely competent managers feel called upon to do. A manager instructs subordinates to do jobs: a leader makes them want to succeed. A manager gives out information needed for the task: a leader uses communication for other purposes – to inspire, to build confidence and morale, and to develop his subordinates. A manager gives feedback to correct errors: a leader gives feedback to reward, encourage, and aim higher. A manager takes the individuals and the team as he finds them, and points them at targets: a leader develops the individuals, and strengthens the team, so that they can tackle a succession of higher targets, leading towards common goals. A manager arranges with people to do what he wants, in return for pay and status: a leader blends the aims of his team with his own.

A manager's style

The way task authority is exercised very often determines the climate of a group, and a manager can choose how he wants his own team to operate.

He can vary his style from time to time to suit the needs of the job. Three main factors determine which style to choose:

1 The morale and competence of subordinates.
2 The type of task (timescale, risk and need for quality).
3 The stage of Systematic Approach one is at.

Some of the earliest research into leadership was carried out in America in the 1930s by Kurt Lewin. He was a refugee from Nazi Germany and was much struck by differences between Germany and the United States in the social atmosphere and the way discipline was exercised. He set up an experiment in which groups of boys carried out a task (making paper masks) under three different versions of leadership, which one might describe as autocratic, consultative, and *laissez-faire*. The results were broadly as shown in Table 9.1.

Table 9.1 *Lewin's experiment re leadership*

Types of leadership	Results
Autocratic	
The leader imposed tasks; the boys did what they were told.	Production results were high in quantity, but sometimes faulty in quality.
The leader kept them in the dark about the next move, but revealed his plan stage by stage.	When the leader left the room, little work was done. The boys took the opportunity to break up what they had made.
	In some groups the level of aggression was very high, channelled towards the leader or other outsiders, or towards a scapegoat. In other groups aggression was very low and they seemed apathetic and dependent.
Consultative	
The leader helped the group to make plans and decide how they were going to work. He gave information when needed, but left delegation to the group.	Production was less in quantity but higher in quality. The boys regarded their product with pride. Work continued, even when the leader left the room. The boys were better able to deal with frustration and to direct aggression towards the true source of annoyance.
Laissez-faire	
The leader offered no help and exercised no control.	Groups lacked direction and were much less productive. Lots of suggestions were made but very few were implemented. When the leader left the room, production sometimes actually rose – perhaps because some able boy took over. Aggression was highest of all.

Another well-known experiment in communication throws light on the effect of management styles. The participants are placed round a table in individual cubicles, and allowed to communicate with each other only by passing notes. They are given a problem to solve, one which requires that everyone should contribute a piece of information that only he has. Two forms of communication are tried: the first, in which each participant may pass notes only to neighbours on each side of him; the second, in which all communications must be through one 'star' man at the centre. In the first version everyone is involved and feels it is his job to bring out the answer; however, there can be a good deal of paper flying around, and although the decision is usually of high quality, it may take a long time coming. In the second experiment the answer tends to come more quickly (provided the 'star' man gets all the information, and has the skill), but while he is up to his neck, the rest of the team feel bored and frustrated, since they do not know what is going on. (See Figure 9.2.)

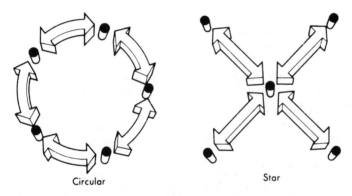

Circular   Star

Figure 9.2   *Circular and star patterns of communication*

These two patterns of communication are obviously related to management style. A consultative manager may sometimes be forced to operate as a 'star' man, e.g. if his subordinates are far apart, or on the move, but he will encourage direct communication between them wherever possible. The autocrat, however, is bound to discourage sideways communication that excludes him, since if he is to take the decisions, he needs all the facts. The communications experiment suggests that consultative management may take longer to get the job done, but the quality of results will be high, and subordinates will have a greater sense of personal fulfilment and achievement. The dangers of autocratic management are that the leader is overworked, communications get blocked and decisions are delayed, while subordinates are frustrated. This does not mean that autocratic leadership is always wrong. If you need results in a hurry, if quantity is more important than quality, or there is little scope for people to use their initiative, one may well need to act in an autocratic way. But do not expect the good results to last forever – and especially not when your back is turned. You must also allow for the effects of aggression – for example, by budgeting for strikes.

Of course, the choice of management style often depends more on emotion or moral feelings than on grounds of interest. The manager who acts like a Victorian ironmaster will no doubt justify his behaviour in terms of results, but he is also fulfilling his own idea of himself and of his place in society. Similarly, a manager who has to keep a department in being can no doubt amply justify a consultative approach, but if he achieves it with conviction, it is as likely as not to be the result of a moral preference. On balance and in the long term, the consultative style scores, both practically and morally; however, it needs more skill, and any shift in approach must be carefully planned, or it may be seen as abdication.

In firms where for years management and employees have been at loggerheads, the effect of suddenly relaxing a highly autocratic control may be that no work gets done at all. Even in firms where there is basic goodwill, subordinates faced with a change in management style need a chance to experiment and adjust, just as the manager does himself. However, as some of the case studies show, a change of style can be made even in unpromising circumstances; and in a society that forbids the cruder forms of coercion, a democratic style is the only sure way by which a sense of energy can be created and maintained.

Management style and Systematic Approach

The style a manager should adopt varies according to the stage of Systematic Approach the task is at. This needs to be considered in some detail.

Aims

Consultative leadership is based on guiding people towards aims they all accept. (If they don't, why should they co-operate, and how can you trust them to use their initiative?) Aims, then, must be on the table for all to see. But since discovering aims for oneself gives deeper insight than just being told, the manager must avoid giving a lecture, but encourage questioning and be open with his answers. Also (and this is the heart of team building) he must understand and support the personal aims of his staff. With autocratic management, aims will not be discussed (though they may be stated) and in general they will be less well known. People can function without knowing the purpose, as long as they are trained to the work and instructions are clear; but they cannot use much initiative, since they cannot tell that the direction they set is the right one. Again, if they lack a sense of direction, their commitment may be low, especially if they feel their own personal aims are ignored. Commitment is high under an autocratic regime only when there is some overriding common aim; people will accept a degree of dictatorship in the interests of winning a war – provided their welfare is given reasonable consideration, or at least there is equality of sacrifice.

Information stage

Under an autocracy, information is often buried, for three reasons:

1 Subordinates try to hide what the boss will not like
2 People see knowledge as power and are reluctant to pass it on, since it may help their competitors for the autocrat's favour
3 Information flow is concentrated through the boss, and he may be too busy to take it all in, let alone pass it out to those who need it

As a result, the grapevine flourishes. Besides circulating facts, its function is to supply meaning, when the authorities do not condescend to explain. No one likes being kept in the dark, so the interpretations people put on the motives of management will often be shrewd, but seldom flattering.

Of course, the enlightened autocrat can do a lot to overcome these problems. (One useful device is the 'briefing group', to make sure that all levels in the company get the facts, at least as they are known to the management.)

By contrast, if the leader adopts an open, democratic approach, people will speak freely; provided he is seen as forward-looking rather than vindictive, rumours will be discussed (which can be important both for the fact of their existence and because they may be true) and unpleasant information will come out in time to do something about it.

Decision-taking

Decisions are not the bogeymen they are made out to be, but they still exist. Big decisions, especially on matters of policy, must be taken at the top – which is what the top is for. But rational decision-making depends on having a full range of options from which to choose – in fact on a free flow of ideas and information. Less important decisions are best pushed down the line as far as they can practically go. ('Practically' means where people have the background knowledge, the technical skill and commitment to the company's aims.) This has the following advantages:

1 Decisions are made by people who are familiar with the local facts.
2 Decisions are made by those who have to carry them out. People are stuck with the consequences of their own plans, and committed to making a success of them.
3 The top keeps its decks clear for really important matters.

Of course, any delegation risks bad decisions being made and objectives not being met. To make a success of it, you need to make regular use both of success criteria and review meetings, the dates for which should be fixed as soon as any project is assigned.

This is the pattern of successful management, at any rate in our culture. It is worth comparing the practice in Japan, where important decisions are often taken not by the board but by the company at large. If the question is whether to switch production from motorbikes to cars, this is passed down from the board and discussed: the foreman discusses it, the doorman discusses it, no one taking up an entrenched position, everyone behaving with non-committal courtesy. At length, a consensus is reached, and the decision is implemented. The disadvantage is that a decision may take years to come through – as exasperated Western salesmen find when they try to do business with Japanese. The advantage is that as soon as a decision is taken, it is known and accepted by everyone; the company switches to its new mode of operation, with the minimum of drama and in an incredibly short time. On its home ground, this approach obviously brings results. Its success may partly depend on other aspects of Japanese culture – for example, lifetime employment in one company.

Planning and action

Groups are incompetent planners: it is cumbersome to have more than one person (or two or three at most) to decide the details of actions and timing. Where 'planning' sessions are held, their real purpose is communication – for everyone to hear what everyone else is to do, and see how the parts fit in. This is particularly needed when the members of a team will be separated from each other, or when time is short, and they are facing an emergency. In a real emergency what matters is not that the best of all plans should be devised, but that one plan should be carried out by everyone – fast. A fire-fighting team does not go into committee when the building is about to fall: indeed the great difficulty for fire officers, and people with similar jobs, is to realize that the sort of no-questions style that is essential when fighting a fire is the wrong way to build a team when the pressure is off.

During the action stage, there may not be much difference between the behaviour of the consultative and the autocratic leader; the difference will be in the behaviour of their teams. The members of the autocrat's team will do what they are told – no more and (if supervised) no less. The consultative leader's team – whose members know the aims and the information – may well have useful suggestions to make, and volunteer to take on some of the action themselves; they will be ready to improvise, and alert for ways to improve their own performance or help their colleagues.

Many elderly autocrats adopted their style from what they saw in the forces; and yet, ironically, successful commanders in the field have often used a very different kind of leadership. A famous example is Nelson's 'band of brothers' in the Mediterranean, in the months before the battle of the Nile. Whenever the fleet was becalmed, the captains would come aboard the flagship and dine there, and the afternoon would be occupied with discussions of tactics for the battle which everyone knew would soon take place. When at last it came, the Admiral had no need to make any signal, for not only were his captains ready to work to a plan which they all understood, but since they knew each other so well, they could improvise and improve, even under fire. Such leadership is far removed from the 'do this, do that' of the sergeant-major.

Review

The review stage is similar to the information stage. An autocrat will hardly expect his subordinates to have improved on his plan: he will be looking for deviations – which they will be trying to conceal. Even if they have had successes, they will be shy of coming out with them, in case there is some rule against it. Reviews may well engender a good deal of heat, but not much light. In one company that was trying to change from an autocratic tradition, the board noticed that a branch that had been making a loss for years had suddenly turned up a respectable profit. One of the directors decided to investigate. He travelled down and grilled the local manager, who seemed decidedly cagey about what had happened. The director took him out to lunch and fed him well, and gradually came back to the subject of profits. The manager suddenly burst out, 'Well, look, I'll tell you what we did: but promise you won't let on to anyone. At the end of last year we showed the shop stewards the last three years' results and said to them, "These chaps in London aren't going to put up with us making a loss much longer. If we don't do something quick, they'll close us down." It scared them properly, and that's how we made a profit. But don't pass it on.' In fact there was no earthly reason why the manager should not show his results to the unions, but being used to an autocratic environment he assumed that anything not ordered was forbidden. In a consultative environment, individuals will readily describe their successes and will be less shy of admitting failures.

If a team is working to goals that all its members accept, any members may find themselves momentarily in the lead – making the proposals that get implemented, providing the impetus – through their knowledge or skill in dealing with the particular problem. The one area in which managers should keep the lead, and if possible excel, is that of process. They should be fortified by process authority – and the awareness that lets them adjust their style, both to the needs of the team and the job.

10   Building on success

The untapped resources of the North Sea are as nothing compared to the untapped resources of our people. I am convinced that the great mass of our people go through life without even a glimmer of what they could have contributed to their fellow human beings.

Jimmy Reid, *Reflections of a Clyde-Built Man*

Mechanistic, organic, ethical

In their working lives people operate in several different systems, each with their own problems to be solved and laws to be understood. (A 'system' in this sense is a complex of related facts, governed by laws which are internally consistent, but which may not apply outside it.) Professions have their own systems – lawyers work in one, engineers in another. But there are three systems in which virtually all managers work, which we might call 'mechanistic, organic and ethical'.*

The *mechanistic* system includes everything governed by the inorganic physical sciences and all the products of engineering and manufacture. We can analyse the functioning of a machine or the properties of a chemical substance and predict with certainty how they will behave, knowing that in precisely similar situations they will behave in exactly the same way. Because they are so predictable, the exceptions become important; when faced with a problem, one's normal procedure is to look for what goes wrong, in order to eliminate the cause.

Contrast the second system – the *organic*, which governs the relationship between living beings. The first difference is that of complexity. So many cells make up a human being, so many human beings make up a group, or company, or nation, that they are always, in the terms of cybernetics, 'exceedingly complex systems', since no conceivable amount of human knowledge could unravel the chain of cause and effect. Compared with this, any mechanistic design, even the most powerful computer is simple and predictable. If I hit a computer with a hammer, it will stop working. If I hit you with a hammer, you may respond by bursting into tears, by calling a policeman, or by hitting me back. I might make a shrewd guess at your behaviour if I knew you well, but I could never be absolutely certain.

* For mechanistic and organic systems see T. Burns and G.M. Stalker, *The Management of Innovation* (Tavistock Publications, 1961).

Many mechanical problems can be solved by knowledge alone. If I read the handbook carefully, I should be able to start the motor mower. But with organic problems, because of the uncertainty, book learning can never replace experience, though it may make the experience come quicker. A young man with a degree in social sciences who thinks people will react as the textbook says is a worse risk than a learner driver on a motorbike.

The third system is *ethical*, and that too has rules of its own. A may have good organic grounds for believing that the way to get B's compliance is to hit him with a hammer; he may still have moral reasons for not doing so – though either morality or advantage may win.

People whose training has been in one of these systems may find it hard to avoid applying its rules to a problem in another. Engineers are tempted to treat human beings as machines – which is as grotesque as a schoolmaster trying to threaten his car into starting on a cold morning. Clergymen have a natural tendency to try to decide between two practical courses of action on the basis of some moral distinction, even where none exists.

One great difference between organic (and ethical) problems and mechanistic ones is that anyone facing them is invariably part of them himself. You can conduct a scientific experiment without jumping into the retort; you cannot resolve a quarrel without having your own feelings brought into play, and without attracting some gratitude or hostility towards yourself. Someone applying an organic solution to an organic problem will work with the other people involved and solve it with them; a person applying a mechanistic solution will see himself as in some way distinct from the people involved, perhaps superior to them. He may be a 'do-gooder', devotedly working for other people without any attempt to consider what they actually want. Managers with this outlook often try to lay down rules, and find human situations exceedingly frustrating, because their damned fools of subordinates do not behave as they ought to do. Meanwhile their subordinates, sensing that they are regarded in a sense as subhuman, will detest the manager, however benevolent his intentions. This is one reason why people prefer to have leaders who have obvious – though not exorbitant – human weaknesses, rather than those such as Shakespeare described:

> Who moving others, are themselves as stone
> Unmoved, cold and to temptation slow.

The temptation to use a mechanistic approach comes from its very success, since it has given us mastery over the material world. Western civilization uses a sequential mode of thought, based on the assumption of action and reaction, of cause and effect. If A is done, we argue, then B is bound to result. Human beings, however, do not obey these laws, but have a will of their own. Yet we still try to make sense of them by applying the other logic in which we have been brought up.

One often finds oneself functioning simultaneously in two or more systems. When one drives a car, one is operating a mechanistic system in controlling the vehicle, but an organic system in one's relation with other drivers. This is one of the dangers of driving; shut in your own mechanistic box, you come to expect that other road users will act according to the rules – or rather, according to the way you interpret them. When they do not, you see them as dangerous fools – which is one reason why in heavy traffic drivers so easily become frustrated and aggressive. At work we operate in all three systems at various times, and must remain alert to the organic and ethical problems of dealing with people.

The construction of success

Nothing succeeds like success. This is a cliché, but there is reason behind it; from success one learns what to do, and one can repeat it, but from failure one can only learn one error to avoid, leaving 100 more to fall into next time. An even more potent cause for the repetition of success is its effect on morale – giving you confidence to take sensible risks and move forward, instead of dithering over the unknown. Sometimes in training one comes across bizarre examples of this. A successful manager tackles a new sort of task and fails completely. He reacts by rationalizing his mistake and pretending that he has succeeded; and under the stimulus of this self-deception, he goes on to real success next time around. Of course this attitude has its dangers, and even people with the smell of success about them can have a terrible fall one day; but it is amazing how they can glide over misjudgements that would have disheartened and ruined less confident men. Some generals have the knack of treating every drawn or lost battle as a victory – advancing in full confidence that their opponent will retreat. One can think of the way Robert E. Lee treated the far larger army of McLellan, in the early stages of the American Civil War.

A run of success can be accepted as a gift from the gods – or it can be deliberately created and used to achieve continuous improvement. There are three stages in doing this:

1 Identifying success.
2 Analysing it – to pick out the practices that caused it, and the general principles that underlie them.
3 Applying the principles and the practices next time.

Identifying success is a problem in itself. We live in a world dominated by mechanical things; cars and lights, lifts and sewers are taken for granted when they perform as they should, but rigorously examined when they go wrong. Within the mechanistic system, this is the proper response: it is no good identifying that your car's tyres are a great success, if the brakes do not work. Our upbringing is usually based on the assumption that adults are there to eliminate faults, and it is branded into us that mistakes are what matter, while looking for success means superficiality. Failure too is usually obvious, while success often consists of nothing more dramatic than quiet, steady improvement. Both the value of success, and the difficulty of identifying it can be shown by this story.

The director of a brewery rang up a consultant about the problem of recruiting managers for pubs who would stay. He knew, the director said, exactly what the difficulty was: every manager who left was interviewed, and they all told the same story of disliking the hours of work and the responsibility for cash and stock. The consultant asked him whether *all* their managers left after only a short stay; did none of them stick at the job? Oh, yes, said the director, quite a lot gave no trouble, and had been doing the job for years. The consultant suggested they should examine this point of success – find out from the long-staying managers what they liked about the job. The director agreed, and arranged for a survey. The answers were quite clear-cut, and unrelated to the reasons why other managers left: those who stayed were all married men, and the benefit they saw in the job was that it let them work alongside their wives. The brewery company redrafted its advertisements, offering a job where husband and wife could work together. Of the people recruited this way, nearly all stayed.

This example shows all three stages – identification of success, analysis of the cause and reproduction of the principle. The analysis stage is not to be left out. There is a story by Hans Andersen of 'Careful Hans', who carried a daily load home from his grandmother's house. The first day she sent him off with a puppy, which he carried home in his pocket, and the animal suffocated. His mother told him he was a fool – he should have led it on a piece of string. The next day his grandmother gave him a pound of butter, so he dragged it home on a piece of string and the dogs ate it. His mother told him he was a fool – he should have carried it wrapped in a wet rag. The next day he was sent with a donkey, which he carried wrapped in a wet rag – at which point the King's dumb daughter saw him and laughed herself silly, with the result that they lived happily ever after. Because something works in one context, it does not mean that it will work without adaptation in another. More often than not you cannot transplant the actual practice. You have to identify the principle that led to the success, and find another practice that uses the principle. In a training group, people may find that it helps discipline if the man who is speaking holds a pencil and passes it to the next speaker when he has finished. If they all go back to their companies and try to use the same practice there, their colleagues will think them crazy. What each of them has to do is to identify the principle – only one person should talk at a time – and find a practice that helps their own work group.

Analysis of failure

Just as one can form a habit of success, so one can form a habit of failure, the effect of which can be disastrous. The habit can be self-induced, or imposed by a manager, whether maliciously or because he thinks his job is to pick holes in his subordinates. The effect of repeatedly confronting people with their failures is to destroy their self-confidence, to make them inclined to see faults rather than success, and to increase their dependence on authority – so that they may come to see the manager who is constantly criticizing them as some sort of father-figure. Someone in a spiral of failure cannot cope with even routine decisions, let alone give any sort of lead to his staff.

The function of analysis is to provide understanding, which makes it an important part of education. But the job of business is not simply understanding the past, but doing something about it, and there are times when dwelling too long on the information merely obstructs future progress. 'History', said Edward Gibbon (England's greatest historian, and so perhaps her greatest analyst) 'consists of little more than a register of the crimes, follies, and misfortunes of mankind'. When one analyses the past, one is led almost inevitably to dwell on these and so to see the future in the same terms. The effect is that one can become smug, cautious and dependent, like Gibbon himself, who 'supported with many a sincere and silent vote, the rights, though not perhaps the interest, of the mother-country' (or in other words spent seven years as a tame vote for Lord North, who was busy losing America). If people spend too long on the analysis of their own failure, they may become not only depressed but frustrated. If this frustration is not eased, it may turn to aggression, and they may start looking for scapegoats – the familiar reaction of a country to defeat.

The great asset of the British used to be, not their natural resources or creativity, but the extraordinary self-confidence of a small nation, which had exerted influence upon the history of the world out of all proportion to its size. No doubt this confidence had its unattractive side, and could be seen as arrogance, or blind acceptance of questionable values. Today people are more inclined to doubt their beliefs. This can be valuable if it leads to a humility of approach and to new and fresh thinking; but it can destroy confidence and risk-taking, without which there will be no achievement.

Developing subordinates

The essential component of building on success is an attitude of mind which can be called 'positive thinking' – a predisposition to see achievements, strengths and things that are going right, and to relate these to objectives which lie ahead. This way of thought is a skill, which can be built up by practice and deliberate effort. Try, for instance, consciously observing how positive contributions help any discussion or job forward. Give 10p to charity every time you make a negative statement, or pick the bad elements out of a piece of news, rather than the opportunity. It is helpful to collaborate with someone else – by arranging with someone in your office or your family to point out whenever you or they make a negative statement. The habit can be built up in any aspect of life, however important or trivial, and the improvement can repay the effort in geometric proportion.

One of the most important applications of building on success is in developing subordinates. Successful managers often seen to breed other good managers among their staff – partly because they tend to be more aware of success in others, since they know the symptoms; partly because someone confident in his own ability can encourage other people without feeling threatened if they do as well as he does. Successful managers have no business hiding their light under a bushel. If they know the reasons for their success, they should be ready to explain them. Or if, like many practical men, they find this difficult, they must give others the chance to observe them in action, so that they can draw out the principles and try to reproduce them themselves. Developing success in this way, does not mean inflating one's own ego, but rather demands a sense of humility; it means attributing to other people their true worth – being prepared to accept that they may be better than you, and to encourage them if they are.

One obvious context for building on success is the appraisal interview. Before the meeting, the manager should list half a dozen of the subordinate's successes during the past year, and these then become the basis of the discussion. This does not mean that the manager must not mention things that have gone wrong, but success must have at least as good a chance to be discussed as failure. The art is to look behind a subordinate's successes and identify the qualities that led to them, and then give these qualities a chance to develop. If someone is born a motivator, make use of it, build on it; if they are able planners, let them plan.

When you give someone feedback about their performance, you need to consider two effects; first, the effect on their morale, second, the usefulness of the data for planning and corrective action. The effects on morale can be codified as in Table 10.1.

These effects are cumulative, except that *repeated* failure is most unlikely to be a useful spur. One conclusion is that if you have to give someone evidence of failure, you should at all costs avoid encouraging them to dwell on it – which reduplicates the effect on their morale: you should lead them straight away towards planning improvements for the future, which is after all the *only* way in which the information you are providing can be useful.

Table 10.1 *Feedback and morale*

Effects of feeding back success	*Effects of feeding back failure*
Raising morale, leading to:	Lowering morale, leading to:
Readiness to take rational risks	Caution, lack of self-confidence
Job satisfaction	Dependence
Self-confidence	Unhappiness
High commitment	Low commitment
Some risk of complacency	May sometimes act as a spur, destroying complacency

The best way to do this is to make positive suggestions, and get the discussion on to these. Since the sole use of failure feedback is to enable the recipient to plan to do better, the feedback must be *precise*. There may be some virtue in generalized success feedback since it may improve morale, though it is far more use to specify exactly what was good. But there is *never* any excuse to tell people that their performance was bad, without indicating exactly what was wrong, what standards would be acceptable and, preferably, what could be done to put it right.

If a subordinate's performance is limited by what you see as grave defects, then you and he must try to correct them. But not many defects are so fundamental that they cannot be supported by the rest of the team. Sometimes people just do not realize how large their delinquencies loom in your view; it may be a matter of discipline, which after a suave or a sharp word they can fairly easily put right. But do not assume that because something like time-keeping comes easy to you, it must come easy to them; it may have cost them heroic efforts to turn up only 20 minutes late! Above all, do not hammer away at defects that are not of crucial importance; if you try and grind a creative genius into managing his desk, you will end up with an uncreative genius, and a desk that is still chaotic.

Our strengths are our resources for overcoming our weaknesses: often the best way to cure a bad quality is to develop a good one. If someone is a good observer but cannot plan, let him use his observation to see how other people cope; if he is a good planner but unaware of his surroundings, let him plan to observe better. If you build on success, either your defects may come to seem trivial, or the impetus of success in one field may sweep on to another. There is a young footballer, playing for a first division club, who 3 years ago was regarded as not really first-team material. He had a good right foot, but his left was weak, for all that his manager made him practise on this. Occasionally, when someone was injured, he got a game with the first team but he never did much good, and the question of transfer was coming up. At that point a new manager took over. He watched the player and observed that as well as having a good right foot, he had a turn of speed which was quite exceptional. Accordingly, he planned his tactics round these strengths. He switched the man to the right wing, and taught the rest of the team to bang the ball into space ahead of him. The man would sprint to get there first, and use his strong right boot for a centre or a shot at goal. In a few months' time he was playing for the England Under-Twenty-Three team. Soon afterwards he was heard saying, in a voice of wonder, 'I scored with my left foot last week – and I'm not meant to have a left foot.'

Another example comes from a teacher in a tough school in East London. A boy in his class had a bad record even by local standards – he had assaulted teachers, he was on probation and had every chance of custody next time round. His reading age was that of a 7-year-old, and he seemed to have no constructive interests at all. The teacher, however, suspected there might be something more to him. One day he happened to bring a trumpet into the classroom and put it on his desk. He noticed the boy peering at it, so he brought it back deliberately a couple more times. One afternoon the boy wandered across and began fingering it. The teacher said that if he was interested, he would show him a few notes. The boy said he would not mind. Some months later, with cautious encouragement, he had made fair progress with the instrument, and was trying to organize a school band. What was perhaps more significant, his general behaviour and even his reading and writing standards were beginning to improve. At that point he left school, and the master lost touch with him. A couple of years later he received a visit from a smartly dressed young man – who with some difficulty he recognized as his former pupil – come back to tell him that he had just won a scholarship to the Royal College of Music. In each case, the development of one talent that was burning to be used overcame weaknesses that seemed to make it unusable.

Success and the organization

In any organization, there is a network of controls designed to spot when things go wrong: cash registers and store records to prevent pilfering; books of account and statutory audits to prevent more elaborate fraud; management accounts, budgets and standard costing, to identify the branch that sells too little or the project that costs too much. This control system is reinforced by the avid attention of the hierarchy. In many companies if a branch sells too little, the district manager, the area manager, the regional director and even the chairman himself will see the deviation and want to know why.

Now there is no doubt that these controls fulfil a necessary function: stock records do limit thefts, and proper cost and financial accounts prevent a company lurching into insolvency. But they suffer from a number of drawbacks. First, their cost – clerks, accountants, and computers are expensive, and are quite capable of costing the company more than they

ave. Second, such controls are rigid, since they are based on the
assumption that one course is right, and that deviation should be stamped
out. Innovation may be discouraged; if a manager finds a way to increase
sales at the cost of a few extra miles run by his vehicle fleet, he is as likely to
be blamed for wasting petrol as congratulated for selling more goods –
whatever the net effect on profit may be. The third disadvantage is the effect
on the morale of staff. People who are not trusted are not going to be
trustworthy and this is true both of shop assistants who are surrounded by
controls to stop them stealing, and managers whose weekly results are
scrutinized at board level – in some companies, before they get them
themselves.

Again, in an organization that makes excessive use of controls, the
analysts – accountants and such – will achieve great power. Line managers
are seen as the people who make mistakes that accountants spot. Able men
will tend to shift themselves into an analytical role – staff rather than line,
regional sales adviser rather than area manager. Senior jobs may go to
people like accountants – whose careers have been safe from errors of
judgement and whose professional *raison d'être* is showing up mistakes. If
people of this sort dominate the board, human relations will be neglected
(for what cannot be measured cannot be important),* and the company
paralysed by financial prudence.

Budgets, forecasts and targets are usually set a year or more in advance. If
one was comparing the control system of a company with that of a guided
missile, one would say the target is treated as stationary, the path towards it
is plotted in advance, and the system is designed to spot deviations, and
steer the rocket back on course. The effect can be shown by Figure 10.1.

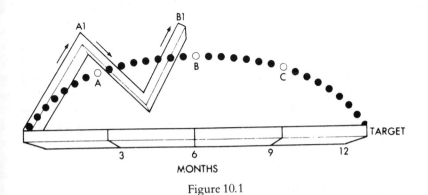

Figure 10.1

* For a discussion of the damage that can be done to the human assets of an enterprise, see
Rensis Likert, *The Human Organisation* (McGraw-Hill, New York, 1967), Chapter 6.

The intended path of the rocket company is represented by the dotted line. If it is on course, it will reach points *A*, *B* and *C* at the end of the first, second, or third quarters. In practice, the missile will deviate, and by the end of the first quarter will be a point *A*1 (one or two branches having done better than they should, others having done worse). Most of the effort of management is concentrated on yanking the rocket back to its planned course. Great attention will be paid to correcting the branches that have failed to meet their target, and this may well lead to overcompensation: if materials ran short before, they will be over-ordered now. The missile may display the behaviour known as 'hunting' – yawing from side to side, in order to get back on track.

There is, however, another way of directing a missile. Here again its position is monitored and its direction altered, but in this case the rocket is not directed back to its original intended path, but on to whatever is *now* the shortest route to its target. Even if the target itself has moved, the movement is spotted and the rocket is repointed at wherever the target may be (Figure 10.2).

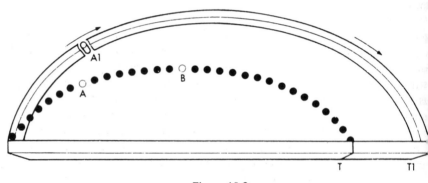

Figure 10.2

Here the missile has once again deviated from its set line and is now too high; but instead of being sent back to point *A* on its original course, it is repointed directly at the target – which itself has shifted its position to *T*1.

This is a fairly close description of the way in which a company should be directed, taking account of two factors which the conventional system ignores:

1 Alteration to the objectives

Circumstances are bound to change in the course of the year as old objectives become unattainable and new opportunities appear to be grasped.

A feedback system that does not cater for this is faulty and may be dangerous. When oil prices doubled, how many companies ploughed on, showing budget variances in fuel costs that were certainly beyond the wit of man to control? This may not matter too much, provided the figures are taken in the spirit they deserve. What is much more dangerous is if new opportunities spring into view but cannot be grasped since the system allows no flexibility.

2 Identification of success

The surest way an organization can improve is by picking up successful practices developed in one unit and applying them to another. Yet, under the traditional system, an unscheduled success is as likely as not to be regarded as a deviation, and even as reprehensible. Even if it is not true, it is what subordinates often fear, just as in the example on p. 97, where the manager was afraid to admit that he had shown the shop stewards his annual results.

A normal feedback system takes information about present difficulties, checks them against objectives, and takes corrective action to put them right. What companies also need is a parallel system for gathering information about successes and innovations, and evolving new objectives and new plans to bring them into wider use, building on strengths that are already there. There may be departments whose job is to survey new techniques discovered by competitors; but new methods and ideas can spring up inside the organization, in any department and at any level – provided there is a way of making them known. This needs a quite different approach from that for gathering information about error. Most progress reporting is through the hierarchy, each manager monitoring his own subordinates and concentrating his attention on lapses and potential bottlenecks. Managers develop great skill in picking out error from a mass of generally successful operations, but their skill in spotting success is usually much more limited. A visit from a superior is often seen as one's cue to appear industrious, obedient, and conventional, rather than as a chance to make new proposals or display new techniques. Therefore many managers are ignorant of successful practices actually in use in their own departments. No wonder they lament the lack of ability in their own people. Meanwhile subordinates are afraid that the practices they have so ingeniously devised will be seen as ways of getting round some regulation – and their fears are often justified. One cure is to appoint people with the prime function of identifying and passing on success. People who do this job need to be:

1 Skilled in conducting reviews and observing success, rather than failure.

2 Not responsible for routine progress reporting, i.e., spotting mistakes; a man's boss, for example, will simply not be allowed to see many of the new techniques that are in use.
3 Imaginative enough to see how a practice that is used on a small scale in one unit could benefit the whole company.
4 Influential enough to be able to propose new objectives and plans, with a good chance of their being adopted.

A team that does this job well may be worth its weight in gold, for the organization will discover within itself huge unknown resources for solving its own problems.

PART 3

Organization Development

The next four chapters deal with the application of training and process consultancy to the task of improving the performance of a company as a whole. While the rest of the book has relevance for most people working in business, this section is more specialized, being of direct use to senior managers who are responsible for human-relations strategy or may find themselves setting up an organization development project, and anyone else who may be involved in it. (People who only want to know broadly what OD is about, should read Chapter 11 and then skip to Chapter 14.)

'Organization development' is a term used to describe the application of various techniques drawn from the behavioural sciences to improving the effectiveness of organizations. It was coined by consultants in the United States to describe their own activities, and there are a number of definitions in the field: Warren Bennis, for example, describes it as 'an educational strategy designed to bring about a planned organizational change'. He goes on to specify that the change agent should be an outside consultant, a behavioural scientist, who bases the education process on 'experienced behaviour' and collaborates with the client rather than advising him from a great height. Most consultants base their work on some combination of training and process consultancy.

It is convenient that a term came into use to describe what Coverdale had been doing for many years. The chapters in Part 3 do not attempt to give a general view of OD, but merely to describe how Coverdale sets about it.

11   The need for change

Behold, they say, our bones are dried, and our hope is lost.
O ye dry bones . . . I will lay sinews upon you, and will bring up flesh upon you,
and cover you with skin, and put breath in you and ye shall live.
                                                                    Ezekiel, xxxvii.

Revival and renewal

The world is full of dying companies: companies supported by one product,
one patent or one captive market; companies where change is feared, ideas
are hated, staff drift in late, wages are low; where industrial relations are a
form of trench warfare; or where everyone is afraid of losing their job, even
though it is not much more than a living death. Companies like these are
often slow to die; especially if they employ enough people for governments
to be willing to keep them alive.

So what makes them live? One way is for the company to be bought up,
its top management fired, its middle managers terrorized into activity.
Certainly this can bring good brisk results. The risk is, however, that when
the top people are sacked, their expertise goes with them. They may have
been hopeless managers, but they probably did know something about
manufacturing nuts and bolts – enough at least to avoid the glaringly
obvious mistakes that people can make if they do not know the business.
Nor are the middle managers, who also know the business, likely to help
since neither their past training nor their recent experience will be of the sort
to encourage them to stick their necks out.

The case I have described is that of a very bad company; far more
common is the run-of-the-mill company, normally profitable, rarely
enterprising, but with a certain basic competence. A company like this may
need reviving – but violent methods of takeover and butchery will do active
harm, since the existing competence will be lost.

For both types of company there is a slower, less brutal way. It depends
on leadership to initiate it, but not on leadership alone. It is perhaps the
most rewarding exercise anyone in business can undertake – financially
rewarding for the company, but also morally rewarding, in that it enables
people who work in it to know a working life rather than mere existence. It
is this process of improving both the muscle-tone and the spirit of the

company that one describes as organization development. Many successful companies use similar methods, not as a way of restoring success, but to make sure they stay successful.

The need for change

Companies face constant change, whether imposed by outside events or by their own desire to grow and improve, and often prepare elaborate strategies for finance, marketing or product development. What they are slow to recognize is that every change will affect the work-force, and that human changes need to be planned just as far ahead: it takes quite as long to recruit or train staff, as to raise capital or set up a factory. People themselves are an active source of change, through their work habits and expectations. For these reasons, any company needs a strategy for human resources – not just what sort of people they will need to employ in five years, but how to train them, and to combine corporate needs with those of individuals. Of this strategy, an OD project might well form a part.

Organizations seem to have a natural progression of growth–stability–decay, controlled by pressures of the environment outside, and human behaviour within. A young company, developing rapidly in a new market, will sooner or later be checked by competition or by the market becoming saturated. At that point, for growth to continue, individuals will have to take risks and diversify; wherever they are reluctant to risk what they have got, a period of stability sets in. In time past this period could last for many years – in the case of some institutions, such as the Chinese Empire or the Roman Catholic Church, for centuries. But sooner or later the outside environment will alter (including the climate of opinion among people from whom staff are recruited) and, if the organization fails to respond, decline will set in. Nowadays, of course, the period of stability tends to be much shorter, but it can still be half a working life.

It is with companies in this stable state that OD is most difficult: changes are bound to come but, the longer the period of stability, the harder the company will find it to respond, as long as there is no immediate crisis which makes everyone see that change is necessary. A new manager or an OD consultant will have to identify some focus of change, some pressure or opportunity, even if only a marginal one, and use that as a spoon to stir the company up and make more changes possible. Otherwise, sooner or later decay will set in, and the company must either be rescued by more violent methods, or go gracefully out of business. This last outcome might well be best for the national economy – the company has fulfilled its purpose, and should pay off its staff and fold its tents; but this is not something that directors or employees are usually ready to accept. A company or department in a period of growth is a great place to work. It is not just that there are opportunities for promotion and expansion: whatever one does is breaking new ground, and abilities are stretched and developed to the full. One effect of OD should be to bring back this climate of growth into the organization. People who are alert for opportunities will find them, people who welcome improvement will make sure it comes; and work will be done in a mood of purpose and hope.

Standards and norms

The way human beings behave is largely determined by internal *standards*, built up by education and other environmental factors. They are often difficult to put into words. A subordinate may find himself in constant trouble, since no one ever explains what his manager's standards really are. We continually compare new pieces of information about the world with our own standards, and where one of them is not being met, it may spark off the objective of doing something to put things right.

In any group of people, there are kinds of behaviour and levels of achievement that are regarded as normal and acceptable. These levels, which we may call *norms*, derive from events in the group's past and from the internal standards of individuals who make it up; in turn the norms will influence the standards of newcomers. There are norms for society as a whole, but also for industries or individual companies or departments. In one office it may be perfectly acceptable to roll up 20 minutes late; in another it may be a serious crime. Norms can relate to technical skill (for example, Rolls-Royce workmanship); morale (regimental standards of courage and discipline); or morality (in some stores it is acceptable to pilfer, in others it is not). They can relate both to what is due to the company, and how the company should treat individuals.

Organization development may be regarded as an attempt to raise or update the norms of an organization. The key to this is probably the norms of *process* – since, when interactive and planning skills are improved, other norms are likely to follow. If, for example, individuals reconcile their own aims with the company's prosperity, they are less likely to pilfer; if they develop their ability to learn from experience, this will directly benefit their task skills. Norms tend to reflect the level of commitment – but not automatically, since a bored professional may have higher norms than a keen amateur. To keep norms high you can either lay down stringent rules and make people observe them, or rely on their internal standards (in practice you probably do a bit of each). The most effective way of bringing new staff to accept the group's norms is to use people to train them whose own standards are particularly high. Some institutions, such as the Brigade of Guards, have initiation periods, during which recruits are driven and cajoled into accepting and taking pride in norms which before they would have regarded as preposterous.

The effect of personal leadership depends very much on how many people are involved, and how much the leader can be heard and seen. A good leader might do wonders for the norms of a group of six, but could do little to overcome the inertia of a whole company. A problem with commercial organizations is that although they do have one generally accepted purpose – to stay in business – it is a pretty uninspiring one, not a serious motivation for employees until bankruptcy is staring them in the face. Sometimes a capable and attractive leader can create a common aim – even if it is merely the aim of emulating or pleasing him. Founders of successful companies may implant higher norms in this way, and their paternalist successors may succeed for a time in keeping them alive. But it is very difficult to keep this up as an organization grows and the effects of the boss's personality is filtered through five or six levels of management.

So how do some companies maintain their norms so that the quality and performance of their branches are consistently higher than that of most of their competitors, in a similar business, employing similar staff? (Employing *much* better staff is self-defeating, since people will not function well in a job which is below them – unless they are given so much extra responsibility that the job itself is transformed.) Companies with consistently high norms are usually those that pay a great deal of attention to process matters. It is also easier for a company to keep its norms high if it has large numbers of similar units – so that norms established in the flagship branch can be used as measures all over the country, while senior management can be alert for successful practices which can applied elsewhere. One disadvantage of diversifying is that it is hard to keep norms high in a range of different businesses.

In the world today, one of the most important norms relates to readiness to change. In some companies, especially those dealing with new technology, this is no problem; everyone knows that their present job will not exist in 10 years' time. There may be general confidence that the company will stay in existence, and will continue to train and develop its staff in whatever skills may be necessary. Other organizations preserve the work habits they acquired in the 1890s, and go broke in the serene assurance that 100 years' experience cannot be wrong.

Norms are reflected not only in the attitudes of employees but also in the company's systems – that is, the pattern of regulations, channels, and practices by which decisions are made and work is done. Systems are in a sense decisions taken in advance, to cover a whole class of events that may occur in the future. If changes are happening in the company's business, technology or style of management, it is essential that systems should be updated in step, or a whole category of decisions will be wrong.

The end-product of OD

If we describe the purpose of OD as being to open a company to change, we still need some picture of how the organization should look at the end of it. The criteria set out below relate not to any particular OD project, but to OD as such – the direction in which it should move any company, besides reaching whatever specific goals are set for the project by management. Certainly this is not the only pattern of an effective company. As Lewin's experiments indicated, an autocratic organization can often be successful in achieving its objectives, providing its management makes allowances for the problems of autocracy.

The reasons for rejecting an autocratic pattern are twofold: first, a belief (for which there is some evidence but which cannot be proved) that today, in Western Society generally, autocratic management finds it harder and harder to get results. One may deplore or rejoice at the change of social attitudes that has brought this about, but one still has to live with it. Second, the company described below will be more in accord with the needs of society at large. Its employees will be free men and women doing their jobs responsibly as a result of rational choice and using their abilities to the full. Political democracy rests on the assumption that people behave in this way in carrying out their civic duties; we should see a better integrated society when we expect similar rights and duties, and similar standards of behaviour, in our working lives.

Characteristics of the well-managed company

Aims

1 The corporate mission is defined and made known to all employees, and accepted by those who have to work towards them. Criteria are set (in terms of money, markets, technology and men).
2 Progressively higher targets are set for staff at all levels, both by managers and by individuals for themselves.
3 People operate in a climate of purpose and whatever they do is in conscious furtherance of some aim.
4 Account is taken of personal aims, especially those directly related to the company, such as job and career satisfaction.

Teamwork

5 The company functions as a network of linking teams. In each team, manager and subordinates alike accept responsibility for its success, and share in the process of closing down aims, setting targets, selecting the appropriate information and determining WHTBD.

6 Responsibility for getting things done is given to people at the lowest possible level – 'possible' being in terms of skill and background knowledge. All levels receive appropriate feedback.
7 A deliberate attempt is made to use and develop the skills of all employees.
8 People operate in a climate of support – for ideas, initiatives and skills.
9 Managers listen to encourage, and give the confidence that comes from recognition of skill and achievement.

Reviews

10 Reviews are regularly carried out, leading to plans for improvement that are in fact implemented. Successes are analysed, spread and repeated throughout the organization. Plans are made in terms of process as well as task.
11 Observation throughout the company is acute, and information derived from it is spread and used.

Change

12 The company, its systems and the individuals within it, are alert to the need for change and welcome the opportunities it provides.

The organization

13 The organization and systems of the company are appropriate to its needs, and evolve in step with them.
14 Fundamentally the company is a co-operative venture with common purposes and shared vision.

Morale

15 People enjoy their work, are stretched by it: look for opportunities, display enterprise, feel they can manage the future and look to it with hope.

12   Managing an OD project

The power which causes the several portions of a plant to help each other we call life. The ceasing of this help is what we call corruption.

Ruskin

The elements of organization development

The aim of an OD project is to make a company more effective, by using the talents of staff – so making it an exciting and satisfying place to work. But none of this will happen unless a company already treats its staff with basic decency. The best-laid OD project in the world will not take off where employees are disgruntled about injustice or low pay, disgusted by their working conditions, distrustful of management or in fear of the sack. It may be possible to persuade them that the OD project is itself designed to put these things right – for example, by improving efficiency so that the company can afford to improve pay and conditions – but to get this accepted, management will have to give some convincing earnest of their good intentions. In some companies management would do better to concentrate first on setting up adequate payment systems, pension schemes and canteens, and come back to OD when they have done the groundwork of acting as a good employer. Occasionally the reverse may be necessary – to grasp the nettle of cutting out overmanning, or of restoring discipline. People are going to do nothing to improve their own effectiveness, if they think it will merely make them redundant, or reduce their opportunities for working some fiddle.

The basic tools of organization development are process training and process consultancy. Process consultancy, the extension of training to practical work on site, is described in the next chapter. Process training is designed to develop the skills of human interaction, such as those discussed in Chapters 3 to 10. This training has the immediate aim and effect of equipping the individual to do his own job better; but the performance of a team depends on the skills (especially the co-operative skills) of individuals, and when the training is applied systematically over the whole body of managers, it goes on to benefit first working teams, and ultimately the organization as a whole. I assume in these chapters that the training element is carried out by means of external courses, but it is possible to envisage the training part of an OD programme being conducted in quite a different way: for example, on site, administered by a department's own manager.

Between training on a course and process consultancy on site there may be an intermediate step; to give people a project, connected with their job and useful in itself, but which is seen primarily as a vehicle for learning. They can start working on it on the last day of the course, under the supervision of their coach. Back at work it can be the first problem which the process consultant helps a participant tackle, persuading him to try out the methods he has learnt on a task that is significant, but where the risks are lower than in his day-to-day work, where the factors are limited and the end result is easy to see.

Training – the individual and the work group

Since the aim of an OD exercise is to develop the organization as a whole, its inception ought to be a board decision. In practice, this is unusual: companies often slip into organization development piecemeal, training first an individual, then a few others on his recommendation, finally his whole work group. If for some reason one of these early training experiments does not work, the whole OD exercise may be stillborn, which makes it important to be aware of the problems of training individuals on their own.

Improvement in performance is only possible within broad limits set by the environment. It is easy for a manager to bring himself up to the level of his colleagues (provided his abilities are not hopelessly below theirs); it is much more difficult for him to improve beyond this level, unless he and the environment can improve in step. Someone who comes back from a course which none of his colleagues has experienced, may find it hard to apply what he has learnt. If he starts asking the purpose of everything, this may be construed as criticism, and it will be worse still if he really does start pointing out the deficiencies he sees around him. Of course, most managers are reasonably receptive and if they send someone to be trained, they will try to support him in using the training. But if he goes back to a really rigid environment, the more he has changed, the worse his problems are, and his unregenerate colleagues may reject him like a graft from someone else's skin. Even if some people are receptive and he manages to improve the way the people in his own section work, the organization as a whole may become hostile and put pressure on them to conform.

People who find themselves robbed of effectiveness will become frustrated and cynical, until their performance slips back to the norm. Sometimes the best thing training does for them is to make them realize it is high time they left their company. This problem of putting training into practice is crucial, since if a participant uses the skills he has learned, he will rapidly improve, while if he neglects them, he will soon be back where he started. If he has some colleague with common experience or similar ideas or, better still, if the members of his work group have all had training, they can support each other in developing what they have learned. For this reason one should train groups of people who regularly work together (boss plus immediate subordinates) over the shortest possible time. They need not all go on the same course – in fact, the manager should rarely go on the same course as his subordinates, since his presence may inhibit them – but wherever possible the whole team should be trained within a space of 2 or 3 months.

The success of training depends very much on the attitude of the local senior manager. It is one of the marks of a good leader that he measures his own success by how well his subordinates develop. (Indeed, purely in his own interests, any manager should make sure he brings some of them up to take over his job, or how can he ever be promoted?) But some managers regard development of their subordinates as a threat to themselves and will not give them scope to use what they have learned. The best hope with someone like this is that he will be carried along in the development of his own peer group, and allow his subordinates to grow with him.

In any OD project, it is individuals that get developed and it is their needs that must be considered. Some foremen and junior managers, especially if they are elderly, may find a residential course a strain and it may affect their learning, at least to start with. A few people have never left their wives or husbands before and may be harried all the week by telephone calls complaining that the hot water has gone wrong. Before anyone goes on a course, he should be recommended as suitable by his manager and briefed by him and a consultant, and both of them of them should be alert for remarks that might indicate stress.

Some signs of successful training within a group – a checklist for managers

1 The job gets done: task results are regularly good.
2 Aims are clarified and people are aware of the whole range of aims being pursued.
3 Measures of success are set, at a level high enough to stretch the group.
4 There is a formal assessment of risk.
5 All the necessary information is gathered before actions are determined (except where the risk is recognized as being low).
6 All discussions are purposeful – indicating an implied use of systematic approach.
7 Task reviews are held and progress is regularly checked against aims.

8 Behaviour is disciplined: in meetings or other business there is awareness of time and little cross-talk.
9 Proposals are supported rather than destroyed.
10 Ideas are not forgotten or lost; other people's ideas (from within and outside the group) are registered and used as a resource.
11 The group is self-regulating – for example, people make spontaneous process proposals, which others support by doing something.
12 People are aware of the skills available and use them.
13 The group is self-developing: it reviews on its own initiative and learns from experience.

Commitment to training

In any organization there tends to be a 'growth point' – a level of management at which action is initiated and new thinking takes place. In the army, for instance, command and initiative in the field is usually in the hands of brigadiers and major-generals, who give the decisive orders and evolve new tactics. The function of higher command, as of higher management, may be to act as a guide, banker and resource. It is more important for managers at the growth point to be committed to the OD programme than for their seniors on the board. From directors you need some understanding, and at least benevolent neutrality; from the two or three ranks lower you need real comprehension and commitment to making it work. As we have seen, training often starts piecemeal and the board is apt to see the success of the exercise rather late in the day. This has at least the advantage that it is seen to be working on a small scale before grandiose plans are drawn up. The main disadvantage is that the board may see OD as something to impose on other people, rather than something to take part in themselves. This can apply even when board members go on courses and come back full of enthusiasm, for unless they actually *use* what they have learned and apply their skill in recommending the scheme to managers one or two levels down, these people may react against it. After all, if managers who are under pressure to produce results, are compelled, for some whim of the board, to spend money sending their staff away for training, they will naturally be irritated.

Another reason why senior managers must apply the training to themselves is the force of example. They cannot expect their subordinates to be free with information or involve their staff in setting objectives, if they themselves do not do the same. In general, managing directors have no business making plans, which is the job of their subordinates; but they have as much need as anyone else to make *process* plans, for their own behaviour and the meetings they take part in. In many companies, of course, senior managers are already pretty good at organizing their own work and skilful in judging their impact on other people. But there is always room for improvement; and at this level a small improvement can have great leverage, if only because of the scale and importance of the work that is done.

For an OD programme to have its full effect, there may be a need for consultancy inside the chairman's own office; board meetings, too, need a time-plan and opportunities for process review. Senior managers who are impatient of applying such discipline to themselves might read Field Marshal Slim's memoirs, *Defeat into Victory* (Cassell, 1972). Consider the enormous care he took to make sure that, both in the 15th Corps and the 14th Army, his headquarters were efficient in the same terms as any other unit, and subjected to the same discipline: the route marches and weapon training for the staff officers, the clerks, the mess waiters; the rule that if any single forward formation was on half rations, headquarters went on to half rations too.

The exercise may also need the goodwill of the unions, and this is one reason for offering places on courses to shop stewards – though not, preferably, before their managers. Shop stewards get where they are because of their natural process ability, and they take to the training like ducks to water. One effect of it is usually to make them better able to spot common ground between the aims of their members and those of the company. Sometimes they are led to rethink their own personal roles: one foreman who combined this with acting as shop steward resigned from the union as soon as he got back, since he now saw his two posts as incompatible.

Where development should start

Where the purpose of OD is simply to raise standards, it may not matter so much where training starts – providing working groups are trained together. But where the company is in a mess or change is inevitable for other reasons, then it is important for those who are going to manage the change to be trained first. Occasionally, training one single senior manager may itself create change. Suppose, for example, that for the first time the chairman begins to examine corporate aims. The effect may turn the company upside-down, while it can be disastrous if he starts imposing process changes (for example, participative management) which he only half understands. A little learning is a dangerous thing, especially in autocrats.

A second question is which individuals, or individual units, to train first. With conventional forms of training, one would expect to start with those who need it most. With Coverdale there is a lot to be said for starting with the most able – those who already have experience of management, a good knowledge of the company and are skilful in getting co-operation. These people will be quickest to use what they have learned, and will provide a standard for the rest. If they are given a slightly more intensive training, they can act as in-house coaches, either on formal secondment or from within their existing jobs, developing their own departments and improving meetings which they attend.

In-house coaches need several weeks formal training, together with some help on site from more experienced consultants. After this, they will be able to coach both on and off courses. This will give them useful training, while at the same time their knowledge and understanding of the company's affairs is fed into the course. They are in a good position to illustrate the concepts of training with local terms and examples, making it easier for less perceptive people to understand what it has to do with their work. Again the mere fact that the training is being conducted by practical and successful people from within the company gives people confidence in its value. Managers who are running the course can build up a relationship with the trainees, so that later they can come back for advice when they run into difficulties on the job. It is a help for internal trainers to be as senior as possible: first, because it will give the project greater standing and their advice more weight; and second, because internal consultants cannot usually advise people higher than themselves, so seniority gives them wider scope.

Patterns of training

The entire management of a company cannot be trained overnight, and there are various ways of making a start. It is important that this is got right, partly to ensure that people who work together can support each other, and partly because there is a risk that people who have been trained may be seen as a sort of Mafia, shutting out the rest. If managers spend a lot of time working with equal colleagues across the organization, it may be best to start at the top and train successive levels downwards. Two other patterns are to be considered – the 'wedge' and the 'core group' – which may be used separately or in conjunction with each other.

1 The wedge

The wedge consists of all those staff (of a level to be trained) who report to one manager, together with the manager himself, and his own superior (Figure 12.1).

It is important that the manager two levels up is trained, since subordinates may well come back keen to make changes that will be out of

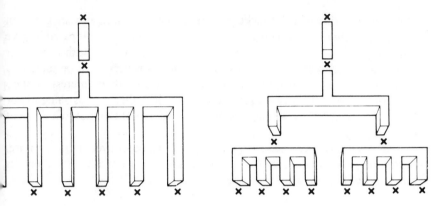

Figure 12.1   *Examples of a 'wedge'*

the scope of their immediate superior, and they will need understanding and support from at least one level higher. The advantage of the wedge is that people who normally work together are all trained over a short period and can reinforce each other. This makes it suitable both for a test sample, and as the basis for carrying a programme through. It is not a good idea for a wedge to form the population of a single course, since people who work together find it hard not to carry their assumptions about each others' roles and capacities into training, and they may be inhibited from experimenting by the presence of people they know. The training of wedges should overlap so that courses have mixed populations. Consultancy, however, will deal with the wedge as a unit.

2 The steering group

In many work units the guiding rules about how people are managed, including matters such as the level of overtime and local systems of payment, are fixed by negotiation with the unions. Within these guiding rules, the works management is preoccupied with organizing day-to-day activities. But no one has the time or the responsibility to consider the future development of human relations in the unit – how to improve in observation, or in sensing and controlling conflict. One way to deal with this is to set up a 'core group', whose functions are:

(*a*) Gathering information and ideas about the future – both hazards and opportunities.
(*b*) Thinking ahead – devising solutions to problems that it sees coming.
(*c*) Small-scale testing of ideas: but not implementation, which is the function of management.

A group of this sort can include shops stewards as well as managers – in each case people whom their colleagues trust enough to be prepared to give their suggestions a fair trial. It will have little or no task authority, so it needs all the process authority it can raise. Its members must be there in a personal capacity, rather than as representatives of their interest; a shop steward, for instance, needs to speak for himself, rather than as a negotiator for shop stewards as a whole, so the group must build up its own sense of loyalty.

A steering group can be set up as the spearhead of an overall OD exercise, or it can exist in its own right. In either case, to work effectively its members will need training in the following skills:

(a) Aiming: envisaging the future and identifying a series of objectives stretching away in time; also reconciling aims which appear to be in conflict.
(b) Operating as a group – listening, support and methodical approach.
(c) Gaining the commitment of others, so that they are willing at least to give ideas a try.
(d) Being able to identify success, even when it is masked by other factors which make for gloomy results.

A steering group can act rather as an internal process consultant to its own unit – with the difference that it will be more ready to provide task suggestions. It is important that it should report to someone senior, ideally the top manager on the site. It needs sharp success criteria and a few early successes to build up their own and other people's confidence.

The benefits of shared training experience

1 From training the work-group

(a) It gives a common experience, which in itself leads to greater cohesion.
(b) It allows individuals to help each other use what they have learned.
(c) It encourages the group to adopt common aims (or at least establish aims which are mutually compatible).
(d) It provides common procedures (such as systematic approach).
(e) It gives a greater awareness of each other's process skills.
(f) It encourages the team to make process plans, to improve the way they work together.

2 From extending training throughout the organization

(a) It gives an individual support from all his work contacts – not merely his own department.

(b) It provides a common language and a common approach to problems, across all disciplines and departments – for example, a common understanding of the significance of the stages of systematic approach. It is a great strength to a company when an engineer from Stockport and an accountant from Southampton, who meet for the first time, find themselves instinctively falling into a common method of working.

(c) It increases people's ability to understand and take account of other departments' aims.

(d) For senior managers, it gives greater understanding of how groups communicate and work together, and how to improve the way they do it.

13   The process consultant

The business of this officer is, where two or more persons are in company, gently to strike with his bladder the mouth of him who is to speak, and the right ear of him or them to whom the speaker addresseth himself. This flapper is likewise employed diligently to attend his master in his walks, and upon occasion to give him a soft flap on his eyes, because he is always so wrapped up in cogitation that he is in manifest danger of falling down every precipice.

Jonathan Swift, *Gulliver's Travels*

The role of the consultant

The best way to make training stick is to continue it on site. On a course, as well as developing his personal skills, a participant will experience being part of a team that works; he must be encouraged to reproduce this back on the job, and Coverdale's way of doing this is to give him support from a consultant, whose role is an extension of that of the coach on his course. Process consultancy of this sort requires a fair knowledge both of business and psychology, combined with a sensitivity to the clients' intentions and needs. It needs a warm human approach, combined with the detachment necessary to analyse the situation and see what has to be done. The consultant also needs plenty of self-restraint, since his art is not to feed the client with answers, but to lead him towards solving the problem himself – so that he builds up skill for the future. The risk is quite high, since if the consultant's guidance is wrong and disasters occur, he will be personally exposed, along with the client he has misled. This risk is greater, since at any one time he will be consulting with a number of individuals. The consultant, like the coach on the course, is never a teacher – his function is to listen, to follow the client's train of thought and identify the needs that preoccupy him, and to seize the opportunity to edge him towards a solution. He may be tempted to manoeuvre the client into doing what he, the consultant, thinks should be done, but the true criterion of his success is always that the client meets his own objectives – which is not the consultant's job to change.

Process consultancy can, of course, take place quite independently of training but, for a number of reasons, consultancy is likely to be more effective where they are combined. First, the training will have given the consultant and the client a common language, common standards of management and points of reference. The client will have a good idea of what the consultant is up to, will be more likely to accept his interventions and to use him in a sensible way. Most important of all, it is very hard for a process consultant to give useful advice, except where the client already sees that help is needed – if he thinks he is perfect, he will not listen. One of the effects of training is to make the client better at seeing his own needs.

The consultant in action

The consultant operates by way of intervention, making comments in order to confirm or question existing assumptions or trains of thought. There are a number of rules he will try to follow:

1 He must build up an atmosphere of confidence and trust. He can do this by being seen to be frank, and ready to put himself at risk at the client's side. At all costs he must not set himself above the client, or talk down to him.
2 He should discover by questioning and careful listening what point the client's thinking has reached on any particular issue, in order to move forward from there.
3 He must encourage the client to learn from experience; otherwise he may get the immediate job done, but not realize that the methods he uses have wider application. Every review they carry out together should be related to aims for the future.
4 He needs to balance his concern for task and process, so that both are improved; and avoid becoming so much wrapped up in the task problem that he fails to see the effect on the client's learning.
5 The client must himself see the need for help: the most the consultant can do is provide information, which may show the client that problems exist. One powerful source of information is the good example of what someone else has done – best of all perhaps, the man's own manager. Indeed one of the most encouraging remarks the consultant can hear is, 'Now at last I understand what my boss has been doing.'
6 The consultant will be judged on how well his contribution meets the client's needs as the client sees them, not as the consultant or the client's boss sees them. Where the manager and subordinate see things in a very different light, a first step is to get them together and try to establish better understanding.

The contract

Both the client and the consultant need a clear common understanding of what the consultant is there to achieve. His brief may be a broad one, as in a large-scale OD project, or it may be limited to one exercise – such as identifying personal skills within a department. In any case, the brief must deal with: the aims of the project; how the consultant will operate; and measures of success. The development of organizations is an abstract process, hard to observe in itself, and the only way for the client to be sure that the exercise is working is to define in clear terms what he wants to get out of it, and how he will know when he has got it. Success criteria should embrace both process objectives (such as improving teamwork) and task objectives (such as increasing sales of product x by y per cent). Whoever is setting up the OD programme must carry his colleagues and subordinates with him; and the best way of convincing them is to have success criteria that are objective and rock hard.

The consultant has a duty to the company, which in practice often means to the senior manager who hired him. He also has a duty to the individuals he works with. If he is told something in confidence, this obligation to keep silent must override any duty to the company – after all, he cannot work with people who have reason not to trust him. But often the decision is not so clear cut. The consultant will gather from the people he works with a whole range of information that he must filter before passing it upwards to higher management: attitudes, opinions, treatment of company regulations, etc. He must use his own judgement in the light of the aims of benefiting both the company and the individual employees.* A more difficult problem is when the consultant forms the opinion, based on observations over a considerable period, that someone is deliberately making mischief or is just not up to the job. In this case he must indicate his concern to the person's boss and encourage him to get full facts and make his own judgement. His role here is like that of any manager, who must support and develop his subordinates, but not beyond the point where their interests clash with those of the company.

There is a worse problem, when it is the manager himself who is incapable. Here the consultant has to adopt a policy, make sure it is known and stick to it. Coverdale's policy (and it is not the only tenable approach) is that the consultant's duty is to the manager who signs the contract or the local sub-contract, and that the consultant gives his best for him until one side or the other ends it. Of course, the consultant should do all he can to avoid signing a contract with someone who cannot do his job and will not learn, but one cannot always identify them in advance. However, neither the moral nor the practical case is an easy one. If a manager is really bad, training his staff may increase their frustration in the short term, since they

---

* An exception to this may be when the consultant's brief is to report on people for promotion, etc. In that case he must make sure everybody he works with understands that he is bound to pass on what he hears. In other cases, when the boss demands a report on a subordinate, the consultant may offer to discuss the man's strengths, but not his defects. He may, if it is appropriate to the manager's purpose, suggest a meeting of all three of them together to explore the problem.

see his defects more clearly and find them harder to tolerate. Sometimes the best result to be hoped for is that the manager will be shown up by contrast with his subordinates, so that management at the top are moved to do something about it. At this stage the consultant's perception of the manager's strengths, such as they are, may be useful in finding him a more appropriate job in the company.

Operation at different levels

The consultant is most effective if he works within one department at several different levels. He will see how their various needs and objectives fit in, and he will be able to pass up the hierarchy information about useful practices and skills that are there to be used. He must also encourage the client to provide his own means for doing this, as part of the necessary management function of spreading success, and he must not become part of the regular system, or there will be an ugly gap when he leaves. One advantage of an outside consultant over an internal one is that people at any level can accept him as an equal, and turn to him as a discreet and independent source of advice. However, a skilful internal consultant can work over about three levels (normally equal or junior to himself), without being regarded either as too senior to confide in, or too unimportant to be worth bothering with.

Examples of process consultancy

The consultant's approach can be illustrated by the way in which he tackles two quite common situations: first, working with one participant fresh back from a course; second, working with a manager and his team on clarifying departmental objectives.

First example: the follow-up interview

1 As preparation for any follow-up interview, the consultant will jot down aims for the meeting (his own and the client's), success criteria, and his outline plan of approach. He should have some picture of how he will operate in likely situations, but the hazard in preparing too carefully is that he may arrive with preconceived ideas. To avoid this, he should plan to listen and probe, rather than talk himself. In a successful meeting, the client will be doing at least two-thirds of the talking.

2 The consultant will lead off by explaining the aims of his visit, which on this occasion will be largely exploratory. He will try and find out from the client:

(a) What exactly is his job? What has he done over the past 2 or 3 months that has benefited the company most? The client will usually be happy to respond, and may come out with problems. The art then is to focus on the one he seems most concerned about (rather than the one he thinks will interest the consultant). Often he will indicate not the problem itself, but only one symptom of it: for example, 'My staff don't come to see me often enough' may indicate that he has a dictatorial style.

(b) How has he reacted to the course? What lessons has he successfully used, or does he intend to use, and what lessons did not seem to work? Are there any points the client would like amplified? The consultant will be keen to draw out the causes of success, especially any that can be transplanted to other parts of the company.

(c) What are his objectives, for work and for himself? What would he most like the consultant to do? The consultant will offer himself as a sort of sounding board, where the client can try out ideas without being compromised.

3 The consultant will encourage the client to apply the themes of the course to work problems, and to construct procedures for meeting the objectives he has defined. He may suggest that he applies aiming techniques and systematic approach in a fairly formal way, so that having proved them in action, he is more likely to use them in future. The main point is to encourage him to think methodically – which, from his detached position, the consultant is in a good position to do.

4 If he judges it will be helpful, the consultant should offer any task experience he may have, in the form of information – ways in which other people have tackled the job. Shared experience of this sort may also help to build up respect. Later, once the client is receptive, the consultant can, if necessary, suggest solutions to task problems. But the client will learn more and be more committed to getting the job done if he comes up with solutions of his own.

5 During the meeting, the consultant should constantly refer back to aims: what end-product does the client want in the time available, and how will he judge his success? He will do this especially when a client produces some vague statement as the agenda. He will explain that he cannot help, until he is clear what the client is on about.

6 The consultant may help the client to improve his own individual behaviour at factory meetings, etc., drawing out the information that the client talks too little, or too much, and encouraging him to plan accordingly. If he is dealing with a manager, he will help him to plan how he will run the meeting (see below). The manager may propose to act during the meeting as an observer; if so the consultant must make sure he knows what he is looking for.

7 The consultant may need to encourage the client to manage upwards,

remind him that a subordinate is not powerless, but has the resources of process authority.

8 Finally, there is not much point in working on task problems if the client's commitment is low, because he has personal difficulties, or because his job is trivial. In such cases, it is much better to work on the personal problem, on improving the client's image, or helping him to get promoted or shifted. It is quite common to find someone stuck in what he sees as a backwater, believing himself (rightly or wrongly) to be regarded as useless. He may start living up to what people seem to expect of him, and become increasingly lethargic. If he has not enough responsibility, perhaps his whole department is short of work and his colleagues and boss are in the same boat, in which case the consultant should make higher management aware of it (warning the man that he is doing so).

Second example: departmental objectives

The second example deals with team-building and objective-setting for a department, showing the balance that can be struck between working with individuals, and with a whole group.

A course often has the effect of making the manager think hard about the departmental aims – sometimes none too soon – and one step the consultant can suggest is to call a departmental meeting to work on them. The meeting may even be held before anyone other than the manager has been on a course, in which case it serves also as an introduction of the consultant and his methods to the rest of the team. Another purpose is to give the manager feedback on his own performance.

1 A day or two before the meeting, the consultant and the manager clarify aims for the meeting, and draw up detailed process plans. They can also clarify in the manager's mind, by discussion, the aims of the department as he sees them, taking into account the aims of related departments, particularly the aims of his own boss.

2 At the meeting the aims are discussed until everyone has the same understanding of what they are (since, later on, when the consultant comes to work with individuals, their main task will be to put *hows* on the departmental *whys*). The aims that come up at the first meeting will mostly be task ones, but someone may well suggest some aim like 'to build an effective team'. This is an important opportunity for the consultant, since, if they do, it allows the whole field of process to be discussed and planned for. Provided enough people present have had training, he can ask what the criteria for the successful team should be, and after a period of silent thought, chart the suggestions. Probably they

will be general process points, such as agreeing common aims, or improving planning, and these can be used as objectives and measures of progress for his own project, which he can review periodically with the manager.

3 After the first meeting, the consultant holds a process review with the manager. Later, this can be built into the meeting itself, as more of the department go on courses.

Third example: two contrasting issues

(a) *'I'm going to sack him!'* The consultant will ask the manager, 'Have you told him?' If the answer is no, the ethical position needs looking at. The consultant will go on to ask 'What is he *good* at? Where in the organization can you find use for this mix of positive skills?'

(b) *'I can't stick this place any longer!'* The consultant will ask, 'What exactly do you dislike about the company, and why? What has held you here for so long, that doesn't apply now?' If the answer relates to higher policy, suggest the staff member carries out his responsibility for managing upwards. If he isn't prepared to try this, perhaps he really should go.

Fourth example – a case study

This study shows how training backed up by consultancy can tackle a problem that at first sight seems to have more to do with emotional tensions and weaknesses than with lack of skill.

The problem occurred in one of the central departments of a large international organization. Its job was development, and the department's role was using land satellite imagery to survey large areas of the world. At the time the technology was developing very fast, and there were exciting possibilities for expanding its use. The department consisted of a manager and three deputies, and below them, about thirty-five staff, many of them highly qualified cartographers, drawn from all over the world. The manager was himself a geographer and a man of some distinction in the field. In spite of this, the department was performing badly: work was not produced on time, and the quality was often poor. The deputy director in charge took the view that the manager couldn't cope, and gave him a time limit to put his house in order. A consultant psychologist was called in to interview the staff, and he uncovered a frightening list of denunciations and complaints: people accused each other of every crime, from incompetence to duplicity, and from sabotage to sexual harassment.

At the time, Coverdale were carrying on a large-scale project within the organization, running a series of courses that included people from all departments. The deputy director called in the senior consultant, and asked him if he could help. The consultant's first step was to arrange for the departmental manager to go on a course, to give him a chance to think through his problems, as well as taking him away from the work environment, which was obviously getting him down. The course included exercises in leadership, and on one of these the manager was designated as leader. He was given half an hour to prepare to brief the rest of the group. To the astonishment of the consultant, he made no preparations at all, and when his colleagues arrived, the briefing he gave was an embarrassing disaster. The problem seemed to be that outside his professional field the manager had great difficulty in visualizing the future, especially where people were concerned.

After the course, the consultant visited him a number of times to help him prepare for meetings, and sit in as an observer. He saw exactly the same thing happening – on one occasion he found himself actually shouting at the manager, 'Look, in 30 minutes you're going to have half your staff in here. What ARE you going to say to them?' Certainly one added problem was that the manager had the threat of dismissal hanging over him, and it did nothing to make his thinking any more coherent. Gradually the consultant was able to coach him into thinking the issues through ('You're going to tell them about X and Y: now what will their reaction be?').

As the manager improved, it became obvious that the problems didn't only lie with him. From the psychologist's report, the consultant diagnosed that the department as a whole lacked two different clusters of skill. The first was being able to distinguish *opinion* from *fact*. People were constantly making misleading interpretations of other people's actions ('He's only doing it because he wants to draw attention to himself'). They needed to distinguish the behaviour they saw from what might or might not be the cause of it. The second cluster of skills needed were those concerned with *listening* and *support*. People tended to listen negatively, to try and pick a hole in any proposal. Accordingly training was extended within the department. The three deputy managers attended full courses, while other professional staff were sent on short non-residential courses, dealing with teamwork, and aimed at developing awareness rather than skill. The consultant checked how many people in the department were potentially problematic, and diagnosed that at least half were trying to be constructive. He arranged for people to be released for training four at a time, and grouped them into pairs – a pair of constructive people with a pair who were less so – all mixed in with people from other departments.

Short though the courses were, they had a considerable effect: trainees learnt the need to listen, and to pick out positive rather than negative points. They took up strongly the need to distinguish between fact and opinion (being trained scientists, they were highly receptive to this, once it occurred to them to apply their professional intelligence to problems of human behaviour). The training also helped the less confident members of staff to become more forceful.

As a result of the general improvement, it became clear that a good many of the department's problems sprang from two individual troublemakers. As staff became more resistant to manipulation, the pair found their influence diminishing, and they decided to leave (one of them having found an academic opening that he had been looking for). From this point on, the performance of the department rapidly improved, and the threat of dismissal was removed from the manager's head.

It can be seen that what the psychologist diagnosed as a nest of emotional problems was sorted out by the injection of skills. By a mixture of training and coaching, the manager was enabled to apply in handling staff the foresight that he had previously reserved for technical problems, while staff learned to consider the evidence before they misjudged a colleague's motives, and to look out for what was positive in their contributions.

14 Functional training – workshops, leadership, negotiation, project management

Process skills are universal: planning and communication are needed as much in a nomad's tent as in the boardroom. The basic Coverdale training can therefore be helpful in almost any situation that requires teamwork or directed effort. Some functions regularly carried out by managers use a particular cluster of process skills, and these can be made the subject of more specific training: e.g. leadership, negotiation, and managing projects, all discussed in this chapter, which begins with a description of the 'workshop' variant of the standard Part I course.

Training workshops

The basic Coverdale courses develop skill, but leave it to the client to apply it back at work. But where courses form part of an in-house programme with specific task objectives, a hybrid form of training has been developed, which allows participants to get to work sooner on the real task issues. The first 2 or 3 days follow the pattern of a Part I course, but from that point on, participants consolidate their skills on tasks that are directly relevant to their job. The key decision for the consultant is how long normal Part I activity should continue before live issues are tackled. In a receptive group 2 days may be enough. Where, however, there are serious problems within the working group – e.g. an autocratic and imperceptive manager, it may not be possible to switch to workshop work until later in the course.

The bridge between the two parts of the course is usually a why/how network, run for the course as a whole. The course director starts the network by posing one of the client company's main objectives for the training: e.g. 'Reduce the level of waste in our plants', or 'Raise morale on the shop floor'. Participants first explore and clarify the company's longer-term aims, then suggest hows for dealing with the problem, their responses being grouped and arranged on the network. At some stage, the hows will define real-life tasks, on which participants can work down to the planning stage (action following back at work).

This sort of training needs consultants who are not only skilful, but also have a deep understanding of the business of the client company; they not only have to understand teamwork in the abstract, but be able to turn the broad objectives set by the company into discrete tasks, defined in a way that will allow participants to make real progress. Consultants must recognize when tasks are outside the competence of the people being trained, and need the help of more senior people or technical specialists. They must be alert to the human implications of whatever is proposed – e.g. the effect on shop-floor employees, and turn these problems into tasks on their own account.

The obvious danger is that participants get so keen on task developments that they forget about the process. It can be quite hard to make them carry out process reviews. However, if the process work is allowed to lapse, the task work will provide no more learning than a normal meeting on site. One way this is tackled is by insisting on two reports from each group in general session – one on process, the other on the task. They are thereby forced to carry out a process review, however perfunctory, and the emphasis soon rights itself, since they realize that it is only through successful process that useful work gets done on the task. Within a day or so, process reviews take up as much time as taskwork.

With this approach, participants gain experience in applying course methods to real problems, as well as making some progress with the problems themselves. They will, however, have slightly less opportunity to develop process skills, and may be less well equipped to tackle difficult process issues with emotional overtones, such as rivalry or restrictive management.

Leadership

Leadership as an art was discussed in Chapter 9. In training for leadership the basic Coverdale format of task and review is maintained, but there are a number of differences. Leaders are appointed by the course director for specific tasks – in a week-long course, each member has three opportunities. If the participants are middle managers, the course must reproduce the world they live in, with tasks and targets being handed down from above. Accordingly all tasks have specific aims (even if these are not obvious), and have tight criteria attached to them. If the manager doesn't know the aim, he must ask, not guess. An important job of the course director is coaching delegates to ask the right questions: not to look for help with the details of the task (like 'Is there a photocopier in this hotel?'), but questions that illuminate what the task is really about, and the result that is wanted.

Leaders gradually learn to approach the task more effectively. To start with, they may virtually finish the job on their own, leaving only a few prosaic chores they instruct the rest of the team to carry out. After a time they learn to pay less attention to the details of the task (after all, they may not be the best person in the group to do it) and much more to getting the best out of their team. They also learn to vary their style with the demands of the job – there are exercises on identifying situations at work where one may need to be more or less autocratic. Most participants experience a shift in style from autocratic to participative, and from concern exclusively with task towards concern with process (Figure 14.1).

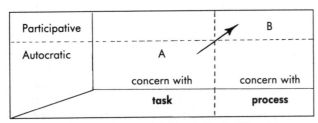

Figure 14.1   *Direction of change of leadership style*

In reviews, although participants are required to be positive, there is a strong emphasis on frankness; given that the leader is being trained for a specific role, he needs a realistic picture of his own performance, warts and all. Again, part of a leader's job is to make people do things they don't want to do; for this reason, some out-of-doors and physical tasks are used: it does no harm if the weather is foul, and leaders have to get their groups out into the rain. The course director is not always a benevolent figure: if the task result doesn't meet the criteria, he will say so. It is not open to leaders to say 'I have fulfilled the aim by doing it in quite a different way' (though they can manage upwards by challenging the course director's criteria).

For newly promoted leaders, the training may be their first taste of standing back from the task, and leaving their subordinates enough space to get on with it. As they become more aware of the skills within their team, they learn the tricky art of managing subordinates who can do their jobs better than their manager can.

Negotiation

Negotiation, like leadership, has a certain mystique about it, since both in trading and in industrial relations, huge sums can be won or lost through a few minutes' skill or ineptitude. It also has overtones of duplicity, and doing the other side down. Certainly this can happen; but as we shall see, when it does, both sides are likely to suffer.

Negotiation might seem the polar opposite of teamwork: after all, within a team everyone's aim is the same, while negotiation suggests conflict – what one wins, another loses. Sometimes this is true. If you are haggling over a carpet, £10 off the price comes straight out of the seller's profit. However, teamwork and negotiation have many aspects in common. As we saw in Chapter 1, any co-operation has competitive elements: e.g. building a team involves negotiation to reconcile the various personal aims. Less obviously, successful negotiation creates a bond of trust and respect between the two sides; and, very often, superficial conflict conceals more fundamental agreement. Management and union may have locked horns over a pay claim, but both sides have even stronger interests in common, such as the survival of the company.

How can negotiations be taught? The basic method is the same as for other process skills – a sequence of trial and review, leading to re-planning. Coverdale first applied its methods to negotiation training in the early 1980s, when ICI Chemicals and Polymers Group was looking for training for senior managers, in order to improve industrial relations. Since then training has been run at every level, covering not only formal negotiations but the implicit negotiation needed to get along with other people and influence their actions, including customers, bosses, colleagues, or subordinates.

Principles of negotiation*

The first rule is to be clear on aims – not only your own, but those of your adversary. It is common for both sides to come out with demands, or 'position statements'. The staff association insists that the office must shut at 4.30 on Friday, to beat the rush hour; management insists that it must stay open until 5.30. But behind these entrenched positions, what are their real interests? Management is concerned that total working hours should not be reduced, and that the switchboard should stay open for orders from customers. Staff don't mind an earlier start in the morning, provided they can get home on time, and there are some people who live nearby and would be happy to work late. If both sides examine their real aims, they can find agreement quite quickly. Reconciling aims may demand ingenuity, and you may need to put your heads together to find a creative solution.

---

* The principles of negotiation are discussed in more detail in *Getting to Yes – Negotiating without Giving in* by R. Fisher and W. S. Ury (Hutchinson 1982). Coverdale's negotiation training is largely based on their work.

A second principle of negotiation is to find a measure or standard that both sides can accept, taking care that it is a measure that happens to suit your argument! If it is a matter of wage negotiations, how is the retail price index going? What do other local firms pay? The more reasoned the discussion, the less you are likely to get into sterile haggling.

Haggling or positional bargaining cannot be avoided all the time. There are cultures where it happens as a matter of course; if you are buying a carpet in the Middle East, you will be regarded as very odd if you pay the asking price. Sometimes principled negotiation can narrow the gap, but there is still an area left for striking a bargain. If it comes to haggling, there are several points to watch. The outcome is likely to be seriously affected by the first bid the parties take as genuine. Very high or very low figures, which are patently unreasonable, have little effect, but you can often steer the outcome by making an explicit proposal that the other side, for some reason, must take seriously. Secondly, you must be careful not to be misled by frequent changes in the position of the other side. A clever positional bargainer might make a series of concessions, from a hundred . . . to ninety . . . to eighty-five . . . to eighty-two and a half . . . , each concession being half the previous one, and the time interval between them becoming ever greater. The implication is that the seller's minimum price is eighty, whereas in fact he might be happy to sell for thirty-seven.

The best defence for a negotiator is to be quite clear about his fall–back position – the best alternative to a negotiated agreement. What happens if you can't do a deal? If the answer is that you can easily go elsewhere, you can hold out for your price and shrug your shoulders if the other side is reluctant. On the other hand, if you *must* do a deal, the last thing to do is to let the other side know it. Some time exploring the alternatives to a deal may suggest fresh options, actually better than those you were striving for. If you are trying to get a pay rise from your manager, and compare rates of pay in job advertisements, you may decide that you are so underpaid that it is better simply to move!

Almost as important as the principles of negotiation is the style in which it is conducted. Often the people you are negotiating with are going to be with you for a long time ahead. There is no conceivable benefit in cheating the union or the staff association, since you have to deal with their members every day. The best negotiators do not play games by having a 'hard' and a 'soft' man, nor go for the other party aggressively. Research by Neil Rackham has shown that they avoid irritating their opponents by pinpricks, and remain calm in the face of personal attacks, though they may point out that an attack is hurtful. If they themselves attack, they do it strongly and suddenly. If a proposal is made, they do not immediately block it by a counter-proposal, but seek to talk round the problem. They look for information by questioning, and check for understanding by giving occasional summaries. They make it easy for their adversary to understand their point of view, by labelling or prefixing – 'I have a suggestion to make'. The exception is that they do not prefix disagreement. Above all, they plan in advance: they consider the full range of options, and the long-term consequence of each, and search for any common ground.

The first aim of negotiating is to reach an agreement that meets your own interests. You want a rapid process that gives a straightforward result (the more complicated the agreement, the greater the difficulties of carrying it into practice). There is, however, a second aim: if you want to go on doing business, it is important that the other side sees the agreement as fair, and that both sides leave with a sense of goodwill. Negotiation based on power, conflict or duplicity may give the first result, but is unlikely to give the second.

Project management

'Projects' come in all shapes and sizes. At one extreme lie vast technological or civil engineering projects, controlled by specialists, lasting many years, and sometimes pushing out into the unknown. At the other end come the minor developments that any manager may have to handle on top of his routine work. Coverdale methods have always been applied to managing projects on a small scale. A manager coming fresh from a course may find it easier to apply Systematic Approach to a discrete project rather than to the day-to-day business of a department. However, running a major capital project is in a different league of complexity: it is a technical subject, having its own professional body (the Association of Project Managers) and calling for sophisticated control procedures and computer programmes. But all projects, big or small, have characteristics in common, in which they differ from normal administration:

• Projects are concerned with change (while in routine administration, change is merely a tiresome distraction).
• Projects are one-off events. With normal, repetitive operations, the way to improve performance is to review the *task*, and plan to do better next time round. With projects, 'next time round' may concern a different task altogether. All that is constant is the *process* of project management, and it is through reviewing process that improvement comes about.
• Projects seldom fall within neat organizational boxes. A project of any size will include negotiation between departments, and probably call on a mixed team of people drawn from different departments and professions. People working on projects often end up trying to serve two or three masters, or having to satisfy departments remote from their own, while still responding to their normal boss.

- Projects are journeys into the unknown. By their nature, they have not been done before, and the result that is envisaged at the start may turn out to be impracticable. Managing a project therefore requires complex aiming skills: to push constantly for a satisfactory result, but recognizing that the result can take various forms, and be achieved in various ways. Aims must be closed down as soon as possible; but not too soon, or the project may shunt itself into a dead end.

There has been a long history of projects failing to achieve their objectives, or overrunning in terms of time and cost. During the 1980s Coverdale became increasingly aware of this as a serious problem for some of its clients, and looked for ways to help. The first study concentrated on large capital projects, but it was found in practice that these were tightly cash-limited, and budgets made no provision for training the management team. In the long term it might be possible to change this attitude, but a better starting point seemed to be smaller, non-capital projects.

The consultants who ran the study were Dr Jack Forrester, who joined Coverdale from ICI, and Gary Willis, who had studied human systems at Lancaster University under Professor Peter Checkland, followed by a spell as a consultant in systems thinking. There one of his clients was the director of research and development of a large engineering company. Together they had developed a complex and elegant system for managing research projects, drawing on both human and computer resources. The trouble was, the system did not deliver the results it should have done. In principle it could not be faulted, but in practice, people seemed uninspired in their attempts to make it work. Either they lacked the will to work together, or the necessary skills.

Given this diagnosis of the problem, Coverdale were the obvious people to turn to, and the senior managers of the research department were persuaded to go on a Part I course. The immediate effects were striking. The tradition of engineering companies in general, and of development work in particular, is one of rigorously analysing errors – not only to put things right, but to assign blame (one of the main requirements of the project-management system had been identifying the culprit when anything went wrong). The managers came back from the course full of the need to analyse success, to set success criteria, and to listen. They set about improving teamwork, and soon the problems with the system seemed far less intransigent. From this and other experiences, Gary came to believe that whenever a sophisticated system broke down, the problem was most likely a human one, to be tackled through training; so he joined Coverdale as an associate.

The consultants felt that they needed to start from first principles, and ask what were the skills and abilities project managers needed, to give a significantly better performance. As a first step, they decided to put together a working group of managers who were faced with this kind of problem. They approached people in a number of large companies, and were pleasantly surprised to find ready support, since many managers wanted to find out the answer for their own sake, and were happy to give some time to the search. About two-thirds of the panel were from existing Coverdale clients, but they were careful to include a leaven of outsiders, to avoid any risk of bias.★

The panel began by looking at two basic questions:

1 What makes projects work, or go wrong?
2 What are the skills of the ideal project manager?

The first question was deliberately left open, to invite both task and process answers. Surprisingly enough, except for matters of budgeting, the answers were all to do with process, especially unclear aims. Projects went wrong not through lack of technical know-how but because, for some *process* reason, the know-how was not being adequately deployed.

Having got provisional answers to this question, the group went on to ask what should be the central themes of any training. Their list included:

- Setting and agreeing aims.
- Managing change.
- Communications – meetings, briefings, and information flow.
- Accountability, authority and responsibility.
- Monitoring and control.
- Managing ideas.
- Skills – identifying one's own, and those of other people.
- Managing time.
- Managing risk.
- Project planning – using a structured approach.
- Managing information.
- Negotiation.
- Setting and managing priorities.
- Working confidently in an ambiguous environment – i.e. one where lines of authority are blurred, or the way forward is ill defined.

The group looked at which of these abilities were capable of being developed through training, and they concluded that they all were, except perhaps the last, which some people felt was a matter of temperament.

★ Companies represented were British Gas, Celltech, Courtaulds Engineering, Davis Langdon and Everett, Esso Petroleum, Grand Metropolitan Retailing, ICI Agro-Chemicals, Shell Chemicals, Synapse Computers, St. Helen's Metropolitan Borough Council, T. P. O'Sullivan, the Wellcome Foundation, and Wolff Olins.

When the panel had done its work, the next stage was to design a training programme. The first course was treated as an experiment, and places were provided free to companies who had collaborated. Subsequent courses have followed the same broad pattern, which is based on a simplified version of the well-known Beckhardt model (Figure 14.2).

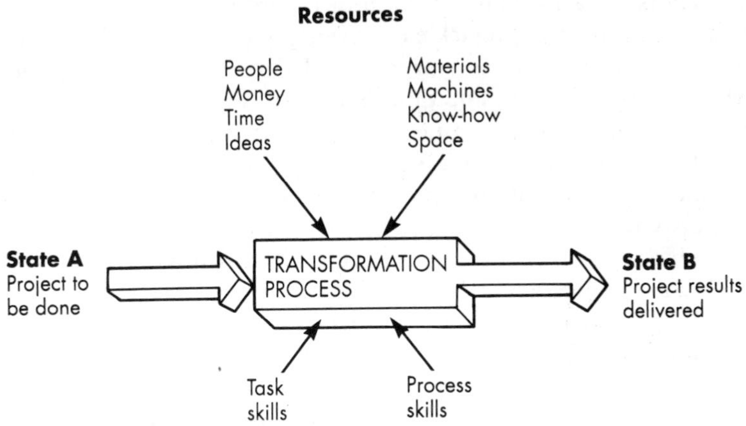

Resources

People   Materials
Money   Machines
Time   Know-how
Ideas   Space

State A   TRANSFORMATION   **State B**
Project to   PROCESS   Project results
be done   delivered

Task   Process
skills   skills

Figure 14.2   *Model of a project*

The training course itself is treated as the 'project', and the first need is to identify the 'State A' of participants. For this purpose, they are sent in advance a detailed questionnaire, designed to give a picture of their competences and training needs, as they see them.

The course lasts 5 days, plus one consultancy day on site, to support the client in putting plans into action. The programme begins with a compressed Part I course, introducing the main process themes (clients who have already taken a Part I course can develop their skills further). The tasks escalate rapidly from simple to fairly complex. Groups are required to work without a leader, however difficult they may find it. This forces them to think about the functions they would like a leader to perform, and the first phase of the course ends with the production of a list of qualities a leader needs.

The second phase starts after lunch on Tuesday. The whole course becomes a 'project organization', with a series of results to deliver. Team leaders are appointed by the course staff, and at various stages they hand over to someone else. Individuals can thus gain experience of either starting up, continuing, or finishing off a project, and the associated processes of hand-over and briefing, according to their training needs. Participants decide who will work on each project, through a negotiation procedure that raises a whole series of issues, such as managing priorities and conflicts of demand, understanding needs for skill, and negotiating. Reviews concentrate on topics that are relevant to the phase of the project, such as 'leadership', or 'negotiation', so that there is a planned development of the course themes. (The course is interested in process only where it has an impact on project results; it is not concerned with self-development for its own sake.)

By Thursday afternoon, all the projects are completed, and the whole course comes together to tackle one large project – on producing a course newspaper. The project has a manager and a number of sub-managers, who together control the organization. Since the course has to break up into sub-groups, several new issues are brought out, such as managing a hierarchy of aims and activities, communication between departments, and roles and functions within a project organization. The last day is mainly taken up with back-at-work planning, with coaches working as consultants. This role is continued during the follow-up day on site, which is included in the programme package.

For this course Systematic Approach is extended, into a form called a 'project agenda'. The differences are:

1 A project consists of a hierarchy of tasks and sub-tasks, linked together on a why/how network. Systematic Approach has to be applied to each of them.
2 Information has to be looked at in terms of different *levels* of Systematic Approach. Does it relate to the main project, or to some task within a task?
3 In setting success measures, a distinction has to be made between *performance* criteria (how well the work is carried out) and *quality* criteria (how good the result is).
4 The What Has To Be Done stage normally produces a list of 'desires' for doing the job. For project management, it is necessary to use systems thinking, following a structure that leads into procedures for estimating, monitoring, and control of the task.

A number of in-house programmes have also been run, usually for larger organizations. Here the aim is to develop not merely individual skills but a project-management system to meet the needs of the organization.

PART 4

The Themes in Action

15 Some detailed problems

Principle and plan

Where people work together, any problem is complex in that it calls for both task and process. Take an example such as 'reducing paper work'. At first sight this looks like a straightforward task issue, calling for task solutions: cutting out unnecessary checks and circulars, installing a computer, or operating through exception reports. But in practice, although bad systems may contribute, too much paper is often a symptom of some *process* sickness in the organization, which needs to be tackled at the roots. The real issue might be:

1 Lack of delegation: subordinates too rigidly controlled.
2 Service departments forgetting their purpose (to provide a service) and so producing reports in an unusable form.
3 Too much formality: people not being able to drop in on each other to give or ask for information.
4 A mistrustful atmosphere: people want to put it on record that they made a particular proposal on a particular date.
5 People feeling a need for power – or merely to keep busy.

Seen in this light, paper work stops being something you tackle by calling in the experts. It is more likely to be cured by the efforts of everyone individually, thinking twice before they send a memo, stating what the aim is and, if it is going to cause a lot of work for the man who receives it, pointing out what are the advantages for him. It may well be that any methods study is best done by individuals, on the paper that they themselves receive or generate. If the manager analyses the written material he receives from his subordinates, this may lead him to issue guidelines on what he wants to know, or to think again about how much he delegates.

This chapter gives some examples of how the themes of this book can be applied in some common situations. They are process plans (or rather, strictly speaking, closed-down WHTBDs, since a plan must take account of local circumstances) which have been found generally useful. Applying them is of course more difficult than merely understanding them. It needs a ready familiarity, so that the right approach springs to mind. It needs something like what in solders is called 'an eye for country' – an ability to size up the strengths and weaknesses of a situation, and the way to approach it. It needs the ability to take some principle of human behaviour, or some open generalization derived from it (for example, that to get co-operation, aims need to be reconciled) and close it down to a plan that will actually enable people to do it. It may need skill to put the planned behaviour into effect.

The examples fall into two main groups: managing oneself (staring work in a new job, and projecting one's image), and conduct of meetings. These are problems which nearly everyone in employment has to face at some time and in which good process planning is the key to improvement. The plans given below can serve both as examples of what a process plan might deal with, and as specific suggestions that can be adapted and tried out when occasion arises.

Managing oneself: starting work in a new job

Most people start a new job with enthusiasm. Often it turns out not to be what they expected, and they begin to think they do not fit. (Of course, with good briefing and induction, this should not happen, but often it is left to the new incumbent to arrange the most important parts of his own induction, and to manage his own manager to make sure he gets it.) The first need is to make a planned effort to talk to your new boss, subordinates and colleagues, and discover the sorts of information listed below. On many of these points a direct question will hardly be appropriate, and you have to form your opinion on the basis of indirect evidence. In any event, getting answers is going to take some time. For this reason it may be worth using a checklist of questions, and jotting down answers (tentative or final) as you get them.

People involved

1 What are their skills?
2 What is their attitude to you?
3 What was their attitude to your predecessor? How are you different?
4 What are the politics, and who are your allies (and enemies)?

Your own position

1 Why were you chosen? For example, to be acquiescent, or dynamic?
2 What are your useful skills? What, in particular, can you contribute which no one else can?
3 Where do you want to be in a year's time?

The job

1 Discover what is regarded as the essential purpose of your job.
2 Get clear success criteria. These should relate not only to the job's result, but to how you do it. Are you expected to be always out and about? Is it frowned on if you work at home? You are in effect setting criteria for the 'hows' as well as the 'whys' of your network.
3 Discover from your new staff how they tackle their own jobs.
4 Get proposals from them on how working can be improved and what they would like to see done. Make sure that at least some of these are put into practice (if for nothing else, for the sake of morale).
5 Discover the extent and the limits of your authority.

Avoid the temptation to make an immediate splash, which often springs from insecurity; unless, that is, you judge that you were appointed with some sort of crash programme in mind. If you are young and aspiring, try not to frighten your manager or new colleagues by making it seem that they are stupid or slow. They will do nothing to help or develop you, if they are afraid of you. Make sure you get sufficient feedback of your successes and failures and whether you are fulfilling the expected role. If you do not get enough, you may have to get your boss to set tighter criteria, or propose them yourself.

There are two special cases to be looked at.

1 Where the last incumbent is your new boss

This can be awkward. Both he and you may feel insecure in your new jobs. He may not be sure what are the limits of *his* authority, and how much he should interfere with yours. He knows he can do parts of your job better than you can, and he may find it quicker to do the job himself than to explain. He may judge you on your methods of work, rather than the actual results you achieve – regarding any changes you make as errors, or even criticisms of himself. With all this, the very last thing to do is to try to shut off your department and keep out of his sight. Instead, go to your boss and get from him an indication of:

(a) His skills: where he would most like and most be able to help you
(b) His priorities: what are the most important parts of your job as he sees it
(c) What he would like to be told about – in addition to the various decisions which you are bound to submit to him.

Invite him to help with particular points. People are usually pleased to be consulted (provided it is not too often) and this will let him keep in touch with what is going on, but at your discretion.

2 Where your job is ill-defined

You may find when you get there that no one is precisely sure what your new job is. They feel a general need but they have not defined the role. In that case, you will have to develop your job yourself.

(a) Get as much information as possible on the nature of the need that was felt.
(b) Look further up the hierarchy and discover the company's aims, as they relate to you.
(c) Cast about for things that need doing. Check that they are seen as appropriate to your job (and make sure they are suitable to your skills) and then make proposals and carry them out.

Projecting your own image

The aim should be to get people (boss, subordinates, colleagues, customers) to value you in accordance with your real strength. In this you may have specific objectives – such as getting promotion, or merely getting people to listen to you. You may need to overcome some sort of reverse 'halo' effect – that is, someone undervaluing you because of one characteristic he finds objectionable. The first stage is of careful self-analysis. Take a pencil and paper and jot down:

1 What do people want and expect of someone in your position? It may be useful to have a look at someone who is conspicuously successful. But pick up what they actually do and how they do it, rather than merely their surface characteristics.
2 What strengths you have that people will find useful.
3 What characteristics put people off.

When you know this, make a plan:

1 To provide people with what they want.
2 To use and display those strengths that are relevant.
3 To do whatever possible to alter (or at least avoid displaying) your negative characteristics.

Having adjusted your behaviour, you still need to make yourself noticed, since people will judge only by what they actually see.

1 Let people know what you are good at. If you do not get a chance to show it, tell them. If you have a talent that is not used, go away and provide a sample of work, if necessary in your own time. It is very charming being modest and British, but it can be a thorough nuisance if you hide a skill that other people need.
2 Avoid saying you are bad at anything – even if you are convinced that it is obvious, or as a joke. Apart from anything else, others around you may well be worse.
3 Never begin a report with a failure. If your manager/customer starts analysing, he may never get to the success. If you have to report failure, do not dwell on it or make excuses. Accept criticism and get on to something else; or better still, make your report in the form of a proposal to put the failure right.

Respect other people's prejudices – unless they conflict with a genuine conviction of your own. Conform in minor matters, such as dress, with what people expect of you, not necessarily with what they do. Pay particular attention to the impression you make on anyone you are meeting for the first time (who will judge largely by externals).

Sometimes people will form their impression of you from what they see at meetings. There are a number of things you can do to be seen to best effect:

1 Arrive precisely on time.
2 Start off by listening.
3 Be quite clear about the aims of the meeting, and of other people present.
4 Consider what is likely to concern them, as well as what they say.
5 Try to consider their aims sympathetically, both in order to identify common ground, and to avoid being unnecessarily provocative.
6 Be clear about what you are trying to get done, and its full implications.
7 Suit your language to your company.
8 If you have important points to put across, there are two distinct ways of doing so: first, by making definite proposals and pushing the meeting along; second, by providing information carefully stressed to lead to the

outcome you want, and drawing out the conclusion by leading questions. If you use the first approach injudiciously, you risk being seen as a know-all; the danger with the second is that you may be seen as ineffectual (or as Machiavellian). Your choice must depend on the mood and what sort of people attend the meeting.

Relations with your manager

Your manager is a piece of information. Think what you know about him: his wants, his standards, his skills and his prejudices. Choose what information you are going to pass on to him, in order to find ways of involving him, while keeping his nose out of your business. Try to identify his priorities. You can then relate your proposals to them – either in so many words or by letting him work out for himself how your proposals will help him. This is particularly appropriate where systems appear to be rigid, or where the boss himself keeps saying 'no'. If he blocks any important proposal, analyse it to see the advantage to him and use this aspect to sell it. If he looks always for what is wrong, present him with successes. If you have just held a successful review, send him the details. If it is an acceptable risk, invite him to attend one of your own departmental meetings. If your boss thinks openly, with very long-term objectives, help him to close down: 'It would help if we could agree on what I need to do tomorrow.'

One occasion for image-making and breaking is when some big man comes down on a state visit to your department, trailing clouds of executives behind him. Here, liaise with your immediate manager to discover what he is after. Is he merely showing the flag, or having a quick look at life at the sharp end? Or is there some local project or problem that has reached his ears? When you know what he will probably be interested in seeing, think what you want to show, and steer him towards the items which are in both categories.

Relations with subordinates

Your subordinates will probably know you so well that your image is close to reality. If you act like the Czar of Russia, you will have the image of an autocrat, and nothing is going to alter it. But make sure that none of your staff (your secretary, for instance) is giving a false impression, through their own self-importance or because they want to protect you.

Avoid adopting roles like the great dictator – exuding efficiency from a stately office to which people come cap in hand, or the whiz kid – inviting them to participate, then dazzling them all with your own brilliance; or the anny – going too far down Systematic Approach, and giving out a plan where you need merely set aims.

Beware of assumptions of what is expected of you, or of what your image really is. One consultant had a telephone call from the managing director of a large textile firm. 'We have a chap,' he said, 'been here for years – by far the best man on the technical side. The trouble is, he's an autocrat – thinks he's still in the 1930s. Do you think one of your courses would do anything for him?' The consultant was dubious, but he said, 'At least we can get him out of your hair for a week.' The man arrived on the course, and proved to be mild, serious and co-operative, particularly interested in the work on using other people's skills. At the end of the week he said, 'You know, I've enjoyed this enormously: it's the way I've always wanted to operate. The trouble is, our managing director – he's one of the old school; he'd never put up with this democracy . . .' Ten minutes' discussion could have saved 20 years misunderstanding; one value of process training is that it provides a language in which discussion like this can take place.

Conduct of meetings

Introduction

At lower levels of management, the first and most obvious success of process training is in improving the quality of meetings. This comes about not because of new procedures, but because individuals have become more skilful – in listening, supporting, clarifying, sticking to aims or in the use of a chart. Training that concentrates on formal procedures for meetings is not likely to help, except where the chairman and some other members already have a fair degree of personal skill and self-discipline.

The term 'meeting' can cover a wide range of encounters, from formal committees to one-to-one interviews. They can also take place for a wide variety of purposes, including:

1 Clarifying aims.
2 Exchanging information – for example, 'Monday morning meetings', and job selection interviews.
3 Progress reviews.
4 Decision-taking, or authorizing proposals (for example, board meetings, or local government committees).
5 Briefing.

Most meetings combine two or more of these purposes, e.g. annual appraisal interviews combine information exchange and WHTBD.

The agenda

Classify agenda items as:

1 Information – giving.
2 Information – wanted.
3 Decisions; it may be worth distinguishing low-risk from high-risk.

State items for decision in a positive way: not 'There is too much rubble', but 'Task – to remove rubble'. You may also find it helpful to set out success measures. Send out agendas at least one week ahead, together with all the relevant information. Items should have notes beside them, giving the reference of any memos, etc., to which they refer. Avoid handing out documents at the meeting. If you must do so, allow time to read them. At the meeting, chart the agenda, then ask for any other business and chart that. The advantage of doing this is that it lets people know that in due course the point that concerns them is going to come up, so that in the meantime they can concentrate on the other items. However, too much other business can be a nuisance, and it may be necessary to restore discipline by threatening to ban it.

Procedure at the meeting

At the start of the meeting, agree its purpose. It may help to pin up a chart headed 'Why have we met?' – on which people can write their answers or initial other people's. Set a time for closing the meeting and, when possible, stick to it. One can also set times for the discussion of each item: it may not be possible to keep to them, but at least it makes the meeting aware when lesser items take up too much time. When points are raised out of their correct sequence (side issues, not necessarily red herrings):

1 Ask the purpose in raising them.
2 Record them as 'bin' items on the corner of a flip-chart – together with their purpose.
3 Deal with them later as appropriate.

Who should attend meetings?

In general, invite only those who have something to contribute, or something to learn that they need to know. Keep down the number of visitors. Do not ask people to attend the meeting merely in order to be nice to them: ask them to lunch instead.

Use of an observer

In a large meeting, it may be useful to appoint an observer. This could be a trainee, or someone who is not concerned with the particular item under discussion, or it could be the meeting's secretary. If your own secretary is present taking minutes, it can be a good way of enriching her job. Another approach is where the manager appoints himself as observer, and leaves his staff to get on with it.

The observer (and the rest of the meeting) need to understand exactly what he is looking for and how often he should intervene. Some possible roles are:

1 Process observer – reporting back during formal process reviews.
2 Conciliator/synthesizer – an observer may be able to sort out conflicts, or spot ways of combining two people's ideas or points of view.
3 Coach – when the manager himself acts as observer, stopping the meeting if necessary to indicate where something has gone well, or why they are stuck.

Other more specific jobs may be to point out when items overrun their set time, or when important issues seem to skip through without proper discussion.

Process reviews

Whether or not you have an observer, you may well need occasional process reviews. You can hold them at set times (not always at the end of the meeting, if you want to make use of the points the review brings up), or whenever the meeting gets into a tangle.

The chair

There is no need for the senior person present to act as chairman. It can be good training for all concerned (including the manager) if the chairmanship rotates. Since the chairman's chief concern is process, avoid making someone chairman if he/she is the task expert in the matter being discussed.

Minutes

The purpose of minutes can be:
1 As a record of decisions.

2 As a repository of useful facts.
3 As a reminder to individuals of what action they must take.
4 As instructions, or an account of the meeting, for people who were not there.
5 As a reminder to the next meeting of where matters were left – sometimes, to act as an agenda.

Not all meetings need all these points. Points 1, 2 and 5 can often be dealt with by preserving a flip-chart. Reminders for action can themselves be a snare, since people stop listening if they think they can catch up through the minutes. You need to decide what the purpose of the minutes are, and deduce from that what form they should take.

Special kinds of meeting

1 Routine information meeting

This may be known as a 'morning meeting', a 'departmental meeting', a 'production meeting', etc. It occurs at fixed intervals (usually daily or weekly) and all the staff of a section are expected to attend. The purpose is the exchange of information that is relevant to the section's aims and on which future action may be based. The only conclusions that should come out of it are:

(a) Simple WHTBDs, allocated by the manager to individuals.
(b) More complicated items, for the agenda of a future policy meeting.

The types of information that need to be exchanged are:

(a) Anything likely to affect operations before the next meeting.
(b) Anything of wide general interest – for example, developments within the company.
(c) Anything likely to affect morale – that is, good things to make use of; bad things to deal with quickly.

All planning should be remitted to individuals (or pairs, if that makes more sense). A few points to watch are set out in Table 15.1
   Some success criteria are:

(a) The meeting is short.
(b) Information is either relevant to the week's activities or is important background material.

Table 15.1 *Problems with meetings*

Hazards	Remedies
Meetings drift on.	Chairman allows information, but cuts out discussion. Set maximum time. Hold meetings standing up – no chairs provided.
Individual hogs the meeting with his pet subject.	Chairman invites him to discuss the point with him later.
Chairman does all the talking.	Rotate chairmanship. Elect chairman into observing role.
Lack of commitment: people try to get out of coming.	Review the usefulness of the meeting every 6 months.
The group starts planning.	The group should listen to plans made by individuals; members can then advise on points which should be built into the plan, such as 'involve the shop steward'.
Sniping – for example, between sub-sections.	Make sure all points are factual and relevant to the task areas of people present. Draw attention to aims common to both sub-sections.

(c) People talk freely, and all relevant information is welcomed, however unpalatable.
(d) People learn all they need at the meeting (or through other proper channels) rather than through the grapevine or the shop steward.

2 Technical meetings

The *purpose* is usually to review progress and agree WHTBD over a wide range of items: there may be thirty or so on the agenda. Board meetings are often of this kind, especially where directors are reluctant to set direction, but plunge into detail instead. Local government committee meetings have a similar pattern, though they have the added dimension of political argument, and on some items the aims of members may be directly opposed to each other. A common characteristic is that not everyone who attends is concerned with every item. The sort of difficulties you find are:

1 Important items are glossed over, while long discussions take place on minor matters.
2 People lose their way in the agenda; or switch off and come to life at inappropriate moments.
3 Pairs or small groups get into heated discussion of trivia, while the rest doze off.

The chairman should start with a well-defined plan, which he declares (and probably charts) at the outset. This should arrange for items to be taken in order, in such a way that:

(*a*) Important matters come high; related items are grouped; and people not concerned with particular sections can be released.
(*b*) The purpose of the meeting should be recorded and checked each time.
(*c*) If the meeting is long, physical breaks should be arranged to prevent people getting tired.
(*d*) The chairman should be prepared to cut short contentious dialogues and get pairs to solve their problems at another time and place.
(*e*) The chairman should also get other members to support him by carrying out particular functions – for example, time-keeping (getting through the agenda); checking that proper weight is attached to important items; process issues; the environment – keeping the room aired, arranging tea, etc.

Useful success criteria are:

1 People go away with useful objectives and WHTBD.
2 A timetable is set and broadly kept to.
3 No one is left with nothing to contribute for a long series of items (unless he is there to learn, and in this case he may be useful as process observer).

3 Briefing meetings

Two sorts of briefings can be distinguished: briefing where the manager gives out a closed WHTBD or a plan; and briefing where the manager merely sets the objective and prescribes success criteria. Each needs its own approach.

Briefing closed-down plans

To get commitment, you need to bring the people you are briefing up to your own level of understanding of the problem. Using the chart, begin with the aims and specific objectives and go through all the information which has led towards the plan. End with success measures. If you are ruling out major changes in the plan, say so tactfully at the outset. You can do a lot of harm by pretending that this is a participative exercise, if it is not. But be ready to accept minor changes and suggestions. The characteristics of such a meeting are plenty of information volunteered by you, and fairly few interventions by your staff (except reading back to show that they understand).

Briefing open objectives

Chart objectives and propose (or elicit) success criteria. There will normally be much less material (since information is still to be sought). Force the meeting to go on clarifying, till they fully understand both the objectives and success criteria, and the implications for getting on with it ('so that will mean actually having it done by Wednesday'). Respond by saying 'You know the constraints and you must use your own judgement. The decisions and the action are all up to you.' Remind them that you are available for information or clarification – and make sure you *are*. The characteristics of such a meeting are a consultative style and plenty of silence.

16 Coverdale on the shop floor – Whitbread Cheltenham and Shell Carrington

The two projects described in this chapter, at Whitbread's brewery at Cheltenham, and at the Shell petrochemical plant at Carrington, both dealt with the extension of training to manual workers on the shop floor. The Whitbread project also shows how Coverdale training can be used to support a programme of Total Quality Management.

Total quality management

TQM is an idea developed by the Japanese. The basic principle is that every activity within a firm has some impact on the quality of products and services that the customer receives; this applies as much to support staff, like typists, as to people directly engaged in design and delivery of products. The aim is to go beyond merely competent performance: to provide customers with a high quality of service that 'delights' them. To do this it is not enough to look only at the final product, at the point where the customer takes delivery; if quality control starts here, goods can pass through the complete chain of production and distribution, only to be rejected at the last moment. The result can be appalling wastage – in some industries, 25 per cent is not unknown. What is needed instead is that as each department passes the goods down the line, quality is observed at every stage. The recipient department must itself be regarded as a customer, to be 'delighted' with the service it gets.

TQM therefore means that everyone in the organization must achieve the right standards. First, the needs of customers, both internal and external, must be understood by everyone in the supplying department; second, the operating procedures required to meet these criteria must be documented; and third, training and monitoring must be good enough for the criteria to be met. Any defects must be spotted at once, usually through statistical sampling of the output; and if goods fall below standard, the cause of the variance must be quickly identified, and necessary improvements made. The motto of TQM is 'Get It Right First Time'. If an operation needs two or three attempts, there must be a brisk review to find out why, followed by the establishment of working patterns that will avoid the need in future.

Until the late 1980s, Coverdale had not dealt specifically with the search for quality. Other consultants specialized in installing quality systems, and arranging statistical controls. However, controls and systems on their own will never make TQM work; what is essential is *commitment* – every staff member must be committed to upholding the standard of the goods that are passed on.

TQM at Whitbread

Whitbread is one of the largest brewery companies in the United Kingdom. In recent years, the pattern of beer sales has been changing very fast. The Mergers and Monopolies Commission produced a report ('The Supply of Beer'), which pushed strongly for a loosening of the traditional ties between breweries and pubs. Its aim was to increase competition, reversing the world-wide tendency for large breweries to dominate the market through economies of scale. This has generated new problems for brewers. Beers have always competed at the point of sale – people know which brand they prefer. But pubs are more and more served by wholesalers, which, if they cannot get their first choice of beer delivered promptly, may well switch to a competing brand. TQM is therefore an important concept for brewers, particularly as excise duty is levied on the total volume of beer that is brewed, and there is no rebate for any that is wasted or scrapped further down the line, in packaging or distribution.

Whitbread started with the concept of TQM, but soon saw that quality of service was as important as quality of the product itself. If a wholesaler ordered 200 barrels for 10 am, that was what he must have, not 150 today and the rest tomorrow. Whitbread's distribution company had already set up a programme called 'Service Challenge', and when in 1990 brewing, and the distribution and marketing of beer, were brought together in one integrated company (called 'the Whitbread Beer Company'), a company-wide scheme called the 'Quality and Service Initiative' (a name that made a good deal more sense to staff) was started.

Coverdale had worked with Whitbread for many years, and the company had built up a policy of using Coverdale training to support the development plans of newly appointed senior managers. When David Hudson took over as general manager of the brewery at Cheltenham, it was decided to use Coverdale to introduce quality and service management. Cheltenham is a traditional brewery, small compared with the modern giants with which it has to compete, engaged in making both keg beer and older-style ale in barrels for a range of Whitbread brands. It employs about 150 staff. Management saw from the start that the main need was to get the work-force's commitment – which raised the question, 'How committed were they now?' To check this, a survey was carried out, based on interviews with 25 per cent of the staff, and asking the rest to fill in questionnaires.

The picture that emerged was not altogether favourable. Shop-floor employees saw the main weakness as being the relationship between managers and themselves. In the past, brewery management had tended towards benevolent autocracy. Not only the style must change, but its past effects would have to be eradicated. Eighty-five per cent of those interviewed saw morale as being 'low to very low'. Various causes contributed, including the uncertain future of the brewery and a recent move to a shift system. Another problem was a change in patterns of work over the years. In the not-so-distant past, breweries contained many simple manual jobs, and appropriate staff were recruited to do them. In a modern brewery, jobs like rolling barrels around have largely disappeared, and older staff, who had been taken on for this kind of work, were having to master operations of much greater complexity.

As a result of the survey, the targets adopted for the Coverdale programme were to improve relations between managers and shop-floor workers, and to encourage greater involvement. The project ran for 2 years, from the beginning of 1989 until Spring 1991, and consisted of a series of workshops, for staff of all levels. Most managers had already undergone Part I courses and the more senior ones had done Part II as well. Accordingly, training took the form of 3-day workshops, which (after a brief recap of process themes) concentrated on task and organizational problems. Some questions examined were the role of the supervisor, and what could be done to improve morale. This last exercise led to a number of changes, such as new uniforms, a new bleep system, and a revised pattern of staff briefings. Participants also worked directly on the Quality and Service project, e.g. identifying the customer–supplier chain for particular areas of the brewery, and identifying quality criteria for each link in the chain. For first-line managers, progress was maintained through off-the-job review sessions called 'Away Days'.

The next, more radical, stage was to extend the workshops to the shop floor. This would be an unusual step in many companies, especially in an old-established industry like brewing, where management has traditionally been hierarchical and paternal. Since operatives had had no previous Coverdale training, their workshops lasted 4 days. The first 2½ days were spent on neutral tasks to develop the skills of teamwork. The course then went on to explore the relationship between customers and suppliers, and how standards could be raised by planning. Finally participants tackled some real-life tasks (previously agreed with managers), such as 'How can we improve the quality in the filter room?' or 'How can we improve the relationship between beer-runners and the keg line?' For the first 3 days participants worked in mixed teams, but on day 4 they went into their normal departmental groups.

The reactions of operatives changed as the course went on. At the start, many were resistant to the basic message; they were not used to the idea that they should help make decisions – they saw decision-taking as the job of management and their own place as carrying out instructions. There was a natural feeling that if they were being asked to think more, they should be paid more. After the first couple of days, however, there was growing interest, backed up by a great increase of confidence, and a sense of pride in tackling matters that had always seemed the managers' prerogative. They began to see managers in a new and more human light – 'They are merely the blokes who know how to organize process'.

It was the supervisors who felt most threatened by the new change of style. By background and experience they tended to be doers rather than managers, and when they realized that they would have to delegate nearly all the doing, some of them felt uncomfortable, especially as the logical outcome – even if never realized in practice – would be self-organizing teams of operatives in managerless workshops, the role of management being limited to 'unblocking'.

A training programme for the whole staff is an ambitious undertaking, especially when operatives are expected to produce initiatives as a result. From the second workshop onwards it was realized that to get results, the programme would have to be highly structured. The pattern adopted was as follows:

- Workshops ran from Tuesday to Friday. On the Monday before, participants were given a briefing by their shift manager on the concept of 'quality and standards'. It was pointed out that quality means fitness for a *purpose* – a Rolls Royce and a Landrover are very different kinds of vehicle, but each is of high quality. Operatives were also introduced to technical matters, such as methods of sampling, and the British Standard 5750, as it applies to the production of beer. A Coverdale consultant would then have a talk with each of them, to allay any worries about the course.
- Each workshop was introduced by the general manager. On the last day he came back, along with departmental managers, to hear the results of the syndicate work – what participants thought should happen in the brewery. One of the managers had the job of taking away the charted material, getting it typed, and circulating it to the participants, as well as to members of the management executive. He remained responsible for seeing the job through, up to the review session 6 weeks later.
- On the next Thursday, the management executive reviewed the

proposals with a Coverdale consultant, and produced a statement of 'Next Steps'. Since it was stressed to operatives that they must come back with *workable* solutions, there were few instances where their proposals could not be put into practice.

- Through normal briefing procedures, the staff of the brewery were all told what the outcomes of the workshop had been.
- Participants coming back from the workshop formed 'quality improvement teams', to put as many as possible of their plans and ideas into effect.
- Six weeks later, each workshop team met the consultant, to carry out a review. Feedback was sought both on achievements, and any blocks and difficulties encountered: what had changed and, more pointedly, what had managers *not* done anything about? Up to this stage, the whole process remained the responsibility of whichever departmental manager originally took it on.

Benefits of the training

At the time of writing (January 1991) the programme is still under way, and it will be some time before the full benefits become apparent (various measures of success will be applied, including a follow-up attitude survey). It was decided that quality improvement teams should first work on the problems that they themselves had selected. Apart from tangible improvements, the aim of this was to develop skill and confidence in problem-solving. As a second stage, teams will go on to tackle more fundamental problems that managers have identified. All the same, some valuable results have already been achieved:

(a) Throughout the long, hot summer of 1990, there was no single case of microbiological trouble with the beer. While it can't be proved that this was the result of training, the obvious explanation is that it reflects both greater awareness of the need for hygiene, and greater care in using equipment, making sure it was sterile before any process took place.

(b) As a result of the 1990 drought, the brewery's main source of stable, chemically pure water, a spring in the Cotswolds, began to run dry. Managers emphasized the need for water-saving, but it was operatives themselves who identified several points in the process where ordinary tap water could be substituted for the purer source, without any loss of quality. Operators also devised a way to recycle the water used in the filtration process.

(c) As production increased, more employees had to go on to shift work. At the same time management sought to broaden the job of warehouse operatives so as to make them totally accountable for their own loads.

This could well have caused difficulties, distribution staff not always being the first to welcome change, but because there was plenty of open discussion beforehand, the change was accepted without any friction.

(*d*) In a process like brewing, short breakdowns have a serious affect on the total production of the plant, since lost time cannot be recovered. Even though most breakdowns are minor, delays can occur because it is not clear whether a fault is electrical or mechanical, or because a fitter or electrician is not immediately on hand. Accordingly the company introduced new training for craftsmen, called 'extended skills'. This consisted of giving electricians some basic mechanical skills, and fitters some electrical skills, so that whichever was called upon could put right simple problems, even though they might not be part of their speciality. The training was fully documented, and certificated by the Engineering Industry Training Board. It made up a series of modules, and operatives who successfully completed them were given an increase in pay. Some craftsmen, already in their sixties, were not keen on undertaking further training, or 'going back to school'; it was arranged that if they agreed to co-operate by giving cover, etc., they would receive a proportion of the increase.

(*e*) The jobs of operatives are being systematically documented for purposes of quality improvement. Only too often such documents sit in the office and gather dust, but here the emphasis is on keeping people aware of what parts of the job are *critical*. Operatives have fully co-operated in this, and have themselves identified what they see as the critical parts of their job, their proposals then being agreed with management. The list of critical tasks is kept on hand, stuck up on a wall near the work position.

Shell UK – Carrington Site

A second example of training designed to cover the whole of an industrial work-force was at Shell UK's Carrington site. Carrington is an old-established petrochemical plant, built after the Second World War. At its peak it employed over 3000 people, but it was heavily hit by the first oil crisis, and later by more modern plants coming on stream. By the time the Coverdale programme started, staff numbers had fallen to 1200, and they were to be further reduced to below 500.

By the mid-1980s, Carrington was under severe pressure, and needed a survival plan. One model of good practice was a new Shell/Esso project at Mossmoran, which, starting on a greenfield site, had been able to introduce new working methods, unencumbered by demarcation and restrictive practices. A plan was therefore put together to introduce what was called 'the new Carrington'. The organization was to be restructured, levels of management above the shop floor being reduced from six to three. The distinction between craftsmen and operators would be abolished, all work being done by multi-skilled technicians. To achieve this, there was an intensive task training programme, which lasted for more than 2 years. The work-force accepted the change, and people who were going to be made redundant were even prepared to spend their last 6 months running the plant while staff who were remaining went off to be trained.

So far, the changes had gone through smoothly, but the job now was to make the new organization work in practice. Decisions had to be moved down the line, to the level where the real information was available – from plant manager to shift managers, and from shift managers to team leaders. Teamwork had to be improved, and the relationship between different levels of management worked out. All this had to be done quite quickly, or there was a risk that either unions or technicians might find pretexts to claw back the flexibility that had been so hard won. Shift managers were faced with all sorts of new problems. For example, given that they had a team composed of ex-electricians, ex-fitters, and ex-riggers, how should they deal with an electrical fault? By sending an ex-electrician, who could do the job quickly, or someone who needed the experience to develop their skills?

The company decided to tackle these problems through training, and Coverdale was selected to run it. The first course was a 6-day workshop for the site manager and his six immediate subordinates. The main issues were the site's aims, and the new management and working practices they implied; and how these could be passed down the line.

The next stage was to extend training to all managers and potential managers. The site manager worked in a highly consultative style, and didn't want to force training on staff. The programme therefore took some time to get under way, but the time spent in getting acceptance proved to be well worth while.

At the start of the project, Coverdale asked the site to provide in-house facilitators. They insisted that they did not want trainers, nor people who just happened to be available; they wanted people of shift-manager level, well equipped with process skills themselves, and aware of the process: people who were good at their jobs and so credible guides for others, able to stand back from the immediate task and take a longer view. This caused a good deal of rethinking by the client, but Coverdale stuck to its guns, and the choice turned out to be one of the project's great strengths. A number of potential coaches were included in the first course, and the most suitable were picked out, and seconded for 6 months, to do full-time consultancy work. They were trained while the earlier courses were being run, and took a full part in coaching the later ones. The essence of their job was supporting managers, and eventually technicians, in putting the lessons into practice.

When all the managers and professional staff had been trained, the next phase consisted of working with technicians. Because of the working pattern of the plant, it was possible to get a whole shift away for 4 days' training, along with the shift manager and other managers concerned. The courses were run at the same hotels as management courses had been. For the first 2 days, the technicians went through the normal training, while the managers were trained separately in leadership. On the third day, technicians continued with their Part I course, but with the managers sitting in as observers – by this time, technicians' groups were well established, so they were not inhibited by the managers' presence. That evening the managers joined the technicians' course, and managed a project carried out by the course as a whole. All the way through, reviews continued in the normal way, with the effect that managers' leadership came under scrutiny from their own technicians. (Having had 3 days' leadership training beforehand, they were used to getting robust feedback!)

This pattern of training was much bolder than the one used at Cheltenham. It was also rather short, since operators spent only 3 days working in their home groups. As many of them began the training in a mood of cynicism (not surprisingly, considering the traumas of staff reduction that the site had been through), this didn't give much time to build up new patterns of working and thinking but it was all that the shift system permitted.

All the same it did a great deal to change behaviour on site, backed up by the facilitators, who joined the course on the last day, and built on this to ensure that learning continued. It was a great advantage that they knew all about the task activities, even if they sometimes found it hard to stand back, and avoid second-guessing a manager's decisions.

Results of training

After their course, each manager tackled a special project, and the results were carefully monitored. They were of three sorts, concerned with procedures, plant performance and product quality.

Savings from the procedural projects couldn't be quantified, though five were regarded as successful and only one as a failure. The plant performance tasks were estimated to have saved more than twice the costs of training, and those from product quality tasks three and a half times the costs of training. The in-house facilitators reported a range of other benefits. Managers were more likely to provide support, rather than merely laying blame. There was greater awareness of other people's ability to contribute, and more confidence all round, especially at junior levels. Reviewing was becoming a habit, and the lessons were being applied. There were problems too: as a result of staff reductions, the organization was a lean one, and some of the back-at-work tasks caused overloading. It was also important to identify the people's priorities rather than letting them be guided by enthusiasm.

Shell's policy is to move more senior staff around the company, and within 2 or 3 years most of the senior staff at Carrington moved on, including the site manager. His successor had worked at Carrington under the old dispensation, and now agreed to undergo both Part I and Part II courses before taking over. He spent the first few months observing the way the system was running before making any changes. In the event, this change of management was all to the good. 'New Carrington' was itself becoming established, but the fresh impetus made sure that improvements did not stop there, but became a continuing process.

17   Architects and scientists – John Brunton and Courtaulds Research

This chapter describes some of Coverdale's work with professional and scientific staff, including, in the case of John Brunton, the top levels of corporate management.

John Brunton

John Brunton is a firm of architects, established in Bradford for over 100 years. By 1955 the firm still had only two partners, but over the next 20 years it grew very fast, and was incorporated in 1982. However, growth did not bring profitability: the quality of the architecture was not matched by management skill, and by the mid-1980s the firm was in serious financial trouble. With the help of its bankers and accountants, a recovery plan was put together. An important part of it was the establishment of a proper management structure, including a non-executive chairman. At the same time, one of the directors, Brian Blowers, was appointed chief executive.

The first 6 months after the chief executive's appointment were traumatic. There were staff redundancies, and directors had to take large cuts in salary. However, everyone seemed to realize that without some drastic and unpopular actions, the firm was finished. The new board quickly established patterns of financial discipline and control, but something still seemed to be missing. Architects are creative, imaginative people and their 5-year university training is geared to developing these talents. However, they are rarely taught anything about management or business, and this can be a serious handicap. They need to manage not only the projects under their control, but their own studios and staff. They need to distinguish clearly between the professional function of designing buildings and preparing drawings, and the management function of organizing day-to-day tasks within the office, sorting out personal problems, and leading a team or a studio. The former partners, now directors, had their own lessons to learn: setting long-term strategy requires skills that are quite different from either operational management, or professional expertise. The board realized that the firm's business weakness was more the fault of the structure than of the staff. As Brian Blowers observed, 'In the past, the directors had seen themselves as responsible for everything, from the hiring and firing of staff to the purchase of paper clips. As a result, everyone else was put in a situation where they dared not take any decisions.'

One of the firm's clients was a small business centre, which had been set up to provide workshop accommodation for new and growing firms. The manager of the centre was Jack Forrester, who combined this job with working as a Coverdale consultant. A chance conversation between him and Brian Blowers led to Jack describing the training, which he did to such effect that Brian sent himself on one of Coverdale's senior management courses. He was sufficiently impressed by the experience to organize an in-house workshop for directors and managers of the firm. People could not be spared for a whole week, so the workshop was broken into two sections, each of 3 days, running from Thursday morning to Saturday evening. The risks with this approach are that after 3 days working, groups may not have settled down into effective teams, or there may be doubts and difficulties left in the air. On the other hand, the advantage is that lessons can be tried out at work, before the second part of the course; the results can then be reviewed, and learning pulled out of the experience. Here the pattern worked well: participants were warned that the second session would begin with a review of progress, so that they were on their mettle to get something done in the meantime.

Brian Blowers concluded that the experience must be extended to other professional staff. Cost was a problem: the budget for training was limited, and the firm decided to cover professional staff gradually, starting with the most senior, by holding one workshop a year.

One characteristic of an architect's job is that, in the course of a project, even a sole practitioner may find himself in the role of leader – harnessing the contributions of other professions, such as quantity surveyors, planners and structural engineers, and controlling progress as the building goes up. Even when the architect is not formally in charge, he often has to persuade, and bring people up to his level of understanding. Accordingly, on the last 2 days of each course, exercises in leadership were introduced, with emphasis on 'steering and joining'. On the Saturday a complex organization with changing work-groups was set up, to carry out four projects in the course of a day. The problems tackled were of real interest to Bruntons, the chief executive and directors being the 'clients', at the other end of a telephone. Each workshop finished with a presentation to them of the results.

The training brought various benefits. One of these was in dealing with clients at the start of a project. This is often the most interesting part of an architect's work, since it gives a chance to think creatively and exercise professional skill. Unfortunately, this stage is often pre-contract, and so the work is unpaid, and the architect has to strike a balance between the effort ᵗe puts into understanding the client's needs and producing preliminary ᵗesigns, and the pressure to keep costs down. It often happens that a client ᵗas only a general idea of the use he wants to make of his site; it was found ᵗhat a lot of time could be saved by systematic exploration of the clients' ᵗims in putting up buildings, and the standards of quality they were looking ᵗor.

During the years following the first Coverdale courses, John Bruntons ᵗxpanded rapidly. It was decided, as a matter of policy, that twenty or so ᵗrofessional staff were enough for any one unit, so the expansion was ᵗnatched by the establishment of three new studios, which were treated as ᵗeparate profit centres. This brought problems as well as benefits: one ᵗtudio might be inclined to hang on to its own clients, even when another ᵗould do the work more effectively; again, if work was passed across, it ᵗnight be neglected, in favour of the work for the studio's 'own' clients. However, the top–down pattern of development meant that within the first ᵗouple of years, the senior people within each studio had all been trained, ᵗnd from then on co-operation improved markedly, both between studios ᵗnd within the individual office.

Another useful practice was to send newly joined senior staff on the first available workshop, in order to give them an immediate insight into the way the firm operated. This applied not only to architects, but to people from other professions, such as an accountant, an interior designer, and a structural engineer. On one occasion when a senior architect joined the firm, the benefit was exactly the reverse: the man was wedded to an authoritarian style of management, and was so shocked by the participative style suggested by the course that he promptly resigned!

Another benefit came in making presentations, which was the subject of a 1-day seminar. Here the emphasis was on planning in advance: in the past, architects had often underestimated the time needed to put a convincing presentation together, so that work had to be rushed and the effects on the client too little considered.

Brian Blowers summed up the effects of the programme in the following terms:

At first it seemed very difficult to quantify the benefits of the Team Workshop approach. However, the very first gain seemed to be that people started to talk less about the problems, and more about the opportunities coming out of the difficulties, whatever aspect of the business they may have been in. The main board began to set objectives and these can now be summarized in the Mission Statement. From these followed a series of policy guidelines and a business plan: but whereas formerly we would have rushed into setting out the first thing that we thought of, we now took time at all levels, clearly defining the task we had to do and regularly reviewing the results against our written success criteria. There has been a shift from day-to-day management to planning longer term, and regularly reviewing those plans.

The second gain was the ability of a group of people from different offices or studios to come together, speaking a common management language, and quickly settling down as a team to tackle the project.

Another successful area was the change in staff morale. It was clear that people began to see that the company meant business; that it was determined to succeed; was setting targets which were attainable, and was achieving them. As a result more responsibility was given to architects and project managers, and this in itself improved motivation.

Since 1985/86 the company has trebled its turnover, increased its studios from four to eight, and is now entering a joint venture with a Paris architect, as it tackles the opportunities of the Single European Market.

We have certainly made mistakes; now we recognize them and tackle the matter quickly.

Thanks to the Coverdale approach and the way we have developed this training within the group, we have, over the last four years, certainly improved the quality of our design, improved the morale and motivation of our only main asset – the people who work with us. And finally, the firm has moved from a loss of £90,000 to a profit of £500,000.

Courtaulds Research Department

Architects are creative people, but a good deal of their work consists of managing construction projects. Research scientists are in some ways the antithesis of managers. A manager's job is to get things done – a research worker's to find things out. Managers typically work with clear purpose, to achieve tangible results, within a tight timescale; their main problem is the pressure of petty decisions and demands on their time. Research workers, by contrast, sometimes have extremely open tasks ('find a new product for the company'), with loose time-scales, and are free to concentrate on their research. There are often differences of personality – researchers are highly specialized in their education, intelligent, creative and often introvert, whereas many managers are generalists, down-to-earth, competent, and good with people. Managers are motivated towards practical achievement, and rising in the company's hierarchy: pure research people aim to expand knowledge for its own sake, and to make a name in the world of science. This is not to say that the divide cannot be crossed – research departments are often a valuable breeding ground for future senior managers – but it is nonetheless a real one.

One might therefore suppose that Coverdale training, with its feet firmly on the management side of the fence, would have little to offer scientists.

However, the essence of Coverdale is its emphasis on *balance* – on finding a happy medium between the pressures of thought and action, between getting the best solution, and getting something done on time. Many Coverdale client companies (such as ICI) are science-based, and have used the training with research people on a very large scale.

Coverdale has long had a connection with Courtaulds, originally through its central management training function, later through direct contact with individual businesses. Many research people had been sent on teamwork courses for managers, to the extent that managers themselves began to grumble about their disruptive effect: researchers kept 'opening up' the task and asking why, just when managers were more concerned with closing down and getting a result (both sides probably benefited from the contrast).

The business of Courtaulds was largely built around fibres and textiles. Over the last 10 years, however, there have been dramatic changes: the company has been moving out of capital-intensive processing, fibres and wood pulp, and has had a demerger of its textile interests. Instead it has been acquiring speciality materials businesses, based largely on new technology. All of this has put a considerable strain on its central research department.

In 1982, when David Giachardi was put in charge of the department, one of the questions he asked was, 'What sort of training do our people get?' When the name 'Coverdale' cropped up, it meant nothing to him, and he asked what it was. He got two kinds of answer: the first was that the training was about personal development; the second was 'We send people because the Chairman told us to several years ago, and no one ever told us not to.' He got a very clear answer from his own second in command, who said it was a waste of time. This surprised him, because other people's views had been quite the reverse; and he later found out that his deputy had never been on a course, but had formed his opinion after seeing a presentation, some years before. His first reaction was, 'If this is what we do, at least let's get some mileage out of it.' It seemed to him that up till then the department had been using the training rather like a sheep dip: treating individuals one at a time, so that when they got back to the flock, they were reinfected with the old ways of working. The training might not be a panacea, but if it was part of the firm's culture, they should get the most out of it. Accordingly he went on the course himself, and subsequently persuaded his Number 2 to go, so changing his mind about the training's effectiveness.

From his experience of the course, David Giachardi saw two potential benefits: first, a development of the skills and knowledge of individuals; second, a common language for the organization. Courtaulds had tended to see the training as a matter of individual development, but what research people needed most was teamwork. After all, able young scientists spend 20 years in the education system learning to compete, and yet industrial research is very much a matter of co-operation. He arranged that all graduate staff who joined the department should undergo a Part I course within their first 2 or 3 years, and go on to attend a specially designed Part II. Special post-Part I courses were designed for leaders of small research groups.

Soon after David Giachardi took over, he began to question how far the research department was in fact meeting the objectives of its customers – the various businesses within the Courtaulds group. Were they in fact 'delighted' with what they were getting? He asked Carrie Spender, the leader of the Coverdale team, to design and run a survey on how user companies saw their research needs, and how well these were being met.

The survey covered work in five countries and three languages, and was based on interviews with some seventy senior managers. Its findings were somewhat disconcerting. The company's strategy on research was not well understood. Customers valued the development work carried out by the research department, but some senior managers saw little point in the more fundamental research. Customers rated the research people they met very highly, and the flow of individuals from research into jobs with customer companies was seen as a valuable resource, even though there was no counter-flow. Both the research department and customers were agreed on the profile of an ideal researcher: 'Someone who is capable of real innovation, both scientifically and in response to market opportunities, and yet is thoroughly practical and can regularly translate new ideas into products and processes which work in our factories and markets.' Obviously such paragons would be hard to grow or recruit (although a few did apparently exist!); but it was a more practical target to develop *teams* with these characteristics. Although customers valued the contacts they had with individual researchers, they did not have much confidence in the department's systems, in the sense of having an organized, accessible fund of information, which could constitute the company's scientific and technological resource base.

One persistent finding was the need for closer contact: research people had to develop a real understanding of the needs and pressures of customers, and of the kinds of opportunity that research could deliver. One respondent said 'Send to the research teams the message that they are a central part of the business, not a contract supplier of science; so that central research becomes like a scientific club, where researchers go to find information and expertise.'

As well as tackling the department's external relations, David Giachardi questioned its internal organization. It employed some 500 people, organized into long, hierarchical chains in the manner of the Civil Service. People were grouped together according to their scientific disciplines, e.g. chemists or engineers. David saw that what was needed instead was to set ιp multi-disciplinary teams, each dealing with one fundamental product, ,uch as viscose or acetate. These teams could be market-responsive – the ιwork of each of them could be paid for by the appropriate Courtaulds zompany, which could make sure they got value for money. There was also ι need for certain shared services, such as analysis, and these became ,eparate sub-departments. (This resembled the system David had been familiar with in his previous role as a management consultant.) Coverdale consultants played a part in these changes, helping people understand the ιnderlying rationale, and taking them through the effects on their own ιoles. They could also make sure that individuals did not suffer, e.g. ιhrough changes in career structure. In this, they had the enormous ιadvantage of being seen as neutral, outside the system.

The old hierarchy made it difficult to pay first-class researchers an appropriate salary; in order to square the system, people had been awarded such job titles as 'Senior Section Leader with Special Responsibility for . . .' This was now replaced by two separate career ladders. First, there was the managerial system, leading from individual researchers to group managers, research managers, and finally the research director. Second, for extremely able scientists and engineers who were either unsuited to climbing the management ladder, or weren't interested in doing so, a parallel hierarchy was set up, representing scientific status rather than authority – leading from Associate Fellow, to Research Fellow, to Senior Fellow. The job of Fellows was examined, and it was found that even though, unlike managers, they did not normally need the skills of leadership, they did needs the skills of 'steering', persuading, and briefing other people about the work they were doing. Training was provided through the Part II course, backed up by 'surgeries' in which Fellows could think through the effect of changes in their role, and how they could get the support they needed (from management and customers) for their work.

As the organization developed, Coverdale was asked to carry out periodical attitude surveys, to check management's perception of the effects of these changes. Each survey showed the need to pay more attention to communications, even though, as a result of earlier surveys, they had improved by leaps and bounds. Carrie Spender and Robert Gordon continued to meet the director of research and his deputy for what were called 'kick round meetings' – the purpose being to look at any problems, and the effects of proposed changes on teams and individuals. They also held regular 'surgeries', at which any member of staff who had been trained could book time, and come with a problem to be tackled. Problems came in all shapes and sizes, from lack of funding, or the interface between different departments, to personal relations with a boss or subordinate. As always in such consultancy, the aim was to get the client to look logically at his/her own problem, open their thinking to a range of solutions, and find the confidence and determination to do what had to be done.

The consultants had the advantage of being able to work at all levels of the organization. In this role, they must never act as messengers; instead they can encourage people at the lower level to make their preoccupations known to management, and equally make sure that senior managers disclose their interests to people lower in the hierarchy. Consultants can also give feedback to senior managers of a sort they might not otherwise get, such as on the effects of their own behaviour. Being a multi-level adviser can have its problems, e.g. having confidential information that could, if disclosed, reassure some lower level members of staff that their worries were misplaced. The great benefit is being able to ring up people, at any level, and say, 'I feel we need to talk about X.' The only way to get to this position is for one's discretion to be trusted, and to have a reputation for delivering results.

One typical problem concerned one of the specialist research groups, which had grown very fast, with many growing pains. (David Giachardi now takes it as a maxim that no small research group should be allowed to grow by more than 20 per cent a year.) There was a lack of communication and some distrust of management, as a result of which decisions were either postponed or resented. The manager himself called in the consultants, first to talk to members of his staff, then to set up meetings in which these problems could be discussed. As a result, the necessary changes were agreed by consensus, rather than being imposed by the boss.

David Giachardi drew a number of general conclusions about running a research organization, and the kinds of training that scientists need. First, the style of management has to be consensual: it is no good trying to run a research group autocratically, since staff are highly intelligent, and usually well placed to find another job. Again, any research organization must be able to flex, since too much rigidity will not allow it to respond to changing priorities. At the same time it must be stable enough for customers to know who they should deal with, on what subject. Scientists are by nature conceptual thinkers, with a long timescale: one of their skills is a very open kind of thinking (what if we did this or that?), and they are reluctant to close their thinking down, even though the timescale demands it. A problem in this work is the lack of feedback: they may work at a problem for years before they find the answer, and they need all the help they can get in measuring their own effectiveness.

In industrial research there is inevitably some tension between the scientist's assumption that he is there to do long-term research and the demands of users for immediate solutions to pressing problems. Fundamental researchers must be to some extent protected, or they will not make any real progress. But they must still get out and meet people in factories, and provide answers to their more fundamental doubts and questions – not so much what to do, but the scientific reason behind it.

The training of scientists can be looked at under four main headings:

Technical, e.g. updating in infra-red spectroscopy.
Knowledge of other aspects of the business, such as profit and loss, and marketing.
Training in skills for specific applications – giving presentations, or writing English.
Personal development, both as individuals and as members and managers of teams.

This last is of great importance: after all, there are few other business contexts where large teams operate in pursuit of objectives that are often unclear. In research the people who run tightly knit teams are often of considerable seniority; after all, where the 'operative' is a PhD, the first-line supervisor ranks correspondingly high. By contrast, people in general management of equivalent status are not so much running teams as co-ordinating activities across an organization as a whole.

Training of this sort is concerned with the ways in which scientists are managed, their relationship with their customers (normally within the organization) and the structure of their own departments. It has little impact on the way the research itself is done. After all, the essence of scientific discipline is reviewing and drawing lessons out of what has happened, and planning experiments to test any new insights. (Coverdale methods have, however, been used – though not at Courtaulds – to rationalize sets of experiments, helping a team work through coherent stages towards a research goal.)

In training research people, one advantage of Coverdale is that it is severely practical. Researchers' background is in the 'hard' disciplines of science, and they respond to something they can use. (There is a contrast with the response of other professions, such as lawyers, who are happy to be given broad, high-level principles to apply, without being too much concerned about the evidence on which the principles are based.)

Since it is extremely difficult to evaluate the effectiveness of an R & D department, it is even harder to put a value on Coverdale's contribution, other than its effect on human relations and the ability of people to cope with change. Looking at Coverdale's work with Courtaulds as a whole, David Giachardi saw that in getting value from the training, the crucial step was to get the active support of senior managers. Line managers themselves had to 'own' the project – indeed Coverdale seemed to flourish where it was furthest detached from the company's training department.

18　Work with children's charities

Coverdale has always set aside a proportion of its budget for charitable activities. This has sometimes meant offering free places on public courses to people with special needs, or from charitable organizations, and has also included offering complete projects at a reduced rate. Two such projects were with national children's organizations: The Children's Society, and the National Society for the Prevention of Cruelty to Children. Apart from the charitable context, some points of interest are the lessons listed by the Director of The Children's Society (an example of the personal insights that can lead to major changes of style), and the process plans adopted by the senior management team of the NSPCC.

The Children's Society

The Children's Society (formerly the Church of England Children's Society) is more than 100 years old. It employs about 1200 staff, spread over England and Wales, engaged in about 130 active projects. It is concerned with the whole range of children's needs, but concentrates on five main sources of deprivation or injustice:

- Poverty.
- Exploitation and abuse.
- Being denied choice and control over their own lives.
- Being removed from their own homes.
- Being in custody.

A good deal of the Society's work is done in partnership with parents to improve children's lives, e.g. by forming voluntary playgroups. The staff who run projects are not simply social workers, but may be acting as leaders or facilitators in the local community, and need a great deal of management and process skill.

Ian Sparks, the Society's Director, joined the Society in 1981 and took up his present post in 1986. Over this period it came to be recognized that the Society had certain management problems. Staff were spread across the country, and there was no common approach to the work they were doing. Another unusual problem the Society had was too much creativity: its aims were broad, its staff intelligent and highly committed, and the result was a surge of ideas, without systematic implementation. The Society's motto tended to be 'Try it and see'. Sometimes this produced admirable results – e.g. the valuable work with young runaways started with workers seeing a need, and getting straight into action. There was a great deal of vibrancy and excitement, but also lack of clarity about where the Society was to go next. The need was not to reduce this energy, but to harness it and make it more effective.

The answer seemed to be some sort of management development programme. Unfortunately, the first two attempts at training fell flat, and Ian recalls a sense of despair at the results. The consultants who were brought in underestimated the complexity of project leaders' jobs, and applied training packages that might have suited first-line supervisors in industry, but not the staff of a charity trying to intervene in the community. Besides, the training caused no discernible change in the way people actually managed. What was wanted was not some pattern imposed from outside but a real partnership between the Society and consultants.

As a last attempt to find the right approach, a steering group was set up to look for a suitable pattern and they proposed a partnership with a specialist organization. Four firms were invited to make presentations. Coverdale's was felt to have three advantages: first, it concentrated on task work, and actually getting the job done; second, it proposed to encourage a common language throughout the organization as a whole, while others were limiting their role to the senior staff; and, finally, it was felt that Coverdale had more in common with the values of the organization than some of the other firms. Rosemary Jackson, the Coverdale consultant concerned, was a social worker by training, and so had considerable knowledge of the task of the Society. She appreciated the problem it had of getting the mixture of staff (those concerned with social work, including residential care, and those concerned with fund-raising and finance) to adopt a common approach.

For the first 6 months Rosemary worked with the Society's directors (the Society's Management Team), beginning with a 2-day workshop to introduce the method of training, and give participants a sense of what Coverdale was about. The workshop followed the pattern of the first 2 days of a Part I course, and uncovered one problem in dealing with charitable staff – that, being highly committed to the work they are doing, they are unusually reluctant to tackle training exercises that have no direct *task* relevance to the Society's objectives. (The same problem has been found with teachers – see Chapter 19).

The next stage was to run a formal Part I course for the Society management team, together with the next tier down. The training was not all plain sailing. At the start, people were suspicious of a body that appeared to be saying 'We can solve your management problems.' Suspicion was increased because of doubt about what the actual content of the course would be, since with training of this sort, one cannot provide a detailed syllabus. Once again, there was reluctance to tackle non-work tasks, leading to a minor rebellion on the second day. However, as always happens, the relevance of the work became apparent as groups began to knit together, and by the end of the week opinions ranged from cautiously favourable to ecstatic.

The director was in a group that chose to go the whole week without any formal leadership. Towards the end of the course, there is a session in which groups observe each other in action, and the other two groups, which had devised elaborate processes for appointing the right leader for the task, were indignant to see that a leaderless group could get as good results as they had – indeed, some of them put it down to sheer fluke.

A year after the first course, a Part II was held for senior managers, and the last exercise of this was a turning point of the project. The Society Management Team had devised a task of real importance to the Society, concerned with ways to implement the principles that had been learned during the week. One key principle was the idea of 'tight/loose management': being tight on Aims and Criteria, but loose on Information and What Has To Be Done. (In the past staff had seen senior managers as the reverse – vague on aims, but fiddling with the details of planning.) In the event this exercise turned into an object lesson in how not to manage. The four divisional teams worked as separate groups, shutting themselves up in separate boxes and passing information up to senior management, which then took all the decisions unilaterally, falling straight into the trap they were trying to avoid. However, out of all this came something of a revelation – that managers should define the purpose and criteria, and then be prepared to stand back. During the review, and as a result of this conclusion, one of the managers asked to make a statement on behalf of all her colleagues. She thanked the Society Management Team for being ready to delegate responsibility; she and her colleagues saw their responsibility as taking that authority and using it.

People left the course with mixed feelings, but it changed the way the Society worked, especially the Society Management Team itself. The invariable practice is now to get aims clear and tight and let people get on with it – subject to rigorous review.

In the meantime, training was extended to first-line managers, such as heads of community projects. For staff at these levels, the programme was modified, Friday being put aside for participants' own managers to join the course and work with their staff on live problems. In addition, since many of the participants worked as individuals rather than in teams, more emphasis was given to co-operation rather than teamwork, and 'steering and joining' exercises were used, involving passing tasks on from one group to another. This is a close simulation of the work of first-line managers in the Society, who move in and out of different groups, and need to obtain commitment wherever they go.

One example of steering and joining in practice was in designing a sex education programme for young adults with learning difficulties. Sex education always presents problems, because there are many different personal views about what message the programme should convey. Here the programme design was started by three members of a team, who then planned how they could take account of views of the other team members, so that the whole team 'owned' the result.

Training is now being extended to administrative staff, and the intention is to train a number of in-house coaches so as to go right down to volunteers, such as workers in shops.

Results of the training

The most important result was a greater sense of common purpose within the organization, particularly at the local level, between fund-raisers and social workers. In most charitable work the two sides have very different preoccupations, and tend to be wary of each other. Now appeal organizers have links with local projects, so that they can speak with personal knowledge of what is being done, or can get a project manager to attend and speak at fund-raising events. Systematic Approach can act as a framework for co-operation, e.g. checking the purpose of any interaction between the different people. Social workers are often suspicious of charity advertising, seeing it as manipulative, and exploiting the needs of children; while fund-raisers are apt to respond with defensiveness. The Society's new campaign, 'Putting our values first', has won the support of all staff groups, and expresses what the Society is really concerned about. Although produced at a time when the economic depression has put charities under pressure, it avoids the appeal of showing children looking miserable, but tries to present a positive picture of what can be done.

As Ian Sparks remarked: 'We never wanted Coverdale to come in and solve our problems: but we needed a way of doing our own job better, and in a more organized way, and this is now beginning to happen.'

The training has sometimes been criticized within the Society for expense – due to the length of the course, and the fact that it is residential. Opinion also remained divided on how necessary it was to use non-work-related tasks for developing process skills. A few people saw the programme as a waste of time, because they didn't see any changes in particular individuals who worked closely with them. One problem was the need, for financial reasons, to space the training over a 3-year period, since staff not yet trained tended to regard the enthusiasms of those who had been with some suspicion. Others, because of the 'cascade' method of implementation, saw Systematic Approach as a badge of authority, or a way of exercising power and control. But most people had quite a different concern – how to reinforce the learning, and keep up the momentum within the Society.

The director himself found that the training gave him a number of personal insights:

- In writing papers and memos, he had the habit of setting out arguments in a very tight way. One of his staff remarked that his memos were like manhole covers, a perfect fit, so you couldn't get your finger in. He realized the need to give more information, and allow space for people to get inside his thinking.
- He was struck by the way in which reviews can so easily start from what went wrong, and stick there. The Coverdale tag, 'review *in order to improve*' is a powerful phrase, in that it makes criticisms positive. Once it is generally understood that the function of review isn't to put people down, it is possible to look at recurrent problems *more* critically than before.
- In reviewing, if an observer makes some vague, judgemental statement, such as 'He was a bad leader', a good coach's response is always 'What did he actually *do*?' A description of the actual behaviour is the first vital step towards solving problems in the way someone works.

The National Society for the Prevention of Cruelty to Children

The NSPCC is a national charity, established for over 100 years. It employs some 1500 staff, has 220 fund-raising branches staffed by volunteers, and helps over 50,000 children a year. Its role includes both investigating cases of cruelty, and helping and supporting the victims. From the time of its foundation, it has been the pioneer in the battle against the abuse of children: e.g. it established the first specialist teams in the country focusing exclusively on child abuse. It is unique among charities in that its child protection officers have statutory powers. It is under Royal patronage, and its guiding committees include people of great distinction. But its work sometimes attracts a good deal of press publicity, making the job of managing the Society an exposed one.

The problems of the NSPCC were partly those of success. In 1984, its centenary year, the Society launched an appeal for funds, which was so successful that, from being financially overstretched, it was able to expand its activities. Over 3 or 4 years, there was a rapid increase in numbers of staff in the field, and the central management functions were hard-pressed to keep up. These problems were made greater by difficulties of communication between the centre and workers in the field. The style of central management was formal and inclined to be autocratic: as Chris Brown, the present director remarked, 'Even buying a tin of paint took six layers of decisions.' There was a great deal of internal paper work, and an active discouragement of informal contacts between staff at different levels. Decisions were made at head office, while staff in the regions were subject to rigid regulation.

These problems were compounded by cultural differences between social workers and fund-raisers (the same problem identified by the Children's Society) and the voluntary helpers who provided the resources. The then director, who had presided over this rapid expansion, was aware of the difficulties, and made various organizational changes, including the appointment of a finance director and a human resources director, and the appointment of regional child care managers to take charge of children's services. The Society had also been gradually setting up child protection teams, to replace the traditional pattern of inspectors working on their own.

In August 1989 the director retired. One of his successor's first acts was to arrange a 2-day meeting for the five members of the directorate, at the Society's training centre at Leicester. The meeting saw two urgent needs. The first was to update the Society's aims and targets, to take account of changes in the world – not least the development of local authority social service departments. The Society needed to clarify both the job it was trying to do and its image in the world. The question was passed upwards to the Society's governing executive committee, which agreed that there should be a fundamental review of its Society's functions. It was decided to employ outside consultants to help with this work.

The second need identified by the directorate was to develop the teamwork of the top management group itself. One problem was the very different backgrounds of the people who composed the group: the fund-raiser came from the voluntary sector, the child care director from statutory social work, and the finance director from the commercial world. The team needed to build up common assumptions and a common language, as well as setting standards of leadership and management style for the rest of the Society. Once again it seemed sensible to look for independent advice. The human resources director drew up a shortlist of consultants to make presentations, and Coverdale was selected.

Team-building for directors

The first Coverdale event was a 3-day workshop for the directorate. It looked at the contributions made by different members and the strengths that each of them brought to the team, so turning their diversity of backgrounds into a positive strength. People felt they were able to 'dump baggage' and get personal problems off their chests. They learnt to be more sensitive towards their own behaviour, and to call on the help of their colleagues in improving their style. One director, who had always known that he was bad at listening, came to see for the first time the effect this had on discussion, and what he could do about it.

Because this work was found valuable, extra training days were added on over the next year, to improve teamwork further. The first plans were straightforward, such as ways of dealing with potential conflict, a key phrase being 'Can we stop and review?' (rather than 'Listen, you!'). These led on to process plans of greater subtlety and formality. The members of the workshop drew up a list of kinds of behaviour that would show that a review was needed: e.g. people deviating from the point, monopolizing the discussion, or getting heated. The review was then structured round a checklist of questions. Another step was to identify a list of 'ritual roles' – pieces of behaviour that individuals were in the habit of repeating, whether or not they were appropriate, and which could stand in the way of judging a case on its merits: one member of the team would claim the moral high ground, by speaking 'in the interests of children', while another would affect a hard-nosed, commercial attitude. Once these patterns were identified and labelled, individuals could avoid falling into them, while the group could give them a gentle reminder if they did.

These procedures were consolidated into a checklist that provided a common approach to a wide range of problems.

CHECKLIST FOR MEETINGS

AGENDA

- Human spot to share feelings.
- Review the agenda – check priorities/time allocation.
- Plan breaks in the timetable – and take them!
- Produce a one-page proforma for every item, in order to:
    - clarify its purpose/nature,
    - capture the essence of key issues,
    - use it as the basis of a process review at end of meeting.

EVERY TIME

- Be clear about purpose – use Systematic Approach.
- Decide who should chair – see chairing checklist.
- Are we driving or being driven by events?
- Would a vision statement or brainstorm help?
- Is the decision clear and appropriately recorded?
- What communication/consultation is needed?
- Are there wider issues to be addressed in implementation?

- Check that the plan covers who/what/when and how.
- Set people up to succeed.
- Watch time-keeping.

ANY TIME
- Do we really need to be doing this?
- Are we looking at the broad picture, or too specifically?
- Can we establish policy/constraints, and then delegate?
- Is it good enough?
- Speak up and be explicit about thoughts and feelings.
- Are you/am I OK about this?

STOP AND REVIEW
- Does this have priority call on our time?
- Is the discussion getting locked, or excluding others?
- Haven't we already agreed and moved on?
- 'Bin it' – important and interesting, but not for this discussion.
- Are we agreeing or disagreeing for the sake of it?
- Too much verbosity?
- 'Ritual mode'.
- Non-verbals – state what you see!
- Any relevant lessons from team-building?

HANDLING CONFLICT
- Use consensus checklist if necessary.
- Non-participants must identify what's happening.
- Identify common ground.
- Be explicit about underlying worries/needs.
- Postpone, and those involved do further work outside meeting.

Another plan dealt with consensus:

CHECKLIST FOR ACHIEVING CONSENSUS

1 Go for consensus except where:
  (a) The chief executive has made the decision.
  (b) The chief executive will make the decision after discussion.
  (c) The decision is the responsibility of another member of the group.
2 Assume there is consensus, unless objections are voiced.
3 Allocate time for achieving consensus. (If it isn't achieved by the end of the set time, the group will decide how to resolve it.)
4 Questions to ask:
  What (specifically) are the issues (aims and information)?
  How important is the decision to the organization's objectives?
  What is the strength of feeling?
  Do I have a particular interest?

Am I representing others? If so, whom?

Who is directly responsible for the outcome of the decision?

What are the implications of the 'wrong' decision. How easy will it be to change?

5 How do we know when we've got it?

(a) By building in a (brief) review of any decisions.

(b) By subsequent behaviour and activities (showing 'ownership').

In judging the effect of these procedures, one must remember that the value of process plans often comes not from following them slavishly but from the effort of planning itself. Defining the way you ought to behave helps you behave in that way. A successful plan is not a restraint but a signpost, to point the direction and be a reminder if you deviate. In practice (as observed by Rosemary), presenting agenda items in a format based on systematic approach saved a lot of time, since people were clearer about what should be brought to the meeting, and the exact point to be decided. The other procedures were more concerned with personal behaviour. While these were being developed and internalized, the effect was to slow the meeting down. From the start, however, they made people stop and think when they were heading in unhelpful directions, and be more aware of other people's needs and reactions; and, with practice, the effect on the team was strongly positive.

The fundamental review

Meanwhile the review of policy was not going so well. It was a huge task, since it was essential to draw on the views of as many people as possible, both in and outside the organization, and there was a background of suspicion and anxiety, about people's roles and relationships and possible changes in authority. The consultants who had originally been called in were providing valuable information, but they seemed readier to push their own strategic conclusions than to work jointly with the Society's management. Coverdale's style, being more consultative, seemed to suit the exercise better, and accordingly they were called in instead. The exercise included sending out thousands of questionnaires to all staff members and a great many volunteers. Key figures in government, the academic world and social services were also approached. When the proposals were in draft form, nine regional conferences were held to get people's views, while a review action group kept everyone informed of progress by means of regular bulletins.

The strategic plan enabled the organization to review its position, and develop a clear sense of direction. One effect was that a good deal of valuable work that it had been doing, such as the 'Listen to Children' week, was now seen as peripheral. It was decided to concentrate on the core work of preventing child abuse of the severest kind. The outcome was a statement of goals that people could unite around, and which could serve as a basis for developing an appropriate organization.

Coverdale's role in this was not to impose a solution, but to challenge and discuss, and to make sure that the consultation was a real one: that people who had problems could put them across, and that everyone had a chance to be listened to by the top board. One demonstration of this was the radical changes made between the first draft of the statement of aims and its eventual form, which included a definition of the Society's values. An essential ingredient in getting the job done was the new-found strength of the management team. As the director remarked, 'We might have had real difficulty trusting each other under pressure . . . We could not have begun to cope without the support of a really strong team.'

19   Coverdale and education

All change in schools

In Britain there is a wide gulf between training and education. Education deals with the ability to think and understand: training deals with action. Education is seen as broad, liberal, and not required to be immediately useful: training, as narrow, down-to-earth, and concerned with specific tasks. Trainers and educators don't read each other's literature, or take much notice of each other's methods. In truth, however, this gulf is largely a matter of prejudice, and training in process skills goes a long way to bridge it. It is, after all, broad rather than specific in its aims, 'liberal' in its intention, and with as profound implications for the way life should be led as anything in education. It is therefore not surprising that Coverdale training has much to contribute to the education system, and that it has become widely used in a very short time.

This has happened at the two ends of the scale: first in training people in education management, such as education officers, inspectors, head teachers, and chairmen of governors, and second, in developing similar skills at a different level of performance among children in primary schools. Among management the training has spread fast, so that over a 2-year period, a quarter of the education authorities in England and Wales made use of it. The catalyst was the Education Reform Act 1988. Under this Act, schools have been largely freed from the direct control of local authorities, and are required to manage themselves. Each school will have its own budget, controlled by its own board of governors, and administered by the head teacher. A whole range of decisions can now be taken on the spot; and within the limits set by the national curriculum, schools are encouraged to go their own ways in educational methods and emphasis, so as to give parents a choice.

Officers at County Hall no longer manage the routine transactions of schools in their area, but exercise strategic control through 'inspectors' or 'advisers'. Many inspectors have a changed role: from being subject specialists they now find themselves giving guidance over a whole range of activities – as well as having the statutory responsibility of making sure that standards are maintained, and the national curriculum followed. The most radical change is in the role of head teachers. From being mainly concerned with teaching and discipline, they are now more like the managing director of their own company, with new responsibilities for administration, finance, public relations, and marketing, and wide scope for educational initiative – provided they can carry their governors along with them. Many officers and teachers regarded these changes with dismay, even though tempered (in the case of heads) by satisfaction at being able to take decisions on their own account.

During this time of change the morale of teachers was generally low. The Act itself was creating extra stress, just when the new national curriculum was causing a vast amount of work. Teachers were also concerned about their professional status, and getting a good deal of criticism, both individually from parents, and collectively from the press.

Newham

The first authority to approach Coverdale as a result of the Reform Act was the London Borough of Newham. There were two coincidental causes: first, the appointment of a senior inspector who had taken part in Coverdale training when working for ILEA: second, two members of a staff development team that had been set up came across Coverdale's presentation at a training exhibition and were impressed. Accordingly, a project with the following aims was initiated:

- To develop teamwork skills, and help people in different roles work together across the authority.
- To mobilize energy, and help get results.
- To develop skills needed to implement the Education Reform Act.
- To provide a system for identifying and spreading success.

The first hurdle was funding. Fortunately, Grand Metropolitan Retailing had a programme for building links between education and industry, and through its generosity a number of free places on a Coverdale course were offered to head teachers. The mixture of attitudes provided a stimulating contrast. After this first experiment, a 3-day workshop for heads, advisory teachers and inspectors examined how to help head teachers in primary schools to manage the changes that were imminent. One major task was to produce a 5-year training plan (in this, Newham was ahead of the government, which later required all authorities to carry out a similar exercise). One product of the workshop was a wall-planner for schools, letting them see at a glance the critical dates for implementing the Act, and plot their own progress towards them.

The next stage was to run courses for primary heads, together with advisers and deputy heads of secondary schools. There was continuing support from Grand Metropolitan Retailing, together with some economies in Newham's other training, while in-house coaches were trained, to help reduce costs. At Newham primary schools were already grouped in local 'clusters', and through this structure head teachers could support each other in using the training.

The programme is still under way (June 1991). In reviving the training, it has been found that heads could easily use the approach as a way of achieving process objectives, such as raising morale. They have found it harder to see it as a way of managing change, or getting tangible task results, and this is the focus of the next stage.

Greenwich

Greenwich was a new authority, set up after the dismemberment of the Inner London Education Authority (ILEA). Here the main impetus came from Rod Sharman, the newly appointed chief inspector. In his days as a head teacher he had found that very little attention was paid to the head's role as manager; it was assumed that if you could manage a classroom, you could do the same for a group of teachers, or even (as in his case) a school with 600 pupils. Rod realized he had a good deal to learn, and managed to send himself on various short management courses. In 1982 he joined ILEA as an inspector. Here the same assumptions ruled – an inspector had been a senior teacher, and so must be a good team member. In practice, there were thirty inspectors in the primary schools 'team', but their only team function consisted of meeting once a month to deal with a straggling agenda of fifty or so items. Since it was obvious that teamwork needed to improve, the ILEA chief inspector made contact with Coverdale, and thirty inspectors were sent to Worthing for a Part I course.

Rod found the experience salutary, and noted that those who gained, gained a great deal. Some people, however, had less fruitful experiences. They felt that the relationship between trainers and trainees was not spelt out clearly enough, and that the trainers seemed to assume that inspectors worked as a team, which was far from the case. Some inspectors felt threatened by the prospect of their performance being commented on by their peers (however favourably). There were reactions such as, 'Why do I, an experienced teacher and inspector, have to learn about management?' 'Why do I have to take part in childish tasks, which bear no relation to my job?' Some of them accused the coaches of manipulation. 'Why can't you come clean and admit what you're doing to us?' But the course still had valuable effects, particularly in empowering the team to make decisions, rather than leaving them all to individuals.

But ILEA was already on its way out, and soon afterwards Rod was appointed chief inspector for the Borough of Greenwich. He saw that to meet the requirements of the Education Reform Act there were two strategies open to the inspectorate. In the first, each inspector would act in a dual role, working on problems of management in a small group of schools, and at the same time covering a subject speciality such as history for a much larger group. He rejected this model in favour of one in which half the inspectors stuck to their subject specialties, while the other half, all former head teachers, dealt with management; each school would have one management inspector, plus six who covered individual subjects. For this to work, Rod decided that he must put in an extra layer of management (three senior inspectors), and train the whole inspectorate in teamwork. In the normal way the management inspector might have little contact with subject inspectors; in Rod's system, their relationship was to be a close one.

Rod looked back on his Coverdale experience with mixed feelings. He felt that the course had worked for him but caused problems for others. However, the new team certainly needed a common training experience. He weighed up the risk, which he saw as very high, but decided to call Coverdale in. This time, however, he and Coverdale arranged that each inspector should have an interview with the consultant beforehand, to sort out any doubts or anxieties. Certainly this reduced tension, although the 'neutral' tasks still caused a certain amount of difficulty. A second topic of controversy was 'risk': the normal policy of education is to play safe, but the message of the training is that rational risks should be taken.

The course took place in May, during the team's first fortnight at work. It was clear that if they were not to forget what they had learned, they must put it into practice right away. The job of inspection during the summer term was planned as a team task, to be carried out by sub-groups. Process reviews were scheduled in advance, and it was arranged that all team members should work with each of their colleagues. A number of procedures were adopted for meetings:

(a) Agendas were kept short, care being taken to distinguish what could be decided on paper from what needed discussion.
(b) A flip chart was used.
(c) Process reviews were built in. This made it possible for people to say 'Stop, we're going down the wrong road', without it being seen as a personal attack.

After the summer holidays a whole day in September was set aside to review the team's use of Systematic Approach. It proved to be well-timed:

organizational tensions were just beginning to build up, and they could be dealt with on the spot. One success of the day was that the team agreed to delegate various jobs to sub-groups, which could work concentratedly, and produce high-quality solutions that the whole team accepted, even though they had not themselves taken part in the discussion. Following this first meeting, it was decided to hold one every 6 months. For future training, it was decided that Greenwich needed in-house trainers. Two members of the team were selected, and sent to CAID (the Centre for Adviser/Inspector Development) for a course on distance learning. It was found that the combination of CAID for task training with Coverdale for process training was a strong one.

The next step was to extend Coverdale training to head teachers; in the summer of 1990, a pilot course was held for twenty-five heads, and the training is now to be offered to heads of primary schools. The question now is, given the considerable cost, how to continue to use the training. Should Coverdale be seen as a pump-primer, on the assumption that benefits will work down to people who have not themselves been trained?

Rod Sharman's view is that, within the education system, three levels of training must be distinguished:

(a) Teachers new to the profession, who need to develop self-management.
(b) Senior teachers looking after two or three other people. These are 'steerers' rather than genuine line managers, since their function is to guide rather than command.
(c) Head teachers, who have a genuinely managerial role.

There is also a range of special issues that need specific training modules (one example is management of time, on which heads and inspectors have received joint training). Although it is difficult to plan ahead while the government is still changing the requirements, Greenwich intends to provide a series of modules, which will be accredited jointly by the Thames Polytechnic as building towards a diploma.

In various other authorities, Coverdale methods have been used for many different purposes, ranging from designing training for school governors to planning strategy for the authority as a whole. One effect of this work is to bring under scrutiny aims that people have only partly defined. In one borough there was a well-known voluntary school, that parents and governors alike wanted to turn into a city technology college. However, the LEA directorate was opposed to the idea of city technology colleges, nor did it want to see the authority lose schools. At first sight these reactions agreed with the LEA's defined aim of producing high quality education within the borough. When it applied Systematic Approach, however, the information hardly bore this out. Did it need the secondary places the school provided? In fact, no. If it kept the school, how many local parents would choose to send their children there? Not many. How much would it cost to keep the school? Over £1m. And what else could be done with the money? Spent it on other schools, whose upkeep had been neglected. In other words, the LEA's own defined aims implied letting the technology college go ahead.

The directors were at first dismayed by this conclusion, but later excited by it; they realized that they needed to see things as they are, rather than merely looking at labels, and that there might be other important decisions that had been taken more by instinct than reason. One cause of this breakthrough was a deliberate choice to spend 3 hours on the question, sitting down together to see it through. Without this approach, problems can recur as regular agenda items, and be no nearer a solution years later.

Teachers and managers

There are several differences between working in education and working in commerce or industry. The first is that the 'product' of schools is undefined. One obvious answer is 'a well-educated school-leaver' – but how do you decide what this means, and, still more, how do you measure it?

A second difference is that education has been remarkably stable in its methods: there has not been much new technology since the invention of printing, and even the evolution of teaching methods has been cyclical rather than in one direction. A change such as the Education Reform Act comes with revolutionary force.

A third difference is the amount of time teachers spend as sole operators, facing a class on their own. Co-operation is an occasional need, rather than the essence of the job. Particularly at secondary level, the process of teaching consists mainly of exposition and analysis, with little action.

Given all this, the way teachers reacted to training was naturally rather different from managers. They were highly committed to their work, and very willing to be trained; at the same time they were unused to the task-review method, and impatient with the slow development of skill, expecting rather a constant flow of new ideas. Occasionally groups of teachers would behave almost like their own pupils, playing tricks and trivializing the tasks, or would react in an emotional way. Teachers were quick to grasp concepts, and, in terms of the Systematic Approach cycle, strong in aims and information; on the other hand, they found it harder to get into action, or produce the sort of informal co-operation that comes naturally to managers. One exercise that had a powerful effect was identifying the skills of other members of the team. The idea of picking out their own strengths – rather than faults – came as a revelation to some; others remarked that they felt more valued in their training team than at any other time in their teaching careers. Again, to many teachers, the idea of self-improvement was a new one: they were used to seeing children develop, but were less conscious of the possibility of developing themselves.

One perceptive view of the project comes from Christine Archer, an advisory teacher working for Newham, whose special subjects are equal opportunities and history. Christine went on a Coverdale course and became an in-house Coverdale coach.

Her first observation was that at Newham training was cascaded from the top. In some ways this is an advantage – a boss who has already been trained is more likely to give subordinates scope to use their initiative, and support in putting the training into practice. The disadvantage is that training may be seen as something handed down from on high, or as the badge of a select club. Again it may bring up the question of equal opportunities, since senior staff tend to be white and male; it worried participants to find that a course dealing with teamwork should have so few ethnic members. The authority recognized the problem of inequality, and part of its 'positive action' was to arrange a Diploma of Management Studies course for non-white teachers. However, Christine questions the value of a DMS, since it deals with *theory*, while what teachers more urgently need is management and teamwork *skill*.

A second problem was some participants' rather starry-eyed reaction. The phrase went round, 'Have you been Coverdaled yet?', implying some sinister process of personality change. This was compounded by the distrust felt by a number of teachers towards the private sector: the training could be portrayed as 'American-type', slick, and concerned with producing automata whose only aim was to get the job done. Besides, what could a management consultancy possibly know about education? Coverdale has the normal apparatus of a logo and leaflets in company style, and these too were regarded with suspicion. Some participants arrived on Part I courses with a very wary attitude, and this may have inhibited learning during the first couple of days. Christine later attended a public course for managers, and was struck by the contrast – managers arrived in a mood that was cautiously favourable, and took the house style in their stride.

The training itself sometimes ran into difficulties. In Christine's first group a senior and experienced teacher took charge, and acted for the first day and a half in a very high-handed manner, until other members made their views clear and there was a pocket revolution. On another course a senior and highly intelligent participant dominated the group throughout, so that other members felt themselves shut out. This was all the more frustrating, in that the other two groups on the course were obviously having a stimulating and enjoyable experience, in a much more democratic atmosphere. Christine observed that education, which thinks of itself as a democratic and forward-looking profession, is actually, compared with industry, rather backward at teamwork, hierarchical in structure, and autocratic in style. However, teachers are quick learners, committed to

etting high quality task results, and prepared to take risks to do so. In spite
f Christine's initial qualms, she saw the training as valuable for education,
) the extent of volunteering herself to act as an in-house coach.

Coverdale in the classroom

One reason Coverdale has caught on with such speed in education is that it
  radically *experiential*. For a long time British education has aimed to
evelop children who are capable of thinking for themselves, and to
ncourage, rather than to repress, nonconformity. In practice, however,
1any schools have remained autocratic environments, where teachers have
)ught – not always successfully – to maintain a tight control. One
ontribution of Coverdale is that it can free teachers from this slavery of
aving to rule. It does this through developing strong teams, which, in the
1ost democratic way, impose their own discipline. Coverdale can also be a
orrective to another characteristic of English education – its concentration
n internal skills, such as analysing and memorizing, rather than the ability
) co-operate.

The first experimental courses for young children were run by Candace
Keenan, the wife of a consultant, in the course of research for an Open
University doctorate. One reason for choosing this project was her own
xperience of failing Eleven Plus, but still ending up with a first-class
legree. The pilot project was a small trial at the St Thomas More and
William Fletcher Primary schools in Oxford, and work was continued at St
Peter's, Cassington, a village school nearby, with three teachers. The
nethods used were much the same as with adults; after all, the training is
active, co-operative and fun, very much what children enjoy doing
anyway. As a way of learning, it was instantly popular. As Virginia Makins
eported in the *Times Higher Education Supplement* (15 December 1989),
When the children were asked what they would do if they could no longer
work in this way, one said "I'd run away and get a sick note to say I'm sick
and I just wouldn't come back to school again"; Another said, "I'd write a
etter to the Queen and ask her to get it back".'

The tasks children tackled included making newspapers, posters and
videos; writing stories for younger children; and planning, and helping to
build, the school pond. Tasks can not only provide process experience, but
contribute directly towards the national curriculum, though it is in the field
of process skills that the main benefits come. Children develop their
co-operative skills, learn to organize themselves and solve problems, and
develop the pattern of learning from experience. They can use Systematic
Approach, having no great difficulty in understanding the stages. These
skills can then be applied to other lessons; and through managing their own
learning, children become committed to succeeding, which is often a radical
change of attitude.

Children, parents and teachers have alike commented on the change. One boy told his teacher, 'In your group, it's like working as one happy family.' A parent noticed that since starting this method of class-work, her son wanted to do more with his sister and other children instead of playing alone. Teachers found that children enjoyed their work so much that they often carried on through play-time, and when they arrived in the morning asked when they would be doing a group task. Teachers also found that their class management skills improved: while children were concentrating on tasks, they could find more time to coach groups, observe individual children, and help those with special needs. A head teacher saw the value as helping teachers to plan the next stage of pupil learning, and to assess the pupils better against predetermined criteria. Pupils, she observed, could now both 'own' their work and understand its purpose – relating it to long-term aims, through a chain of asking 'Why?' This last skill can sometimes cause trouble: more than one child starting secondary school was rash enough to ask 'What is the purpose of this lesson?'

The approach is being used within a number of education authorities, but it has not spread as fast as management training. The main reason is cost. Government funds are readily available for training head teachers in how to manage, but not for experimental methods in the classroom. Moreover, teachers themselves need to be trained; research seems to show that they need a full Part I course, followed by a workshop on applying the method in the classroom, before they can operate effectively. Even though Coverdale cuts costs to the bone, this still means an outlay of several hundred pounds per teacher, and without support from industry, this is not generally forthcoming.

Bangladesh – the agricultural management development programme

In 1981 Coverdale learned that a large-scale training project in rural Bangladesh was being considered by the International Development Agency (IDA – the development funding source of the World Bank). Two consultants went out to Bangladesh to consider the problem. As well as having discussions with the relevant ministries, they went into the countryside, to meet people who would actually be doing the development work (they were, as it happened, the only consultants do to this). At the Department of Agriculture, they were able to talk to the permanent secretary, who was quick to appreciate the potential of the training they were proposing, and gave the project his immediate support. As a result, work got under way very quickly, and consultants enjoyed the advantage of being financed directly by the World Bank, and so controlling their own budget.

The main aim of the training was to get IDA-funded projects implemented more effectively and on time, by improving management skills and co-operation of all levels of staff. There was also a longer-term aim of setting up an institution to continue the work of management development, making Bangladesh self-sufficient in this. The underlying theme was building on the country's human strengths, to make the best use of its limited physical and financial resources.

The first training course turned out to be an occasion of some hazard, since it was introduced by the permanent secretary in person, and included members of his immediate staff. The consultants had no advance warning of this, but fortunately the course went well; and, as a result, training was extended within departments, down the various levels of the hierarchy. Part I courses were followed by departmental workshops, designed to tackle task problems and attended by the departmental head, together with all his staff in the two or three levels below him. It was thought unusual to have people of such different status working side by side on the same task. One purpose of these workshops was to develop methods of monitoring the progress of projects, and participants themselves developed new action timetables and disbursement target tables. Senior officials remarked that these workshops were the most practical ever to be run in Bangladesh.

In some departments training was eventually extended further still, down to the managers of local branches. Language was less of a problem than might have been expected: the earlier, more senior, courses were all run in English, while for the later courses, local course directors and coaches were trained, and hand-outs were translated into Bengali. Lower-level groups tended to work in their own language, but general sessions were held in English, with occasional translation of complicated points. Courses tended to be lively and noisy, discussions in general session being enthusiastically chaotic.

The project got under way in May 1981. Over the next 3 years, over 3000 managers, ranging from joint secretaries to forest rangers, were trained.

Progress and responses

The response of participants to training was affected both by the different work pattern of civil servants compared with managers in industry, and by the national culture. Systematic Approach was learnt avidly, and used with great skill; scientific workers in particularly adopted it as a standard method for dealing with people, parallel to the scientific method in which they had been trained. Other participants took to the Approach readily, because they had seen their own bosses using it. By training, civil servants are skilful at dealing with information but inclined to be cautious in action: after all, in civil adminstration, the risks of making a mistake are usually higher than the rewards of initiative. This caution may be reinforced by the facts of life in a Third World country: the status of public servants is very high, but there is no comfortable safety net for those who fall. Again, civil servants are more used to spotting errors than identifying things that have gone well, so the need to review successes came as something of a revelation. Once more, local culture may have reinforced the effect, since giving praise in public is unusual, and can be embarrassing for the recipient, while bystanders may suspect some ulterior motive.

Another theme of the course that was new to participants was that of learning from doing: they were well used to applying theory, but much less used to pulling theory out of what happened in practice. Some parts of the course were seen as very high risk, especially the exercise in which each group watched the other groups working (participants were afraid they might be picked up as performing badly). There was also some resistance to the idea of success criteria. To set a specific target is to give a hostage to fortune – if you fail, there is no glossing over the fact. Some people found it more natural to muddy the water, so as to make sure the result could *not* be judged!

On each course managers were asked to reflect on the learning of the day and pick out useful lessons. Some of these were:

- 'We have to bear in mind the inconveniences to the other groups/ individuals whose co-operation is sought, and we should let others know our purpose ahead of time to allow them to think over the matter before we join them.'
- 'No particular style of leadership is universal; the leader must be able to decide what style is appropriate at the time (autocratic, democratic, participative).'
- 'While giving assignments to others who will execute it, ensure that the assignment is understood clearly and properly, i.e. the same understanding you have: and recheck (ask the person what he understands it to be).'
- 'Before starting a big project, have a small-scale trial run first (pilot project) in order to avoid failures. This reduces the risk.'
- 'If we know the skill of an individual and we assign the job in that area, then the team can have trust.'

Results reported

In follow-up workshops and consultancy visits, managers were able to quote many examples of how they had applied lessons of the course to their own job. For example:

1 Preparing and carrying out a mangrove afforestation project.
2 Building staff housing in the forests.
3 Advanced planning to ensure timely procurement of pumps, fertilizers, and pesticides.
4 Extending the acreage of wheat planted during the winter season, and the proportion of this land covered by a second irrigation, during the growing season.

Among the problems that were identified on the initial courses was a backlog of millions of dollars of unclaimed reimbursements.

In follow-up interviews, participants were asked to describe any successes they had achieved that they were prepared to attribute to the training. Some responses were:

- 'Before, members of co-operatives were trained in cottage industries. In one month they learned three or four handicrafts but did not become skilled in any one area, so that they were unable to use it as a trade, and their finished products were not marketable. Now the focus is directed to one specific area in which the members show natural skill, so that they can use it as a trade and also train other people.'

- 'Four of us in my division have received the training and now have a common language, so that I do not have to spend as much time explaining things to them – they understand the language I am using – because we all understand Systematic Approach. I used to be authoritative about assigning work to others. Now we decide who can best fulfil the needs of the job, and the supporting assistance needed by other staff is also decided voluntarily.'

- 'In gathering information (about pending disciplinary procedures), we used to send circulars and we depended completely upon the field officers; we did not set a timescale – we sent casual reminders. There was no follow-up, and progress was not known. Now they comply to our needs because we set a specific date for receiving the information. We send out special messengers, and ask them to send their information back by special messenger, to ensure it gets to us on time.'

- 'In training people to help farmers carry out surveillance of pests in fields, we used to say, when you see an insect, just kill it! We did not identify priorities. No one knew that predators were beneficial, and they used to kill them as well as the pests. After the course, we made a joint decision about which pests to survey. We chose only three predators, because they are easy to identify in the field, after discussion about what farmers will be able to recognize. We never asked (people being trained) to go to the field and see what is there; we used to give lectures. People did not have any knowledge about surveillance. Now we have trained the district level people in the use of this technique and training will go right down to farmers.'

Making trees grow

Within the Forests Department, the Plantation Circle is responsible for managing the existing Sunderbans Forests on the Coastal Area of Bangladesh, and for carrying out the biggest afforestation programme in the world. The target in the 5-year period 1980–5 was to plant 100,000 acres of new trees. Apart from the huge task of raising seedlings, planting, and maintaining plantations, the project included building houses for forestry staff, acquiring boats to improve transport, setting up radio communications with remote areas of the country, and improving public relations. The work can be difficult and dangerous: many forestry officers have to live in remote areas, where there may be shortages of fresh food, drinking water and schools for their children.

Following his own Part I course, the Chief Conservator of Forests decided to extend the training to the next two levels of his staff (assistant conservators of forests and divisional forest officers), and to run shorter programmes for supervisory staff, including forest rangers, deputy rangers nd clerks. His aims were to improve co-operation between administrative ind field staff, and to spread a common approach among staff at all levels; ilso to improve the preparation of detailed plans, and meeting time chedules. Between October 1981 and January 1983 240 people attended :ourses, and received follow-up in the form of individual interviews (or :hort workshops for headquarters clerical staff). Some results reported by hree divisional forest officers are quoted below.

Plantation and maintenance

'Previously this was an estimate. Now detailed plans are made, with time :argets for each stage – survey, seed collection, nursery raising, planting and maintenance. It will take time to quantify the results, but the benefits so far are:

- No one can escape, because the plan is there.
- A plan for seed collection is made, where to get seed and when; and
- plans are made for planting – specifying the week for planting. (These plans are monitored by wireless by the Conservator of Forests.)
- The right number of seedlings are ready at the right time to meet plantation targets.
- If you sow in time, with proper quality of seedlings, planting can take place at the end of the winter/beginning of summer, so that seedlings get maximum growing time, survival percentage is higher, wave damage is low, and maintenance is reduced.

The target for planting in '82 was 15,000 acres and this was achieved; the target for the next year was 20,000 acres.'

Construction of buildings

'Range officers are now thinking about quality – for example, in buying materials for construction of staff housing, it is better to get the best timber and the best cement. Officers can construct houses for a cost of Tk. 190 per square foot, whereas the current Public Works Department rate in Chittagong is Tk. 275 per square foot. Before the course, purchase of raw material was haphazard; now officers make a plan and purchase all raw material before the construction work starts.'

Team building

'There is an improvement in team spirit, signified by less grumbling, less quarrelling, better co-ordination and an improvement in disseminating

204 Coverdale on Management

information downwards. Subordinates used to say "It is not possible."
Now they say, "I will try."

- We have improved in how we divide the work. I say to my team, "You
  tell me how you will phase the work and what you expect of me – for
  example, what logistic support do you need."
- Targets are set as a result of discussion; it's no use setting unrealistic
  targets.
- Where the weak points of a man are known, then I stress certain stages of
  the work as a precautionary measure.
- Appreciation for good work is given.'

View from a deputy secretary

A. B. M. Abdush Shakoor, a deputy secretary in the Ministry of
Agriculture, who is also a well-known playwright, commented as follows:

> I was aware that in principle every next man has something of importance
> for me, and yet in practice I continued to be wise in my own conceit. The
> course . . . made me critically aware that indeed every individual did
> have something of value.
>
> Coverdale asked me to critically appreciate my earlier success in·order
> to build on it later, when for life I was taught to probe into my previous
> mistakes with the sole purpose of avoiding them. The course made me
> see that even when consciously I was keeping from talking I was not
> really listening; I was only marking time for talking and waiting for the
> cue. This was a revolutionary discovery for me, and I have ever since
> been cultivating the art of effective listening with surprising results . . .
>
> Coverdale develops favourable situations where the trainees
> themselves create knowledge dialogically necessary for their 'problem
> solving'. Such training is not easily forgotten, as the creator is the last
> person to forget his creation.

Evaluation of Coverdale work in Bangladesh

After the first 10 months of work (concentrating on more senior staff), the
project was evaluated by an independent consultant on behalf of the
Ministry of Agriculture and Forests (MOAF). Below are some extracts
from his report:

> There is no doubt that the first 10 months of [the project] with only about
> 8 months since active training started, has brought about changes in the

attitudes and practices of senior managers in MOAF and associated agencies. This is a small, though significant, contribution to the overall task of improving levels of management in MOAF leading to better implementation of IDA (and other) projects.

The most obvious return for expenditure on the product is the professional training skill of Coverdale – what one might call the classroom skills. But in addition there has been an impressive move forward towards the training goals which plainly were not occurring previously. It is the ability to deploy classroom skills quickly and effectively that have perhaps justified costs higher than usual.

One of the valuable features of Coverdale training has been the training of senior staff members of MOAF development projects as 'coaches'. These officers are consulted about further training and play a part in the actual conduct of courses and workshops.

Economy in time results from study and understanding of plans and procedures, and the eradication of problems by better co-operation and co-ordination. Most influence in this respect is wielded by the more senior half of the bureaucracy, and it is in this area that the human relations training of the Coverdale Organization is most effective.*

★ 'Report on Evaluation of Agricultural Management Training Institute (Phase I) and Proposals for its Future Operation (Phase II)', by Harry T. E. Smith, 21 January 1982.

21 Training across frontiers – ICI and 'Hygrowth Electric'

Coverdale and language: ICI Europe

It is hard enough for different offices and branches to co-operate when they all speak the same language, but for multi-cultural companies the problem is far greater. In the past these have usually been large, sophisticated organizations, able to identify points of friction, and take steps to reduce them. In post-1992 Europe, however, the ability to work confidently across frontiers will be vital for small organizations as well as large ones, and it may indeed be the biggest hurdle Europeans have to leap in trying to compete with the huge single-country markets of Japan and the USA. What Coverdale can provide is a sort of behavioural Esperanto – a common approach for dealing with problems of co-operation and teamwork, which can be translated into any language, understood by people of any culture, and used to explore points of misunderstanding.

This was the thinking behind a series of courses held on behalf of ICI Europe. This organization, largely concerned with manufacturing, faces every sort of cross-cultural challenge: a German working in Italy may manage or collaborate with a Dutchman working in Spain, dealing with each other by telephone, taking part in meetings and project groups. It is therefore vital for the company's success that multi-national teams should work together effectively. Coverdale has had a long and fruitful relationship with ICI, dated back to the 1960s, and a Part I course forms part of the core training of all young graduates. Peter Pay, the training managers of ICI Europe, had himself undergone the training in the UK, and recognized its potential as a way of getting a common approach. As a result, a series of multi-cultural courses were run, and these have continued at the rate of one or two a year.

On these courses people start off by working in national groups. General sessions are held in English (with some translation of tricky points) but groups work in their own languages. From about the third day, participants pend more and more of their time working in multilingual groups, made up on the lines of the traditional funny story beginning 'There was a German, a Spaniard, and an Italian . . .' The immediate reaction of participants is that working like this will be impossible. In practice it often happens that, thanks to the first 2 days' training, the new groups actually do better than the old ones, and people are sometimes amazed by the quality of results. One reason for this is that groups are forced to slow down and clarify exactly what the task or proposal means. Do they all understand the words written on the board, in the same sense? One task was running a 'cabaret'; it is a French word, commonly used (or misused) in English, but what exactly does it convey to a German? People have to find out before they can take the task any further. But problems like this do not blow them off course, because all the time they have the common language of Systematic Approach, leading them towards action.

The groups also make formal plans to take account of the different priorities of different linguistic groups, and the different ways they look at the world. To build on this, towards the end of the course, national groups are asked to list any difficulties they expect in putting the training into action. The lists are then swapped, so that a group of Spaniards has to propose solutions for the Germans' difficulties and *vice versa*. Right to the end of the course people continue challenging assumptions, both linguistic and cultural; and on their return, they not only have a language of action they can use across frontiers but a skill of questioning for meaning, and an instinct for the kind of phrase or situation where ambiguity can happen.

'Hygrowth Electric'

For 50 years Hygrowth Electric (a disguised name) has been a byword for engineering excellence. From small beginnings, it grew very fast, and is now established world-wide. Initially, its products were highly technological, and sold only to large users. However, in the field of electronics, miniaturization has meant that products tend to halve in size and in price every 4 years, until devices that have formerly been extremely expensive now become available to small firms and even the general public.

For Hygrowth, this meant a change in its sales and marketing strategy. Instead of dealing direct with its customers, as one engineer to another, it had to set up a network of dealers, selling to small firms and retail shops, and this business soon came to account for almost half its sales. In this new field Hygrowth found itself facing strong competition. After all, it was a late entrant, its competitors produced models that were similar in price and quality, had similar modes of promotion and could promise similar delivery dates. Hygrowth decided that the key to successful competition must lie in developing its dealer network, particularly in human relationships.

Dealers varied much in quality: at one extreme there were technical experts, who added value by providing advice and consultancy to their customers; at the other extreme there were 'box movers', who had little understanding of the goods they were selling. Between these there were the large wholesaling organizations, which dealt with a wide variety of products of all sorts. Hygrowth felt that it needed to improve its network all over Europe, and it knew that there were wide discrepancies between one country to another. The first thing needed was more information, and accordingly it called in Coverdale, on its reputation in the field of human relations.

The dealer survey

Coverdale's first step was to design and carry out a survey, to find out what really was the relationship between the company and its dealers. Forty Hygrowth people and twenty-nine dealers, drawn from eight countries, were interviewed to discover what were the main successes and difficulties of working together, and what could be done to improve the partnership. Besides the interviews, dealers and sales staff completed (separate) questionnaires, to show how each side saw its relation with the other. Hygrowth people also completed a questionnaire dealing with management issues within the sales force, such as motivation, leadership and stress.

The findings differed from country to country, but some points ran true throughout. It was clear that Hygrowth had been highly successful in building up an effective network in a short time. The reasons for this were first, the quality of its products; second, the reputation of the company for honesty and straightforwardness; and, third, the enthusiasm and commitment of the sales force. Time and again dealers saw sales representatives as doing much more than what would normally be expected in a business relationship, while representatives saw the bond between themselves and the dealers as an important ingredient in the success they had achieved.

On the other hand, a number of weaknesses were uncovered. Almost without exception, dealers felt that the company should do more and better marketing. They were also unhappy about delivery time: it was stressed that if a product couldn't be supplied immediately, it was better to say so frankly rather than producing an optimistic forecast that merely turned out to be wrong. The dealers also criticized the systems for orders and contracts, while the sales force pointed to problems in the method of payment. But for them, a more fundamental complaint was the status accorded to dealer account sales in Hygrowth as a whole. Up till now these had been seen as a peripheral, remote from the company's main targets. As a result, dealer account sales managers had no authority and little influence over the central functions that played a crucial part in obtaining good sales esults – pricing, warehousing and delivery, credit control, and marketing ervices. The problem was one found in many matrix organizations: sales nd production staff were totally dependent on each other, and yet each eported to its own management, and were judged by criteria that were ometimes mutually conflicting. For example, production departments vere expected to keep stocks to the minimum, while salesmen were judged on sales volume, which often depended on having a wide range of goods vailable.

The next stage was to provide training workshops for dealers. Training vas given not only in process skill but in skills such as figure work and ccountancy, consultants being called in to design suitable materials. Hygrowth staff commented with some surprise that Coverdale consultants made no attempt to offer this kind of training – they knew their limits and vere quite happy to share work with other people.

As a result of this work, both company and dealers feel that they have made great strides towards building up an effective partnership. Dealers and salesmen alike feel that the company is aware of their problems and will take active steps to put them right. Dealers are helped to run their businesses more effectively, while the company can rely on its product being enthusiastically sold in this still-growing segment of their market.

Response to the survey

From the survey, the company identified a number of problems to tackle. The first was to improve the relationship between different functions within the company, and here training was an obvious resource. Workshops were designed and run in every country. They consisted of a 2½-day course on basic process skills, followed immediately by 1½ days spent on attacking real issues. An important aim of these workshops was 'boundary spanning' – training sales and production people together, and making them spend time on resolving the various problems that inhibited co-operation. The courses were run over a 2-year period, and had a marked effect on the way people in different departments worked together. These practical changes of behaviour were later given added force by changes in the company's organization, which though not directly inspired by the survey were made much easier by the changes in work patterns already achieved.

The second subject for attention was relations with dealers, starting with formal dealer conferences. Hygrowth's competitors held events that were sometimes little more than lavish displays of hospitality, but Hygrowth prided itself that its conferences were serious working occasions. When the company's staff were asked about them, they replied that the conferences were excellent – 'We tell them all about the company'. When dealers were asked, they said the conferences were terrible: communication was all one way, like parent–child, and, besides, the points raised were all at the salesman's level. There was no chance to discuss the issues that really concerned them, as directors and senior managers. But they added that Hygrowth need not worry – all manufacturers' conferences were just as bad.

Hygrowth realized that this gave it a real opportunity to set itself apart from its competitors. A new-model conference was designed and run by a mixed steering group, consisting of dealers, company staff and consultants. A dealer acted as chairman, and dealers themselves chose topics to work on. Advance training was given to facilitators, who would help to run it. In the first year these were all Hygrowth staff, but over the next 2 years dealers and technical experts on the products were included. The main message of the conference was that the company must listen to dealers, rather than merely the other way round, and after the first year every conference began with a report reviewing the recommendations made the previous year, and explaining what the company had done about them. The subjects for discussion were chosen carefully, as being matters of real strategic importance, rather than minor niggles that could best be sorted out on the ground. Finally, each conference had a keynote speech from some distinguished international figure.

The first of these new conferences caused considerable qualms to higher management, who were afraid that the dealers might spend their time pulling the company to bits. In the event, the result was the opposite – dealers said that the conference was the best they had ever attended, and commended the company for setting it up. With hindsight, the small step of appointing a dealer as chairman was seen as marking a lasting change in the company's relations with its dealers.

Appendix I   Charting

'The horror of that moment,' the King went on, 'I shall never, never forget.'
'You will though,' the Queen said, 'if you don't make a memorandum of it.'
Lewis Carroll, *Alice in Wonderland*

Introduction: what is charting?

Charting is a method of improving the effectiveness of meetings, by continuously recording the process of discussion in a form that everyone can read. Typically this means writing with a broad, felt-tipped pen on a large pad of white paper fixed to a wall or blackboard. Some benefits of charting are:

1 Everyone understands what is being talked about.
2 People stick to the point.
3 Everyone knows what is proposed or agreed.
4 Anyone whose mind wanders has a chance to catch up.

Things that can be charted include:

1 Agenda (whether or not a typed agenda is sent out in advance).
2 Decisions.
3 Proposals.
4 Pieces of information.
5 The progress of discussion through the various stages of Systematic Approach or other formal methods of working.
6 Brainstorming.
7 Diagrams such as why/how charts, or critical-path networks.

Charting is a skill and needs practice. With practice any literate person can do it; and bad charting is better than no charting.

Benefits of charting

A chart has two main sorts of use: as a *guide* and as a *group memory*.

Benefits of charting as a guide

A chart can display and keep in the mind of the members:

1 The topic being discussed.
2 The aims of the discussion – that is, what final result people are trying to achieve.
3 What stage the meeting is at – for instance, if the meeting is at the stage of gathering information, the chart will say so; and people will not start making plans or decisions before the data is complete.

A chart can crystallize thinking. When the writer says, 'What shall I write?' (or charts his own interpretation), a vague conclusion is forced into definite wording. In the same way when individuals realize that what they say is likely to be recorded, they take time to think before they speak, and to put their thoughts into a precise language.

A chart helps to keep the flow of the meeting going. Once a point has been agreed and recorded, people naturally move on to the next one.

A chart draws attention away from individuals and their concerns, and towards the common goal – the task the meeting is trying to achieve. It can, for example, discourage someone who thinks he knows all about a subject from talking at random to air his knowledge. A chart helps everyone to contribute. Even someone who knows little about the subject can follow the discussion, and sometimes make helpful contributions about matters of steering or process – for example, that plans are being made before the information is complete.

Above all, a chart focuses all minds present on the same thing and by so doing expands thinking. This is particularly so when suggestions and proposals are recorded as they arrive; each person's ideas lie on the board for the rest to digest and work on, and the result can be a synthesis of ideas, far more useful than anyone present could achieve on their own. Discarded ideas can be crossed out before the meeting passes on.

Benefits of charting as a record

A chart acts as a memory or the group. For example, if someone has a point which he thinks important, but which is being neglected, he may well hammer away at it, in and out of season, and so hold up the meeting. If, however, the point is recorded to be discussed at the proper time, he will shut up.

When an impasse occurs, a good way to help a meeting forward is by everyone having two or three minutes of silent thought. A chart helps by allowing people to scan all the available data.

A chart acts as an instantaneous set of minutes of the meeting, and as a record – agreed by everyone – of decisions, etc., on which formal minutes an be based. A chart itself, if kept, can be a reminder not only of what was ecided, but also of the stages of discussion and state of mind of the people aking part. It can bring this back after the lapse of a month or so more vividly than a typed summary or minutes.

Special uses of charts

Brainstorming

This technique is a way of solving problems by generating as many ideas as possible in order to choose the best one and develop it. Everyone round the table throws out random ideas – without attempting to criticize or evaluate them. They can be recorded on a chart, for discussion, evaluation and improvement later.

Why/how networks charts (see Chapter 4)

These are a technique for establishing:

1 The underlying purposes of a task.
2 Various ways of achieving these purposes.
3 How the various aims and means relate to each other.

A why/how network can be an individual's working document. It can also be the product of a meeting. In that case, it is built up step by step on a wall-chart from points produced by individuals.

Composite charts

Once items are charted in a particular form or relationship, it is often difficult to alter them, either on paper or in readers' minds. One way of getting round this is by building composite charts from small individual sheets of paper. For example, on a why/how chart, everyone privately writes down hows and whys on small slips of paper. The chairman can then arrange these slips in a network, grouping related points together and moving them round to show appropriate causal relationships.

Charts prepared in advance

A chart is a useful visual aid for public speaking. One can pin up a chart already written, but sometimes it is more telling to build up a chart as the talk progresses. A skilled chart writer can write a chart freehand which will be legible even from the back of a large hall. However, it may be helpful to design the chart in advance, writing in faint pencil or yellow felt-tip –

neither of which can be read by the audience. The speaker can then build up charts apparently spontaneously, by writing over them in a darker colour.

Skills and techniques

Record briefly the sense of what has been said, but do not distort statements or simplify them in such a way that important points are lost. If someone says, 'It would take three men to carry the box upstairs', do not just chart 'Box heavy' (unless the point about the three men really is irrelevant). Summarizing should take place without fuss: people should not be constantly asked to repeat themselves – unless they are being woolly and need to be made to sharpen their statements. They should find that their essential meaning has been recorded, without their having to spell it out.

Leading by charting

The chart writer is in a position of considerable authority. He can select phrasing and items to give prominence, choose which of two contributions to write up first and often keep the eyes of the meeting on what he is doing. He can make statements like, 'So that's settled; who's going to do this and that?' With skill he can direct the meeting (whatever the formal chairman may intend) and do so without being obvious. Therefore it is often appropriate for the chairman himself to chart. The chairman can of course direct the writer by telling him exactly what to write up, but this is often slow and irritating.

Writing and layout

If your writing is good enough, cursive script is much faster than capitals. A skilled writer has in mind a clear picture of where he is going to record different items. It is important to have a heading for each category of contribution (for example, *information* or *plan*). But do not be so concerned with layout that there is delay in getting things written. It is better to start charting, find the format is wrong and restart, than to waste time dithering. When a heading has apparently been concluded, it is important to leave space below, as you may have to go back and fit more in.

Spelling

People are often reluctant to chart because their spelling is bad. In fact, many people make spelling mistakes on a wall-chart because they cannot

asily see what they are writing, and the matter is not of the slightest
mportance. If any pedant draws attention to them, point out how
rrelevant they are to the needs of the job.

Use of colour

Felt-tipped pens are available in a wide range of colours. Use different
colours for different types of input – for example, blue for information,
brown for ideas. Red and green are not easy to read at a distance but are fine
for headings. Yellow is no good (except for underlining and designing the
chart in advance, as mentioned above). Good colours at any range are black,
blue, brown, purple and orange.

Other equipment

Paper can be bought in sizes of 46 × 76 centimetres or, better still 61 × 92
centimetres. This is all the essential equipment. Sheets can be stuck on a
wall by two small pieces of masking tape. (Avoid transparent sticky tape,
since it may damage the paintwork.) This provides a reasonable writing
surface. Clips are available which hold pads of paper and fit on to walls or
the top of blackboards. Completed sheets can be flipped back over the
blackboard; this can be a dangerous practice, as relevant points may be lost.
It is better to tear completed sheets off and stick them up round the walls.

Storage

If there is any likelihood of charts being kept, make sure they are labelled
and dated. Avoid leaving charts full of confidential information stuck up
round the room.

Final points

If you are introducing charting to a meeting where it has not been used
before, do not (unless you are the host) insist on elaborate equipment. Paper
and masking tape is all that is needed. Do not make a great business of it;
just say 'here are a lot of good ideas lying around; let's record them before
they are forgotten'.

On this basis, charting can be introduced to any meeting; it is often most
effective in voluntary meetings, outside offices, where people tend to be
both less businesslike and less disciplined.

Appendix II Human behaviour and purposes

This appendix attempts to summarize the general assumptions about human nature and the human condition on which Coverdale training is based.

Co-operation

1 Man is a social animal; co-operation is as natural as conflict, but fruitful where conflict is sterile. There may be occasions of conflict which cannot be reconciled; but it is in the interests of both sides to assume the opposite. The exception is war, where the aim is precisely to harm your adversaries; but war itself is a kind of co-operation in mutual destruction.
2 Self-interest does not suggest that we should love our enemies, but it does require that we should try to find a course of common action with those with whom we are in conflict, that will suit the aims of both parties. This co-operation, if prolonged, will itself lead to a certain comradeship.
3 Any person is better than I am at something and has something of value to contribute to a team. Therefore the views and skills of anyone are worth considering. I can tell what people are good at only by listening to them, and by understanding their meaning and aims.
4 Every kind of human behaviour is useful in some context. Rightly used, any defect becomes a strength.
5 People are neither predictable nor wholly unpredictable. It is useless to treat them as machines that will react when something is done to them. But it is possible to influence and guide their actions and feelings, if we adjust our own behaviour, constantly observing their needs and responses.

Management and training

1 A manager has a choice between driving his subordinates towards his own objectives, and establishing common aims which his whole team will accept, since their personal needs are taken into account. If he habitually chooses the first alternative, he may snatch short-term gains, but will seldom be successful in the long run.
2 People become committed to solutions which they themselves have helped to devise, will be more patient if they run into difficulty and more determined to produce success.

Enterprise

1 People need not sit still and wait for things to be done to them. They can and should be up and doing in the interests of the aims they hold.
2 Although we are surrounded by external forces, we have some power to direct them. If they are impersonal, we can analyse them and use or control them; if they are human, we can influence individuals and establish common ground between their aims and our own. Through individuals we can influence the whole human environment. It is never a good excuse for inaction to say that the system makes us powerless.

Human thought

1 We constantly make assumptions which are useful, since they are generally true and avoid the need for explorations or discussion. We leave the house at 8.00 every morning, assuming that the train will run on time. Many assumptions we do not recognize as such, but take as facts. These are walls for thought, and we cannot see over the top of them. We must remain alert for the new piece of information that throws doubt on an assumption, and be bold in testing it.
2 The way in which people improve is by building on success. In almost all our activities some element of success will be found. Our need is to identify it, find what may have caused it and can be used elsewhere. Success will tell us what to do; failure will only tell us what to avoid. Failure is useful when it indicates limits or inspires us to greater effort; but repeated failure makes us timid and suggestible. Success analysed makes us confident; success repeated can lead to improvement for which there is no limit.

Appendix III   Some results of training

There are notorious difficulties in evaluating the results of training. If, following a course, participants act differently, this may not be the result of the training as such, but simply of being taken away from their work for a few days, and treated with concern by supposed 'experts' (the well-known 'Hawthorne' effect). A valid scientific experiment requires the use of a matched control group, and (especially with managers) matching is extremely difficult. There is also the problem of what the control group should do in the control period, since whatever experience they have is likely to influence them. For reasons like these, hardly any studies of training achieve the sort of certainty that can be found in laboratory work.

Several large Coverdale projects have had systematic follow-up of a sort which, if not scientific, is at least practically persuasive. At ICI's Wilton site (a case study described in the first edition of this book), T.P. Gray interviewed some 500 managers who had undergone the training, and found that 35 per cent were convinced of the training's usefulness, 35 per cent broadly in favour, and 30 per cent neutral or opposed. The benefits people saw were analysed, and found to vary for different levels of management.

Senior managers saw the main benefits as being steering, gaining commitment, and communicating in complex groupings; and also in concepts of aiming and objective setting. *Middle managers* saw the main benefits as being personal skills (listening, support), identifying objectives, and planning, both for themselves and for work groups. *Supervisors* too saw the main benefit as planning, both for task and for personal improvement.

In Unigate (a study also described in the first edition) a comparison was made of the costs of training, with the savings that could be directly attributed to follow-up projects. The seventeen projects that could readily be costed achieved *annual* savings of £317,000, compared with a total cost of training and consultancy of £320,000. The indication was that from measurable benefits alone the pay-back period was not more than 12 months.

One of the most striking examples of training targets being achieved was at Esso's oil refinery at Fawley. Here safety was made one of the main targets of the Coverdale project, and over its first 7 years the annual numbers of disabling accidents fell from 61 to nil, and of all injuries from 1072 to 58, making the Fawley refinery the safest of Esso's sixty-nine throughout the world. (However, one must recognize that all these studies are open to the same broad objection – that the various improvements may be at least partly due to factors other than training. At Fawley accidents were already on a downward trend. In ICI, although most managers thought the training had improved them, the study gives no evidence of actual changes of behaviour; while at Unigate, it is possible that management might have achieved the savings anyway.)

A more recent study was carried out in the engineering division of the northern region of British Gas. Here some 500 managers and staff had been trained, and the aim of the study was to determine the benefits to the division. The survey was based on five discussion groups, each of eight people, drawn from different parts of the organization, with a skew towards the more senior end of the hierarchy. Groups produced reports listing qualitative benefits, together with difficulties that had been encountered. A wide list of benefits was produced, with few difficulties except in the most junior group, where people felt that the initial enthusiasm had been allowed to fizzle out. Besides these reports, the forty people who took part in the survey also answered a questionnaire, dealing with the extent to which Systematic Approach and the other themes of Coverdale were used in practice. People were asked to identify the last major task they had completed at work, identify how far they had used each stage of Systematic Approach, and how helpful it had been; and how far the training had helped in terms of the various other skills and techniques taught by Coverdale. Answers were on a 7-point scale.

On the general successfulness of the project, the average mark was 5.5 (out of a maximum of 7), while the measure of support for Coverdale averaged 6.0. Once again, responses tended to be less favourable among members of the fifth group. It was, however, notable that every single individual gave the maximum mark of 7 to the usefulness of at least one Coverdale theme, implying that every individual improved in some skill or other, presumably in accordance with their needs. The questions varied in objectivity; it is easier to frame a specific question about the use of techniques, e.g. 'In your last major task, were success criteria set?', than about a skill such as listening, which is exercised continuously.

Obviously a generally favourable picture of the course (perhaps simple enjoyment) could colour the answers. But the exercise produced data of considerable value for comparative purposes with other courses.

A similar though less elaborate means has been used by Coverdale to compare the effectiveness of individual courses (described by David Bettes in an article in the August 1986 edition of *ICT*). Eight weeks after each course, a questionnaire is administered by telephone to eight randomly chosen participants, and also to their immediate superiors. Questions cover the aims of going on the course, and how far they have been met; the effectiveness of the course compared with expectations; and any changes of behaviour or effects on business results. Examples are sought, but respondents also mark answers on a 5-point scale, an analysis of the first twelve courses being used to provide a benchmark for subsequent quality control. It is clear that the training is generally found satisfactory, in the sense of giving results as good or better than expectation. From the point of view of quality control, one drawback is the need to wait 8 weeks for feedback, although this is probably the minimum time needed for the training to make much difference; another drawback is that marks are heavily concentrated around 3 to 4 ('as expected' or 'better than expected'). The results show consistency of marking within each individual course, and also between individual participants and their bosses, even though the telephone-interview system makes it likely that responses are independent.

Two studies were carried out on the effects of training younger people. The first project, with primary school children, is described in Chapter 19. The training used was called Systematic and Cooperative Learning Approach (SACLA) and was based on the view that children need separate training in group work skills in order to work together effectively. Research was carried out in three primary schools in Oxfordshire. Over 200 pupils were involved, aged between eight and eleven. Experimental groups of children trained in SACLA were compared with control groups who did not experience the training. The same pre-test and post-tests were carried out for both groups.

One criterion chosen was the amount of interaction that occurred between children, and whether or not it was related to the job being done (as opposed to merely idle chat). Clearly if the training was successful, children would spend a higher proportion of their time on useful interactions, compared with both idle chat and working on their own. In order to get detailed information about pupil behaviour, a systematic observation instrument was used – 'The Pupil Record', devised by Deanne Boydell during projects in primary education at Leicester.* It was designed for use in informal junior classrooms, where children are seated round tables in small groups and the tutor, rather than talking to the whole class, talks to individual children or their groups. The observer focuses on one

* See Boydell, D. (1974), 'Teacher-pupil contact in junior classrooms', *British Journal of Educational Psychology*, Vol. 44, pp. 313–18; Boydell, D. (1975) 'Pupil behaviour in junior classrooms', *British Journal of Educational Psychology*, Vol. 45, pp. 1229–9.

child at a time and records a sample of his/her activities by coding on a pre-prepared record sheet what the child is doing, before moving on (at a pre-set time) to the next child. By observing in this way, one can measure the frequency of different activities and interactions.

In all, 8618 observations were made of each group – experimental and control – and the results showed, first, that total interactions in the experimental group were significantly higher than those in the control group (78 per cent of total observations, compared with 48 per cent). In other words, children in the experimental group spent a lot more time talking to each other. Second, in the experimental group, the majority of interactions (three-quarters) were purposeful, while working on the task. In the control group, purposeful interactions were only a third as many. There was therefore no doubt that the training achieved what it set out to do – produce a measurable increase in the extent to which children worked together.

The other study, by Taylor, was with YTS trainees.* The training used was not actually Coverdale, but followed the same broad pattern of task-work in groups. The subjects were YTS trainees, aged between 16 and 19. Earlier courses lasted 5 days, those later in the year 4 days. Trainees were followed up between 4 and 6 weeks after the course, to see which of them had been able to make use of the training, or improved in some way. Those who could state general improvements were treated as 'possibles', while those who could give detailed instances of improvements were treated as 'probables'. Probables amounted to 53 per cent, and probables and possibles together to 75 per cent of trainees.

One measure of success adopted was the attitude scale know as 'Locus of Control'. This measures the extent to which an individual regards his destiny as being in his own hands, as opposed to being in the hands of outside forces (such as 'destiny' or 'the system'). People who regard their fate as being within their own control are called 'internals', and internality is generally associated with success. Trainees were measured at the start of training and 6 weeks afterwards, and it was found that those on 5-day courses showed a significant swing towards internality. (Four-day courses were held towards the end of the YTS year, and it was found that those trainees who were still looking for jobs showed a significant move towards the *external* end of the scale, so masking any benefit from the training.) The effects of leadership were examined, and it was found that the groups that kept the same leader throughout the course (whether explicitly appointed or not) tended to produce better results than those that did not. Although doubts had been expressed whether less able trainees would be able to cope with the training, there was no evidence that those who scored lower on intelligence tests benefited any less, and the training was later extended to special needs trainees, including young offenders.

* See Taylor, Max (1990), *Effectiveness in Education and Training*, Aldershot: Gower.

Appendix IV: Coverdale, ethics and Christianity

Ralph Coverdale's Christianity had a strong influence on the design of his training. First, it gave him a belief in free will. He had been trained as a Jesuit, an order which has traditionally opposed the determinist strain in Christianity itself, which is strong in Calvin and St Augustine. Second, Christianity indicates that men and women are individuals, whom it is never right to manipulate in the supposed interests of the collective idea. They are created in the image of God, with points of view others should consider and aims that have as much right to be followed as our own. Third, Ralph Coverdale found warrant in the New Testament for his emphasis on the study of success. In the Old Testament the Chosen People are required to follow a precise code of behaviour and are punished if they go wrong. Since disaster follows hard on the heels of sin, individuals do well to examine where they have erred. This doctrine of salvation by analysis underlies the two most powerful philosophies of our age, those of Marx and Freud, both of whom were brought up in the Jewish faith. Mosaic law sets out in great detail the deviations from righteous behaviour that are forbidden. Indeed eight of the Ten Commandments begin with 'Thou shalt not . . .' By contrast, Christ's two basic commandments to his disciples are positive and *open* – they give aims, which people must decide for themselves how best to fulfil. Men and women are charged with the duty of using their talents for the benefit of God and their neighbour, under the guidance and with the purpose of love.

Holding these beliefs, it is not surprising that Ralph Coverdale encouraged a chaplain from the Teesside Industrial Mission, who came on one of the courses, to be involved with the training and its application with a range of organizations, not all of them industrial. The chaplain, Tony Birbeck, was struck by the close relationship between Coverdale's approach and his own ideas about applying Christian principles. Since then he has worked as a Coverdale consultant on many projects, and has recently become a director of the firm.

Coverdale training has been used extensively in the Church of England, by chaplains from industrial missions and by vicars of ordinary parishes. They, after all, have a constant need to manage by process authority alone. The results have been felt, not in spectacular campaigns of conversion, but at the most basic levels – in developing teamwork between clergy and laity, in identifying and, more importantly, using the skills and experience of members of a congregation, by better planning of sermons or study courses and in the resolution of conflicting interests in a parish.

The way in which a consultant who is also a priest looks on his work can be seen in this extract from the address Tony Birbeck gave, in 1975, at Ralph Coverdale's memorial requiem mass:

Many of us associate certain words with Ralph Coverdale. One such word is 'purpose'. At particular times – and death is probably one of them – we find ourselves thinking about the purpose of life. One way in which Christians have tried to describe the purpose of life is to say that it is to glorify God.

In human terms we find ourselves trying to copy or emulate those whom we admire. That may be considered to be a compliment to the person whom we seek to copy. So it is with God. One of the ways we glorify Him is to work so that His characteristics may be seen in the relationships and situations of life. We glorify Him by bringing out His characteristics so that they may be recognized and enjoyed by others, and that others may grow in those characteristics.

God is love and God is loving. Where we bring about situations where people are taken account of, where their ideas are heard, where individuals sacrifice their own viewpoint or immediate interest in order to care about others and their contributions, then love for those people is seen in action.

God is creative, for God is Creator. Where we make opportunities for people to do things, overcoming frustration and enabling satisfaction and some sense of fulfilment, we are enabling creative activity.

God gives hope. Indeed I believe the Christian religion to be, pre-eminently, a religion of the future, not of reminiscence. To help someone to look to the future with all its possibilities is to turn them from fear and to lead them in the direction of hope and to consider life's possibilities.

God encourages us to build community. The theme of community is like a thread from the beginning to the end of the Bible. The Church is God's community and should reflect His love as a body of people deeply concerned for building community. It is concerned with reconciling, for Jesus's work was basically a work of reconciliation: overcoming the divisions that harm and debase, that are wasteful of human energy.

Reconciliation can happen when different men and women come to share aims and priorities; when they can meet together and grow in mutual understanding and respect. In short, we glorify God when we help people to grow to that fullness of stature of which they are potentially capable as human beings; the stature God would have them enjoy. Ralph's work, as I saw it, was dedicated to bringing about those sorts of things.

Further reading

The books listed below develop further some of the topics covered in the text. Some of them were source books for Ralph Coverdale; others deal with the underlying psychology or philosophy, or discuss applications of the training.

Management style and leadership

Harvey-Jones, John, *Making it Happen, Reflections on Leadership*, Collins 1988.

Likert, Rensis. *New Patterns of Management*. McGraw-Hill, New York, 1961.

— *The Human Organisation*. McGraw-Hill, New York, 1967.

McGregor, Douglas, *The Human Side of Enterprise*. McGraw-Hill, New York, 1960.

Creativity

de Bono, Edward. *The Use of Lateral Thinking*. Cape, 1967; Penguin Books, 1971.

Koestler, Arthur. *The Act of Creation*. Hutchinson, 1964; Pan, 1975.

Scott Williamson, G. and Pierce, I. H. *Science, Synthesis and Sanity*. The Peckham Health Centre, Collins, 1965.

Building on success

Haldane, Bernard. *How to Make a Habit of Success*. Prentice Hall, Englewood Cliffs, New Jersey, 1960.

Maltz, Maxwell. *Psychocybernetics*. Wilshire Book Co., Hollywood, 1960.

Mechanistic and organic systems of management

Burns, T. and Stalker, G. M. *The Management of Innovation.* Social Science Paperback. Tavistock Publications, 1961.

Negotiation

Fisher, R., and Ury, W. L. *Getting to Yes, Negotiating Without Giving in* Hutchinson, 1982.

Psychology and philosophy

Aristotle, *Ethics,* translated by Rackham, H. Loeb. London/Harvard, 1934.
Bandura A., *Social Learning Theory.* Prentice-Hall, New Jersey, 1977.
Coverdale, Ralph. *Risk Thinking.* The Coverdale Organisation Ltd. 1977.
Ellis, H. C. *The Transfer of Learning.* Macmillan, New York, 1965.
Lewin, Kurt, Lippitt, Ronald and White, Ralph K. *Patterns of Aggressive Behaviour in Experimentally Created 'Social Climes'. J. Soc. Psychol.* (1939) 27–99.
Lippitt, Ronald and White, Ralph K. *An Experimental Study of Leadership and Group Life.* In Maccoby, Newcomb and Hartley: Readings in Social Psychology. Holt and Co., 1958.
McClelland, D. C. *The Achieving Society.* Van Nostrand, Princeton, 1961.

Training and small groups

Belbin, R. M., *Management Teams, why they succeed or fail.* Heinemann, 1981.
Babington Smith, B. and Sharp, A. *Manager and Team Development, ideas and principles underlying Coverdale Training,* Heinemann, 1990.
Taylor, Max, *Effectiveness in Education and Training.* Avebury, 1990.

Index

Abdush Shakoor, A. B. M., 204
Acquiescence, 34
Action stage, 58, 96
Afforestation programme, 202
Agreements, verbal, 34
Agricultural development programme, 199–205
Aims:
  closed, 31
  corporate, 52
  establishing, 61
  group, 35–6
  open, 31
  organizational, 49–51
  origin of, 30
  personal, 35–6
  social, 36
  terminology of, 29–30
  and timescale, 30–1
Aims network, see Why/how network
Aims stage, 94–5
Archer, Christine, 196–7
Authority, 87–9
Autocratic leadership, 92, 93, 94, 97
Awareness, 66–7

Babington Smith, Bernard, 7, 11
Bangladesh development programme, 199–204
  evaluation, 204–5
Beckhardt project model, 145
Behaviourism, 12–13
Belbin, Meredith, 16
Birbeck, Tony, 222, 223
Boydell, Deanne, 220
Brainstorming, 61, 86, 213
Briefing meetings, 160–1
British Gas, training benefits, 219
Building construction programmes, 203

Carrington case study, 167–70
Centre for Adviser/Inspector Development (CAID), 194
Chairmanship, 72, 157
Change, need for, 113–14

Character strengths, 12, 13
Charting, 73, 211–15
Children, courses for, 197–8
Children's Society case study, 180–4
Christian principles, 222–4
Classroom courses, 197–8
Coaches, role of, 18, 124
Commitment, 33–4, 89
  in TQM, 163
Communications patterns, 93
Company characteristics, well managed, 118–19
Competition factor, 21–2, 83
Conflict factor, 19–20, 35
Consensus checklist, 187–8
Consultant, process, see Process consultant
Consultative leadership, 92, 93, 94, 97
Control systems, 106–8
Co-operation factor, 21–2, 34, 83, 216
Core group training, 125–6
Courses:
  classroom, 197–8
  company, see under individual company names
  individual, 220
Courtaulds Research Department case study, 174–9
Coverdale, Ralph, 3–8, 11, 222, 223
Coverdale learning system, 3–4, 13
  syllabus, 18–19
  Teamwork Part I course, 15–17
  Teamwork Part II course, 17
  see also under Systematic Approach
Creativity factor, 20

Dealer survey, 208–9
Decision-taking stage, 95–6
Departmental objectives, 133–4
Diploma of Management Studies (DMS), 196
Discussion, types of, 82–3, 85–6

Education Reform Act 1988, 190, 193
Emotion, role of, 79–80
Enterprise, 217
Environment, physical, 73–4
ESSO experiences, 8, 9
  Fawley training benefits, 10, 219
Ethical system, 100–1

Failure, analysis of, 103, 104
Follow-up interview, 131–3
Frustration, 33

Giachardi, David, 175–9
Greenwich, London Borough of, training
    schemes, 192–5

How/why network, *see* Why/How network
Human thought processes, 217
Hygrowth Electric programme, 207–10

ICI Europe programme, 206–7
ICI Wilton, training benefits, 218
Information meetings, routine, 158–9
Information recording, 40, 56
Information stage, 95
Instructions, framing, 32
International Development Agency (IDA),
    199

John Brunton case study, 171–5
Joiner's role, 89

Keenan, Candace, 197
Knowledge (as basis for authority), 89

Language barriers, 206–7
Lateral thinking, 42–3
Leadership:
    consultative, 92, 93, 94, 97
    research results, 92
    skills, 90–1
    training for, 138–9
Learning by experience, 60
Lewin, Kurt, 92
Listening, effective, 81–2
Locus of Control, 221

McClelland, David, 12
Manager:
    autocratic, 92, 93, 94, 97
    as observer, 66–7
    performance, 90
    role of, 91, 217
    skills, 27
    style of, 24, 91–4
    and Systematic Approach, 94–8
Manipulation, 74–5
Mechanistic system, 99–101

Meetings:
    behaviour at, 153
    briefing, 160–1
    checklist for, 186–7
    conduct of, 155–8
    routine information, 158–9
    technical, 159–60
Ministry of Agriculture and Forests (MOAF
    Bangladesh, 204–5
Minutes, meeting, 157–8
Morale, effects on, 80, 104–5
Multi-cultural programmes, 206–7

National Society for the Prevention of
    Cruelty to Children (NSPCC), 184–9
Negotiation:
    principles, 140–2
    training in, 139–40
Networks:
    personal, 46–7
    why/how, *see* Why/how networks
New job, preparations for, 150–5
Newham, London Borough of, training
    schemes, 191–2, 196
Norms, 115–16

Objectives, revising, 108–9
Observation, 66–7
    self-, 68–9
Observer, role of, 157
Organic system, 99–101
Organizational development:
    elements of, 119–20
    purpose, 117
    starting point, 123–4
    training patterns, 124–7

Perception, 65, 69
Planning stage, 57, 96
Planting programme, 203
Positive thinking, 103–4
Process, definition, 70–1
Process authority, 88
Process consultant:
    case study, 134–6
    contract with, 129–31
    examples, 131–4
    levels of operation, 131
    role of, 128, 129
Process planning, 72–5, 78–9, 150
Process problems, 70
Process procedures, 71–2
Process reviews, 138, 157
Process skills, 75–7

rocess training, 119
roject concept, 10
roject management, 142–3
  training for, 143–6
roposals, making, 83–5
sychological needs, 11–12
upil Record, The, 220

Relations:
  with manager, 154
  with subordinates, 154–5
Responsibility, 87
Review stage, 58, 97

chool management, 190–1
cientific method, 60–1
creening, 276
elf-analysis, 68–9, 152–3
elf improvement, 22–3, 150–2
ensitivity training, 6
harman, Rod, 192–4
hell-UK case study, Carrington site, 167–70
ilence, use of, 72–3
kills, *see under* Process skills; Task skills
ocial learning theory, 12
tandards, 115
teerer's role, 89
ubordinates, developing, 104–5
uccess, 109–10
Success criteria, *see* Success measures
Success measures, 30, 47–9
Supportive development, 77, 82–3
Systematic Approach:
  in agricultural management, 200
  benefits of, 63–4
  in classroom, 197
  development of, 9, 14, 53–5
  and management style, 94–8
  in education management, 193, 194
  in multi-language situations, 207
  stages in, 55–8
  in teamwork, 63
  ways of using, 58–61

Task:
  closed, 44–6
  definition, 70
  open, 43
  selection of, 15–16
Task authority, 88

Task problems, 70
Task skills, 75
Teachers, 195–6
Team building, 203–4
Teamwork:
  improving, 22–3, 28, 68, 78
  skills, 9–10
  use of Systematic Approach, 63
Technical meetings, 159–60
Thinking skills, 20
Thinking time, 73
Total Quality Management (TQM), 162–3
  Whitbread example, 163–7
Trade unions, role of, 123
Training:
  benefits from, 23–4, 126–7, 218–21
  characteristics, 17
  commitment to, 122–3
  core group, 125–6
  implementing, 120–1
    checklist, 121–2
  for leadership, 138–9
  for negotiations, 139–40
  principles, 7, 8–9, 14
  process, 119
  for project management, 143–6
  sensitivity, 6
  wedge pattern, 124–5
Training groups, 7, 8–9, 16–17
  behaviour in, 71–2
  checklist, 121–2
Training workshops, 137–8

Unigate, training programme, 218

Vertical thinking, 42

Weakness:
  overcoming, 105–6
  use of, 78
Wedge pattern training, 124–5
What Has To Be Done (WHTBD) stage, 56, 57
Whitbread case study, 163–7
Why/how networks, 37–40, 62, 213
Working groups, 78–9
Workshops, training, *see* Training workshops

YTS trainees study, 221